TECHNOCRACY RISING
The Trojan Horse of Global Transformation

by Patrick M. Wood

*The dark horse of the
New World Order is not Communism,
Socialism or Fascism. It is Technocracy.*

Printed in the United States of America

First Printing, 2015

ISBN 978-0-9863739-0-9
Coherent Publishing
P.O. Box 21269
Mesa, AZ 85277
www.CoherentPress.com

Additional Information & Updates
www.TechnocracyRising.com

Dedication

This book is dedicated to my two daughters, Debra and Jennifer, and my two sons, Joshua and Benjamin, and their children, who may have to live with the consequences of the *Brave New World* of Technocracy, should this present generation fail to reject it.

TABLE OF CONTENTS

ACKNOWLEDGEMENTS

This book would not exist without the encouragement and knowledge of a number of people. Special thanks is given to Dr. Martin Erdmann for his patient instruction and diverse knowledge on these topics; to Carl Teichrib, who co-labored with me in much of the early research needed for this book; to Michael Shaw for his detailed and knowledgeable input on Agenda 21 and Sustainable Development; to the University of Alberta (Canada) for generously granting access to me to study their extremely valuable historical library archives on Technocracy, Inc. Special thanks is also given to those who actually turned this into a book: to my loving wife, Charmagne, who encouraged me every step of the way and whose sharp eye turned up literally hundreds of editing issues; to Gail Hardaway, whose teaching career in English greatly helped in the editing and proofing process; to Spencer Fettig for her youthful and critical proof-reading skills and suggestions that definitely brought more clarity to many passages; and to all my friends at RevelationGate Ministries who encouraged and donated to this project. Above all, I give credit and thanks to the God of the universe who put this information in front of me and then opened my eyes to understand what I was actually looking at, without which I would most certainly still be wandering the halls of intellectual ignorance.

FOREWORD

That which has been is what will be,
That which is done is what will be done,
And there is nothing new under the sun.
Is there anything of which it may be said,
"See, this is new?" It has already been in
Ancient times before us. (Ecclesiastes 1:9-10)

Modern Technocracy and Transhumanism are both products of the notion that science and technology can somehow fulfill the utopian dream of perfecting society in general and humanness in particular. Furthermore, the rapid advancement of science and technology is leading its practitioners to believe more strongly than ever that final and total deliverance from their unenlightened past is but a hairsbreadth away. They see wars being eliminated, poverty being eradicated and society living in perfect harmony thanks to their careful scientific management. However, as you shall see, the desire to reform society and humanity is hardly new but is deeply rooted in both history and in religious substitution; in history, because there are many examples of an elite using their control over some form of technology to subjugate others; in religious substitution, because traditional faith in God as the sole provider of redemption and transcendence has been replaced by a reliance on science and technology to provide the same benefits.

The religious foundations for technological advancement have been either ignored or hidden away from the view of most Westerners during most of the past two centuries. As long as modernity's Positivism – the principal philosophy of what would later undergird the technocratic worldview – held sway over the minds of its adherents, the conscious recognition of a reality other than what naturalism offered could be denied. Postmodernity's recognition of the futility to wilfully suppress the knowledge of technology's religious aspects has not necessarily generated a more realistic view of its advantages and limitations in the world of physical reality. Quite the contrary, the present-day acolytes of technology who serve in the corporate and academic temples of research and development are even more committed than their forbearers to achieve the impossible: perfection in each and every aspect of human existence. The ideals of Utopia have never been more widely hailed as the foundation stones of modern living than by the proponents of a communitarian and technocratic world society.

It should be noted that while the lure of technology appeals to the would-be captains of global hegemony, it also appeals to the lowest echelons of humanity as well. For instance, the philosopher Michael Heim wrote once, "Our fascination with computers... is more deeply spiritual than utilitarian. When on-line, we break free from bodily existence." We then emulate the "perspective of God", an all-at-oneness of "divine knowledge". Once again, technology is being promoted as a means to transcendence and redemption. For some, this is a non-traditional religious transcendence of the body and material limitations in the ephemeral, ineffable realm known as "cyberspace". For others, it is a spiritual quest to transcend our limitations and reacquire personal divinity. On a larger scale, the developers of nuclear weapons, space exploration and artificial intelligence, for instance, may be propelled by religious desires, but they are sustained by military financing and the results of their labours are totalitarian governments ruled by an elite of technocrats.

The reader is urged to make careful study of this book and its primary message, that in the name of science and scientism, technocracy is on the rise world-wide, that it is an age-old deception of the greatest magnitude, that it is not what it appears to be and that it cannot make good delivery on its fantastical promises.

Dr. Martin Erdmann, Director
Verax Institut

PREFACE

The dark horse of the New World Order is not Communism, Socialism or Fascism: It is Technocracy.[1]

I don't know anyone who follows the news who doesn't say that the world seems to be crumbling before his eyes. The American dynasty has seemingly hit a brick wall in every conceivable direction. Wealth is shrinking, record numbers are on welfare, our political structures are dysfunctional, regulations are suffocating the economy, personal privacy has been shattered, foreign policy disasters are everywhere, racial conflict is the highest in decades and on and on.

Don't think that these changes are merely some strange twist of fate or that they are somehow all unrelated. *They are not!*

In fact, the world is being actively transformed according to a very narrow economical/political/social philosophy called Technocracy, and it is impacting every segment of society in every corner of the world. Furthermore, Technocracy is being sponsored and orchestrated by a global elite led by **David Rockefeller's** and **Zbigniew Brzezinski's** Trilateral Commission. Let the evidence speak for itself. [Note: Trilateral Commission member names are in bold type.]

Originally started in the early 1930s, Technocracy is antithetical to every American institution that made us into the greatest nation on earth. It eschews property rights, obsoletes capitalism, hates politicians and traditional political structures, and promises a lofty utopian dream made possible *only* if engineers, scientists and technicians are allowed to run society. When Aldous Huxley penned *Brave New World* in 1932, he accurately foresaw this wrenching transformation of society and predicted that the end of it would be a scientific dictatorship unlike anything the world has ever seen.

Indeed, Technocracy is transforming economics, government, religion and law. It rules by regulation, not by Rule of Law, policies are dreamed up by unelected and unaccountable technocrats

---

1 Patrick M. Wood, "Technocracy's Endgame: Global Smart Grid", August Forecast & Review, 2011.

buried in government agencies, and regional governance structures are replacing sovereign entities like cities, counties and states. This is precisely why our society seems so dislocated and irreparable.

Still say you've never heard of Technocracy? Well, you probably have but under different names. The tentacles of Technocracy include programs such as Sustainable Development, Green Economy, Global Warming/Climate Change, Cap and Trade, Agenda 21, Common Core State Standards, Conservation Easements, Public-Private Partnerships, Smart Growth, Land Use, energy Smart Grid, de-urbanization and de-population. In America, the power grab of Technocracy is seen in the castrating of the Legislative Branch by the Executive Branch, replacing laws and lawmakers with Reflexive Law and regulators, and establishing regional Councils of Governments in every state to usurp sovereignty from cities, counties and states.

Technocracy Rising: The Trojan Horse of Global Transformation connects the dots in ways you have never seen before, taking you on a historical journey that leads right up to the current day. It will show you how this coup de grâce is taking place right under our noses and what we might do to stop it.

When Americans saw through Technocracy in the 1930s, they forcefully rejected it and the people who promoted it. If Americans are able to recognize this modern-day Trojan horse, they can reject it *again*. Indeed, *they must!*

Patrick M. Wood
Author

INTRODUCTION

Technocracy is the science of social engineering, the scientific operation of the entire social mechanism to produce and distribute goods and services to the entire population...[2]

Let me be clear about the intent and scope of this book. My premise is that when it was founded in 1973, the Trilateral Commission quietly adopted a modified version of historic Technocracy to craft what it called a "New International Economic Order". This has been largely unrecognized even to this day. With the combined weight of the most powerful global elite behind it, Technocracy has flourished in the modern world and has perhaps reached the tipping point of no return. This book will explain Technocracy in detail, demonstrate the methodology that has been used to implement it, document the control over power centers that allowed the methodology to be used, and most importantly, expose the perpetrators who are responsible for it. If the reader does not see the importance of these connections, then neither will he see the economic and political dangers in such things like Sustainable Development, Agenda 21, Public-Private Partnerships, Smart Growth, Green Economy, Smart Grid, Common Core State Standards, Councils of Governments, etc. The creation of all of these programs will be laid at the feet of the Trilateral Commission, in the name of Technocracy. Indeed, the Trilateral Commission and its members were simultaneously the philosophical creators of modern Technocracy as well as the implementers as they occupied key positions in governments, business and academia since 1973.

I can already hear the Trilaterals and Technocrats howling in protest after reading just this first paragraph. "Not so!", "Foolishness!", "Lunacy!" I've heard this lame defense for almost 40 years. One of the first lessons learned about liars in my early days, when the Cold War was in full play - and the Soviets were also consummate liars - was to "Watch what they do, not what

---

2 "What Is Technocracy?", The Technocrat, Vol. 3, No. 4, 1938.

they say." So, to all you elitists who might perchance be reading this book, you stand naked before the evidence.

To the rest of the inquiring world, you may not like what you discover here, but if you follow along to the end, you will see all the dots finally connected in a way that makes perfect sense. The term technocracy was first used publicly by W.H. Smythe in his 1919 article, "Industrial Management". During that time in history, academics and professionals were fervently debating various aspects of the industrial and technological revolutions and their impact on society, economy and government structures.

The word itself is derived from the Greek words "techne", meaning skilled and "kratos", meaning rule. Thus, it is government by skilled engineers, scientists and technicians as opposed to elected officials. Technocracy was generally considered to be exclusive of all other forms of government, including democracy, communism, socialism and fascism, but as we shall see, there was some ideological blending of ideas when it suited the person or group doing the talking.

In any case, whenever you hear the word Technocracy, this minimum definition will always apply. As the movement progressed and ideas were expanded, some of those additional ideas were branded backward into the original definition as modifying clauses, but they only added to the original meaning without necessarily changing it.

My interest in globalism and the activities of the global elite started in 1976 when I was a young financial writer and securities analyst. I later teamed up with Antony C. Sutton to study and write about the Trilateral Commission, its policies and members, and their plans for global hegemony. Sutton taught me how to "Follow the money. Follow the power." which has proven to be an invaluable aid in getting to the heart of a matter. Although I would like to write a follow-up book to our *Trilaterals Over Washington*, *Volumes I* and *II*, the subject of Technocracy now trumps all others. If there is a holy grail (or, unholy grail) of understanding on the New World Order, this is it.

In a nutshell, historic Technocracy is a utopian economic system that discards price-based economics in favor of energy or resource-based economics. Technocracy is so radically different from all current economic norms that it will stretch your mind to get a grasp of what it actually means and what it implies for a global society.

However, in order to properly integrate Technocracy into the total picture, I will briefly address some other important and related topics along the way, such as Scientism, Transhumanism and Scientific Dictatorship. That these are not dealt with in full at present is not to diminish their importance in any way; perhaps follow-up works will allow for a more detailed and complete treatment of those topics.

In the 1930s, there was a popular movement called Technocracy that spawned a large and zealous following of hundreds of thousands of members in the United States and Canada. Sadly, history books reveal little about this movement, and so my study of it required a significant amount of time-consuming original research at significant personal expense. As I dug deeply into historical archives and old media, I was increasingly shocked by the impact that Technocracy had then and is having on the world today.

There have been many small crackpot movements throughout history to which we might say, "Who cares?" When a hundred people get together to talk about UFOs, utopian philosophy or whatever, it's just a hundred people getting together. If nothing comes of it, all the folks eventually pass and history forgets that they were ever alive. This is not so with Technocracy for many reasons:

- By the 1930s there was at least a 100 year backdrop of philosophical justification for Scientism and Technocracy.
- The organizers were top tier engineers and scientists of their day, many of whom were professors at prestigious universities such as Columbia University.
- Their plans were meticulously detailed, documented and openly published.
- The impact of their policies and philosophy on the modern global society is gargantuan.

Technocracy is about economic and social control of society

and persons according to the Scientific Method. Most of us think about the so-called scientific method when we think back on the carefully crafted experiments in high school chemistry or biology class. That is not what I'm talking about here. Technocracy's Scientific Method dates back mostly to philosophers Henri de Saint-Simon (1760-1825) and Auguste Comte (1798-1857). According to the global-minded New School,

Henri de Saint-Simon is renowned as the founder of the "Saint-Simonian" movement, a type of semi-mystical "Christian-Scientific" socialism that pervaded the 19th Century. Saint-Simon envisaged the reorganization of society with an elite of philosophers, engineers and scientists leading a peaceful process of industrialization tamed by their "rational" Christian-Humanism. His advocacy of a "New Christianity" -- a secular humanist religion to replace the defunct traditional religions -- was to have scientists as priests. This priestly task was actually taken up by two of his followers -- Barthelemy-Prosper Enfantin (1796-1864) and Saint-Amand Bazard (1791-1832) -- who infected the whole movement with their bizarre mysticism and ritual.[3]

Saint-Simon, along with Comte, is considered a father of so-called "social science" studies in universities world-wide. He was the first philosopher to bring psychology, physiology, physics, politics and economics to the study of humanity and human behavior and the first to suggest that the Scientific Method could be used in the process to discover what made man and society tick. As such, he had no regard for what "little people" thought and highest regard for those enlightened ones of superior intellectual abilities. Human nature was merely an object of dispassionate research and objective analysis.[4]

Auguste Comte was the founder of the discipline of Sociology and the doctrine of Positivism, and many regard him as the first philosopher of science. He was heavily influenced by Saint-Simon. Comte promoted the notion that the only authentic knowledge is

3　　Quoted from The New School website, as of 10/5/2012

4　　The Great Debate web site, http://www.thegreatdebate.org.uk/Saint-Simon.html

scientific knowledge and that the Scientific Method was the only way to arrive at such truth.

If you want to learn more about Saint-Simon, Comte and their followers, there are a multitude of good resources in your public or university library and on the Internet. The point of invoking their names here is to point out that Technocracy's elite way of thinking had been brewing for a long time and was hardly original with modern technocrats. However, since science was rapidly advancing during the 1920s and 1930s (and the Great Depression falsely convinced many that capitalism and free enterprise were dead), they believed that they alone possessed the knowledge to make a scientific society operate successfully and efficiently. Further, bolstered by the supposed death of capitalism during the Great Depression, they figured that their ship had finally come in, and it was time for them to take over, restructure society along scientific lines, and thereby save the world: no more depressions, no more war, no more poverty.

You will soon learn everything about Technocracy that you wish you did not know, and yet there is one more important point that you need to understand to put it all in context. In order for Technocracy to succeed, it is necessary to have in place a comprehensive system for the orderly management of all humans and all facets of societal operation. This includes the economic, political, social and religious. Furthermore, these areas must not be merely compatible; they must be so thoroughly entangled with each other that distinctions among them will not be obvious to their subjects. Indeed, this is the "holistic" approach to global governance. [Note: Governance is a process of regulatory management and does not refer to representative government, as it is commonly understood. The regulators are unelected "experts" who answer to no one, as is the case with the European Union, for instance.]

This is an important point to grasp because it permeates the thinking of all historical and modern Technocrats alike. It is, so to speak, the "glue that binds" these concepts together, rendering them inseparable, interdependent and symbiotic. Unfortunately, in order for you to really get into the Technocrat's mind, I must digress into one more philosophical discussion, but I promise it will be short!

The Greek word for whole is "holos", from which we have a number of modern words such as holistic, holism, holon, holarchy and so on. The philosophical concepts that have grown up around these words have as much to do with metaphysics and religion as they do with politics or economics. In 1926, Jan Christian Smuts (1870-1950) wrote a political treatise called *Holism and Evolution*. Who was Smuts? As a statesman, military commander, politician and philosopher, Smuts advocated the founding of the League of Nations and later was a leading figure in the creation of the United Nations Covenant. In 1917, he was chosen to be a member of the Imperial War Cabinet in England, during which time he helped to found the Royal Air Force. In his native South Africa, Smuts was twice elected Prime Minister after holding several lesser elected positions.

In *Holism and Evolution*, Smuts proposed the "Theory of the Whole" which states, in part, that "what a thing is in its sum is of greater importance than its component parts."[5] Thus, the city is more important than its inhabitants, the state is more important than its cities, and the whole of humanity is more important than cities, nation-states and all the humans therein. The individual is seen relinquishing his or her rights, privileges and aspirations to the greater good. Smuts viewed evolution as an integral part of the holism phenomenon as towns grow into cities, cities into states, states into countries and countries into a global society. From every sub-atomic particle to the entire universe, each smaller part is integral and subservient to the larger. This is an early-modern scientific notion of the earth as a complete organism (whole) that has many interdependent parts (smaller wholes) that are subservient to the larger organism. Holism is also the rationale for regionalism of all magnitudes, whether Councils of Governments within states, or country groupings within continents, such as the European Union.

The philosophy of holism has since matured. Fast forward to 1967 when Arthur Koestler coined the word "holon" in his book, *The Ghost in the Machine.*[6] Koestler suggested that a holon is a sta-

5   Dr. Paul Moller, *Holism and Evolution*, (College of European and Regional Studies, 2006).

6   Arthur Koestler, *The Ghost in the Machine*, (Macmillan, 1968), p. 48.

ble unit within a larger system that is controlled by other holons greater than it, all of which are in a continuous state of evolution to a higher, more complex form. Such a complete system of holons is referred to as a holarchy. Accordingly, "The entire machine of life and of the Universe itself evolves toward ever more complex states, as if a ghost were operating the machine."[7]

Personally, I reject this thinking altogether because man is the pinnacle of creation and not a mere holon that must serve the holarchy. In other words, I believe that man is not to be the servant of nature, but rather nature is to be the servant of man. In the balance of this book, I will make the case that Technocrats, from the 1930s until the present, view all of the holons in the world as little more than engineering projects to be analyzed, debugged and re-engineered according to their Scientific Method. They are an egotistical bunch, to be sure, thinking that they alone have the technical abilities to save the rest of us from our ignorance and archaic beliefs such as Christianity, liberty, and personal freedom.

The Devil in the Details

It is no mistake that there is a decidedly religious aspect to Technocracy. Saint-Simon's "New Christianity" saw a pressing need to replace historical Christianity with a secular humanist religion where scientists and engineers would constitute the new priesthood.

This is in stark contrast to New Testament Christianity where the Bible speaks of the church, for instance,

But you are a chosen generation, a royal priesthood, a holy nation, His own special people, that you may proclaim the praises of Him who called you out of darkness into His marvelous light. (1 Peter 2:9)

Saint-Simon's New Christianity not only redefined the object of worship - science instead of God - but also the priesthood that would serve this new god. However, this same scenario has played itself out innumerable times in the Old and New Testament. When the One God of the universe was seen as abandoned, idols and false gods were created to replace Him and to provide vari-

---

7   Piero Mella, *The Holonic Revolution*, 2009. (Pavia University Press, 2009).

ous ill-defined benefits to would-be worshipers. Some prominent examples in the Old Testament include Marduk, Baal, Bel,
Molech, Ashtoreth, Tamuz, Dagon, etc. In the early period of the
New Testament church, competing idols included Apollo, Zeus,
Helen, Athena, Pluto, Hermes and so on. Each of these idols had
its own attendant priesthood, that is, those who were allowed to
approach their god and who alone were allowed to relay what
their god had to say to his/her followers.

To say that Christianity and idolatry are mutually exclusive
is easily seen in the New Testament where Christians are simply told to "flee from idolatry" (1 Corinthians 10:14). The apostle
Paul goes on to say,

> ...the things which the Gentiles sacrifice they sacrifice to de-
> mons and not to God, and I do not want you to have fellow-
> ship with demons. You cannot drink the cup of the Lord and
> the cup of demons; you cannot partake of the Lord's table and
> of the table of demons. Or do we provoke the Lord to jealousy?
> Are we stronger than He? (1 Corinthians 10:20-22)

Here is the crux of the matter: There is a Devil in the details
of Technocracy. We must be very careful in our examination of
Technocracy to see this undercurrent of religious substitution because it proves to be the basis for global deception greater than
anything the world has seen to date.

Technocracy will be shown to be thoroughly anti-Christian
and completely intolerant of Biblical thought. This has always
been the hallmark sign seen in idolatrous religions and practices!

As stark as the contrast might be upon careful examination, we will also see how threads of Technocracy, Scientism
and Transhumanism are interweaving themselves into the
modern Christian church. Many modern Bible-believing
Christians are quite disturbed and perplexed by this in-
trusion into historic Christianity. For technocrats who see
Technocracy as salvation for both political and economic structures, then certainly it can be salvation for your soul as well.
This is very dangerous thinking and is leading many Christians
and churches into a state of active apostasy, a falling away
from traditional Biblical doctrines, teachings and practices.

Trilateral Commission

In 1978 when I co-authored *Trilaterals Over Washington Volumes I* and *II* with the late Antony C. Sutton, we wrote extensively about a newly formed elitist group called the Trilateral Commission that was co-founded by **David Rockefeller** and **Zbigniew Brzezinski**. They chose about 250 elitists from North America, Europe and Japan in order to create a "New International Economic Order" (NIEO). The membership consisted of people from academia, industry, finance, media and government.

Sutton and I interpreted the NIEO as a reshuffling of conventional economic theory, such as Keynesianism, in order for their members to game the system for their own benefit. After all, the elite have been known for this type of crass manipulation to accumulate money to themselves at the expense of every one else in society. We thought this was the case with the Trilateral Commission.

Brzezinski's 1968 book, *Between Two Ages: America's Role in the Technetronic Era*, was written when he was a professor at Columbia University, yet it was this book that originally endeared him to Rockefeller and other elitists. Sutton and I wrote extensively on Brzezinski's philosophy and conclusions as revealed in *Between Two Ages*, but neither of us had any inkling that the word "Technetronic" might have been a knockoff for the word "Technocratic". Why? Because at that time neither of us had any knowledge of Technocracy or its doctrines. However, as I was researching the history of Technocracy the thought occurred to me to go back and re-read *Between Two Ages* to see if there were any parallels or conceptual connections to early Technocracy. Needless to say, I was shocked: throughout his book, Brzezinski was floating the party line of Technocracy.

Thus, it became increasingly clear to me that the Trilateral Commission's original goal of creating a New International Economic Order might actually mean abandoning status quo economics in favor of a completely different economic system of Technocracy. If this is the case, then it has escaped virtually everyone's attention for the last 40-plus years!

Well, better late than never, I suppose.... I therefore hope that you will make a careful and detailed reading of this book from beginning to end and then do some digging on your own to see if these things are true or not.

In 2009, when I had formalized my research on Technocracy to the point that I could adequately communicate it to others, I contacted a few of my professional colleagues, all of whom are very well educated on various aspects of economic globalization, global religion, science and world politics. Not only was there general acceptance of the research, but the most common response was, "This connects all the dots that we could not previously connect." In other words, Technocracy really is the glue that binds together disparate events, movements and concepts.

On the whole, if this new knowledge collectively drew alarm from them, then I realized that Technocracy was much bigger than I had originally thought. They not only encouraged me to continue this work, but they also put themselves to the task of further research as well. In this sense, I am not writing this book alone or in a vacuum but rather with the concurrence of disciplined minds from different academic genres.

Understanding Technocracy will help you to understand and connect seemingly unrelated topics like

- Agenda 21 and Sustainable Development
- Land and water grabs by Federal agencies
- ICLEI, Smart Growth and Public-Private Partnerships
- Communitarianism, the Third Way and Communitarian Law
- Global Warming/Climate Change
- Smart Grid, Carbon Credits, Cap & Trade

Indeed, all of these modern phenomena have their roots firmly planted in the doctrines of early Technocracy as far back as the 1930s and beyond!

CHAPTER 1

THE BACKDROP FOR TECHNOCRACY

Technocracy did not spring out of nowhere. Rather, there were a host of philosophies co-mingling with each other from at least the mid-1800s through the turn of the century. This cauldron initially produced more discussion than action, but it was inevitable that some strains of thoughts would solidify into society-changing movements. And indeed, they did: Darwinism spawned the eugenics movement; Marxist philosophies led directly to the Communist overthrow in Russia; Fabian socialism was identified with colonialism in southern Africa; the Technocracy movement took off in the 1920s, and so on.

The fact is, "Ideas matter!" What seems like a crazy idea today could just as easily change the world tomorrow. In that sense, the period between 1890 and 1930 was a pivotal time for the future of the world. All notions of Biblical inerrancy and historical accuracy had been discarded by the intellectual elite. Radical new inventions created by scientists and engineers were revolutionizing both the physical and social world. The engineered and mechanized slaughter during World War I sent shockwaves to every corner of the world.

The purpose of this book is to explain Technocracy and not the broader experience of world history. Thus, the following abbreviated statements about prominent philosophies and philosophers of the period can only serve as a reminder for what people were processing in their minds at the time. For the curious desiring more detail, there are a myriad of works available in your local or university library.

Positivism

The Frenchman Auguste Comte (1798-1857) is known as the father of modern sociology and was the founder of Positivism, a philosophy that was very popular in the late 1800s. Comte was considered the first philosopher of science as he elevated science by claiming that the only authentic knowledge is scientific knowledge. This naturally discarded all notions of absolute truth based on the Bible and metaphysical truth based on man's imaginations. Comte believed that his "science of society" could be discovered and explained by applying the Scientific Method in the same manner as it was applied to physical science.

Scientism

Scientism takes Positivism to an extreme by claiming that science alone can produce truth about the world and reality. As such, it is more radical and exclusionary than Positivism. Scientism rejects all philosophical, religious and metaphysical claims to understand reality, since the truth it portends cannot be validated by the Scientific Method. Thus, science is the absolute and only access to truth and reality. Scientism is often seen overstepping the bounds of provable science by applying the Scientific Method to areas that cannot be demonstrated, such as evolution, climate change and social science.

Progressivism

According to one historian, progressivism is a

political movement that addresses ideas, impulses, and issues stemming from modernization of American society. Emerging at the end of the nineteenth century, it established much of the tone of American politics throughout the first half of the century.[8]

Industrialization was enabled by science, technology and invention. As knowledge increased, it was surmised that society must change along with it, or at least adapt to it. Progressives called for bigger government run by qualified managers with diminishing personal liberty and national sovereignty, but they simultaneously fought to reduce waste and increase efficiency in government. The emphasis on efficiency drove many progressives into Technocracy since science appeared to be the only pathway to achieve it.

---

8   Alonzo L. Harriby, "Progressivism: A Century of Change and Rebirth," in *Progressivism and the New Democracy*, ed. Sidney M. Milkis and Jerome M. Mileur (University of Massachusetts Press, 1999).

Darwinism

The philosophy of Darwinism grew out of Charles Darwin's book *The Origin of Species*,[9] published in 1859, which proposed that all life naturally evolved over long periods of time from the most simple creature to the most complex. It specifically rejected the Biblical account of creation and in general all thoughts of intelligent design. By the early 1900s, the concept of Darwinism had expanded to use evolution to describe social change and eugenics theories. Eugenics proposed the artificial manipulation of the human "gene pool" via selective breeding and "cleansing", as ultimately seen in Hitler's genocidal rampages during WWII. With today's advancement in various technologies such as genetic engineering and nano-technology, Transhumanists (Transhumanism and Technocracy both rely on Scientism) are boldly claiming that they are now firmly in control of the evolutionary process and will direct the creation of Humanity 2.0.

Fascism

Merriam-Webster defines Fascism as

a political philosophy, movement, or regime that exalts nation and often race above the individual and that stands for a centralized autocratic government headed by a dictatorial leader, severe economic and social regimentation, and forcible suppression of opposition.

What differentiates Fascism from Communism is its protection of businesses and land-holding elites. Indeed, corporate entities during Hitler's war years were virtually merged with state interests. Today, the term Fascism has multiple nuances, but all point to a totalitarian system where corporatism and the state are seen as functionally equivalent.

Socialism

The doctrines of Karl Marx are seen as the original basis for Socialism as an economic and political model. Socialism eschews private property and the accumulation of wealth through state-ownership of all productive resources and distribution based

---

9   Charles Darwin, *The Origin of Species*, (London: J. Murray, 1859).

on "to each according to his need." As with Marxism, Socialism is described differently depending on the angle of observation, but the common denominator in all cases is a high level of social and economic control through state-ownership and management with authoritarian control over production, distribution and consumption.

Fabianism

The Fabian Society was formed in England in 1884. It held to a form of Socialism (thus often referred to as Fabian Socialism) that promoted a slow and indirect transformation of society instead of a more radical approach. It was named after the Roman General Fabius Maximus who used delaying tactics against the Carthaginian army led by the famous general, Hannibal. Over the decades, many famous individuals became members of the Society, including H.G. Wells, Bernard Shaw, Virginia Woolf and Bertrand Russell. Social activist Beatrice Webb played a key role in forming the Society and later founded the London School of Economics. The Fabian Society has had a profound influence in many nations and continents around the world, including Great Britain, the United States, Europe and southern Africa.

The Influencers

Henri Saint-Simon (1760-1825)

Saint-Simon was recognized as the father of Technocracy by the Technocrats themselves. He could also be considered the philosophical father of the so-called "emerging church" that is becoming prominent around the world today. Saint-Simon was born into an aristocratic family in France, fought in the American Revolution and later turned to a life of writing and philosophical criticism. He developed many radical strains of thought that influenced people after him, including Karl Marx, Jean-Jacques Rousseau and Auguste Comte among others. He proposed a Christian socialism where everyone would be part of the "brotherhood of man", and suggested that private property should give way to societal management by experts, or technocrats. His *New Christianity* also called for churches to be administered by experts who would direct their parishioners into social programs designed to reform the world and alleviate poverty.[10]

Auguste Comte (1798-1857)

Comte was Saint-Simon's most famous student and was the founder of Positivism which was popular in the second half of the 1800s. As the first "philosopher of science", Comte is also credited as being the father of modern sociology. Like Saint-Simon, Comte also placed a large focus on religion by creating the "Religion of Humanity", which some called "Catholicism plus science" and others called "Catholicism without Christ".[11] Comte also followed Saint-Simon's concept of evolutionary history by formulating three stages of societal development: Theological, Metaphysical and Positive, with the later meaning that the laws of science that control the world are fully known and understood.

Thorstein Veblen (1857-1929)

Born in America, Veblen was an economist and sociologist who followed Saint-Simon's and Comte's theory of evolutionary history by combining Darwinian evolution with his own institutional economics. As a prominent figure in the progressive movement, he was fiercely critical of capitalism while he championed a leadership of a "soviet of engineers". In 1919, Veblen helped found the New School For Social Research (today called The New School) that became a seedbed of radical thought. The New School is where Veblen met Howard Scott, the soon-to-be leader of the Technocracy movement in the U.S. In the early 1920s, Veblen, Howard Scott and M. King Hubbert were all members of the Technical Alliance, a precursor to the Technocracy movement. Early Technocrats universally credit Veblen as a leader of their early efforts to define and organize a technocratic movement. Ironically, Veblen died three months before the stock market crash in 1929, which proved to be the catalyst for wide-spread public interest in Technocracy.

---

10   Henri Saint-Simon, *The New Christianity*, (London: B.D Cousins, 1825).
11   Arthur, *Religion without God and God without religion*, (London: Bemrose & Sons, 1885), p. 142.

Frederick Taylor (1856-1915)

Taylor was an American mechanical engineer who became fixated on ways to increase efficiency in manufacturing processes and worked for years studying and making improvements. In 1911, he published his seminal work, *Principles of Scientific Management*[12] and changed the world of business management forever. Because of his expertise and problem-solving skills, Taylor also inadvertently invented the profession of business consulting. As his notoriety spread, the word "Taylorism" became a synonym for Scientific Management. Taylorism was widely adopted in the USSR as a means of increasing production without having to increase education and training.

Edward Bellamy (1850-1898)

The writings and activism of Edward Bellamy, a dedicated socialist, were widely received by the Technocracy movement after his death. His most famous literary work, *Looking Backward*,[13] was a Rip Van Winkle sort of tale where the hero wakes up in the year 2000 and is then shown how society has changed (looking backward) in the intervening 100 plus years; it describes a Utopia where the state owns one hundred percent of the means of production, run by experts, and everyone in society has all his needs met while living in harmony with each other. The book was an immediate best-seller and created an enthusiastic social movement that lasted over 10 years. The Nationalist Clubs, which promoted the socialist idea of nationalizing all business, ultimately had 162 chapters across the U.S., with 65 of them originating in California. Not incidentally, California later became a hotbed for Technocracy meetings and organizations.

The Cauldron

Were these the *only* philosophies and people contributing to the buildup to Technocracy? Absolutely not. These are standouts, however, that help us to understand the complex mix out of which Technocracy arose. Starting with Saint-Simon, it took over 100 years for Technocracy to congeal and finally arise as seri-

---

12   Frederic Taylor, *Principles of Scientific Management*, (Harper & Brothers, 1911).
13   E. Bellamy, *Looking Backward*, (Boston: Ticknor, 1888).

ous academic and social movements. Today, 80-100 years later, Technocracy has increased its grip and influence over the affairs of men. All of this is to say that Technocracy was not some poorly thought out whim of an uneducated crackpot. To the contrary, the progenitors of Technocracy include academic professors, philosophers, inventors, social activists and prominent members of society.

Setting differences aside, one can easily identify some common threads: rejection of capitalism, distributed wealth, state-ownership of industry, rule by experts instead of politicians, historical and societal evolution as guides for the future, the preeminence of science and the exclusion of Biblical Christianity.

If utopian scientists and engineers were thoroughly hooked on the evolutionary progress of man and society by the 1920s, how much more clever are they today as they strive to take evolution into their own hands to create their own destinies? As the prestigious *Smithsonian Magazine* stated in 2012,

> *Adherents of "transhumanism"—a movement that seeks to transform Homo sapiens through tools like gene manipulation, "smart drugs" and nanomedicine—hail [scientific] developments as evidence that we are becoming the **engineers of our own evolution**.*[14] [Emphasis added]

---

14   Abigail Tucker, "How to become engineers of our own evolution", *Smithsonian Magazine*, April 12, 2012.

CHAPTER 2

FROM PASSION TO MELTDOWN (1920-1940)

The basic problem was that the technocrats' social analysis lacked a political theory of action.[15]

The 1920s were not conducive to public acceptance of Technocracy, nor was it even aware that prominent educators, scientists and engineers were zealously laying the groundwork for it. The interlude between the catastrophes of World War I, which ended in November 1918, and the September 1929 stock market crash was a mere 11 years. During that time, all sorts of societal changes would take place that would taint the entire landscape for the next 100 years.

During the Great War, over 9 million combatants died. This shocked the entire world, not only because of the number of dead, but the means by which they died. It was the first technology-driven war in the history of the world: ships, tanks, airplanes, high explosives, machine guns, radio, chemical warfare, etc.

The public got over it quickly enough and threw themselves into the reckless Roaring 20s that were full of hedonistic abandon. Before the crash in 1929, pretty much everyone believed that prosperity and good times would last forever. They had assurances from all quarters that the world was done with war, that everyone had learned his lesson and would never let it happen again. With 10 years of economic boom behind them, they also had assurances that economic prosperity was a permanent fixture. Life was good. Capitalism was great. Peace and prosperity for all. America was living the dream!

However, because of the technology used in the Great War, the engineering profession was suffering from a mixture of guilt and

---

15   William E. Akin, *Technocracy and the American Dream*, (University of California Press, 1977), p. 112.

societal angst. Technology that they had collectively invented had gone terribly wrong and resulted in the mechanized death of millions. Furthermore, they reasoned, society had been fundamentally changed with the inclusion of technology, and politicians were obviously incapable of managing the resulting hybrid society. In their view, technology was certain to continue its transformative pace and if they - scientists, engineers and technicians - were not allowed to run it, then the outcome would most certainly be further disasters. Thus, as theories of engineering blended with various shades of Comte's positivism, the brainchild of Technocracy was born.

The intellectual and philosophical stew that fed this brainchild was seasoned with progressive thought, Positivism, Taylorism and Taylor's Scientific Method of management, Darwinism and eugenics. (According to the *American Journal of Sociology*, "Eugenics is the science which deals with all influences that improve the inborn qualities of a race; also with those that develop them to the utmost advantage.")[16]

Furthermore, thanks to Auguste Comte and his "science of society", the early Technocrats believed that they could engineer society by applying the Scientific Method in the same manner as it was applied to physical science. This was a mistake, but one that was never recognized as such, even to this day. To them, the simple fact that the world was becoming even more techno-centric only fueled the urgency of their discussions and planning for Technocracy. They alone could save the world from itself while politicians were certain to just make it worse.

By 1921, Frederick Taylor's masterpiece, *The Principles of Scientific Management* (1911), had 10 years to influence business, government and society. The essence of Scientific Management was

> *Science, not rule of thumb.*
> *Harmony, not discord.*
> *Cooperation, not individualism.*
> *Maximum output, in place of restricted output.*

---

16   Galton, Francis, "Eugenics: Its Definition, Scope, and Aims", *American Journal of Sociology*, (July 1904).

The development of each man to his greatest efficiency and prosperity.[17]

Taylor's theories not only captivated the U.S. but the entire world, including the U.S.S.R and Germany. Taylor's famous time-and-motion studies proved that workers could be driven to a level of efficiency and production never before realized.

One historian concluded that Taylor

...asked the public to impose scientific management on reluctant businesses and unions for the good of the whole. Taylorites began to argue that the system promised a shift from arbitrary power to scientific administration not only in the factory but in society as well. Such a shift would bring about the realization of social harmony through, as one young Taylorite engineer wrote, "the organization of human affairs in harmony with natural laws"... Such ideas were heady stuff for engineers.[18]

When the Great War started in 1914, Taylorism was reaching its initial nadir just in time to be applied to wartime economies. Factories cranked out weapons with precision assembly lines staffed by robot-like humans performing the same repetitive tasks up to 16 hours per day. Taylor had leveled the playing field, however, because all the various combatants had learned and implemented the same techniques.

Indeed, engineers had a lot to think about in the early 1920s. In the end, they essentially concluded that it was not their fault that technology had failed the world, but rather the fault of ignorant and corrupt politicians who did not know how to handle what they did not understand.

By the fall of 1919, it was Thorstein Veblen who began to call for a revolution of engineers. As co-founder and professor of The New School in New York, Veblen's ideas were not yet well-known by many engineers, but they caught the attention of a radical young upstart by the name of Howard Scott, who would remain an advocate for Technocracy for the rest of his life. In fact, it was Scott who later founded Technocracy, Inc. in early 1934.

---

17   Frederic Taylor, *Principles of Scientific Management*, (Harper & Brothers , 1911).
18   Akin, p. 10

Thus, in 1919, Veblen and Scott started a group they called the "Technical Alliance" to organize a "soviet of technicians". The Alliance failed miserably to attract many like-minded engineers, but Veblen continued to sponsor discussions about his proposed revolution at The New School. By 1921, Veblen was ready to try again and did so with the release of his *Engineers and the Price System* that took all the blinders off. He plainly stated,

If the country's productive industry were competently organized as a systematic whole, and were then managed by competent technicians with an eye single to maximum production of goods and services instead of, as now, being manhandled by ignorant business men with an eye single to maximum profits; the resulting output of goods and services would doubtless exceed the current output by several hundred percent.[19]

Howard Scott was truly a disciple of Veblen at this point but not without even more radical ideas of his own. It was Scott who first proposed that an energy-based value system would eliminate profit motives and provide a purely functional basis for the organization of society.

By 1922, as the early organizing efforts came to an end, Veblen moderated his activism and Scott essentially dropped out of sight. He continued to stump for his radical theories in restaurants, coffeehouses and speakeasies in his hometown of Greenwich Village in Lower Manhattan. Nobody took him very seriously, and many considered him a boorish, yet flamboyant, blowhard. Greenwich Village, known as a bohemian artist and non-conformist community, was perfectly fit for Scott and even led some to call him the "Bohemian Engineer".

Columbia University

In 1932, Walter Rautenstrauch was a professor at Columbia University and headed the Department of Industrial Engineering which he had previously founded as the first such department in the nation. It is not certain how Scott and Rautenstrauch met, but it was immediately clear to both of them that they shared a com-

---

19   Thorstein Veblen, *Engineers and the Price System*, (BW Huebsch, 1921), pp. 120-121.

mon interest in promoting a system of Technocracy run by engineers, scientists and technicians. Scott, being a minor figure from Greenwich Village, latched onto the prestigious Rautenstrauch as his ticket to stardom.

Rautenstrauch approached Nicholas Murray Butler, the president of Columbia, for a green light to complete an industrial survey of North America, which Scott had started years before with his failed Technical Alliance. Both Columbia and Butler prided themselves for being on the cutting-edge of progressive radicalism, and Technocracy was appealing. Thus, with one stroke of the pen, Scott had Columbia's facilities at his disposal as well as its prestigious reputation. It was later revealed that Scott had misrepresented his own academic credentials, never having graduated from a recognized university, so it is understandable why Scott viewed this new association as the biggest break of his life.

In the early fall of 1932, Rautenstrauch and Scott hastily formed the Committee on Technocracy to supervise the industrial survey project. Its members were drawn from other Columbia University educators and included another soon-to-be key player in Scott's life, M. King Hubbert. Scott became the "consulting technologist" on the Committee, and it was his methodology that would be used to conduct the survey. Financial resources were hard to come by during The Great Depression, so one of Scott's colleagues convinced the Architects' Emergency Relief Committee of New York to fund the project by making dozens of unemployed architects available to work on the survey at Columbia. This engineering workforce was likely housed in the basement of Hamilton Hall at Columbia where other temporary projects had been located in previous years.

In a 2006 biography on Nicholas Murray Butler, Michael Rosenthal revealed what happened next:

Enthralled by Scott's messianic fervor, Butler invited him in 1932 to come to Columbia, working in the Department of Industrial Engineering, to conduct research into the history of American industrial development as seen through a complex series of energy measurements. When it became known in August that Scott and his fellow technocrats were estab-

lished at Columbia, interest in Technocracy exploded. A dance was named after it, Scott became a sought-after speaker, and The Nation proclaimed his theories revolutionary. Butler tried to dampen expectations about its potential... but it was clear that he was excited to have captured it for Columbia.[20]

This instant notoriety had a drug-like effect on Scott who already suffered from an over-inflated view of his own importance. After his death in 1970, a Canadian paper ran a feature on the Technocracy movement and Scott's role in it:

Howard Scott, the messiah-like originator of Technocracy, a graduate of Columbia University, acted as Director-in-Chief until his death in 1970 at the age of 80.

He was a genius, Service says with the same touch of awe in his voice. He was a man for another world, a man who spoke to the sum total of conditioned brains in the price system. Scott was the first of many on earth to co-relate the symbols of technology, science and energy into a working system.[21]

It may not have been Scott's idea to position himself as a messiah, but neither did he do anything to discourage it. He was also not a graduate of Columbia University but apparently did nothing to correct that assumption either. Scott was much more the promoter than the engineer, and promoters are often known to bask in accolades and unsolicited attention.

Just three months later in January 1933, the Committee on Technocracy abruptly fell apart. Although the industrial survey was still incomplete, Scott began to reveal his pre-conceived ideas on Technocracy as a social system, being fully convinced that the results of his survey would completely support his conclusions. It is important to remember that Scott's radical ideas about Technocracy were developed and tempered at the feet of his mentor, Thorstein Veblen. Rautenstrauch had taken a different path, studying and applying Taylor's scientific management principles and those of Henry Gantt, who had worked closely with Taylor in the 1890s. Gantt also had experience with Veblen, but not to the extent of Scott. Second, Rautenstrauch was a well-educated

20   Michael Rosenthal, *Nicholas Miraculous: The Amazing Career of the Redoubtable Dr. Nicholas Murray Butler* (Farrar, Straus and Giroux, 2006), p.422.
21   "No Government, No Politicians, No Taxes", *The Montreal Gazette*, Sept. 14, 1974.

and highly respected engineer with a splendid reputation; Scott didn't have a degree at all which also explained the serious flaws in his design skills and methodology. As Rautenstrauch's confidence in Scott was shaken, he was doubly alarmed by Scott's radical ideas being expressed even before the Industrial Survey was completed. For Rautenstrauch, prescribing application for any project was never proposed until all the "evidence" was gathered and analyzed. Third, Rautenstrauch was uneasy with the blazing limelight that Scott brought to the project.

Some reporters began to more closely investigate Scott's background and educational credentials, and their negative findings proved to be the proverbial straw that broke the camel's back. The press subsequently turned on Scott and, hence, Columbia University. The head of Columbia, Nicholas Murray Butler, cherished a positive limelight, but Scott was giving the whole university a very large black eye. The entire project was summarily forced to leave the campus.

It is important to note that there were two forks of Technocracy at this point. Scott would go on to create the more radical Technocracy, Inc., in late 1933 while Rautenstrauch and the other professors stayed on at Columbia with a less-radical form of academic Technocracy that continued the core concepts but not the name; to them, the word Technocracy had become toxic and simply was not used again for fear of being re-associated with Howard Scott. This hush-hush was reinforced by the press when Randolph Hearst, who controlled a significant portion of the nation's media at the time, released a memo forbidding staff reporters from mentioning the word "Technocracy" under penalty of being immediately fired. Scott did salvage one relationship with a young geophysics instructor at Columbia who had been eager to join the Committee when it was first announced: M. King Hubbert.

By early 1933, humiliated and accused, Scott's personal life went from bad to worse, hitting bottom in March 1933. An unpaid judgment of $1,640 that had been levied against him in 1923 came home to roost, and he was called to account. Still unable to pay, Scott testified before a judge that he owned no significant property and that he was currently living at the apartment of M.

King Hubbert in Greenwich Village. He also admitted to the judge that he did not have a college degree.[22]

Casting personal defeat aside, Scott saw opportunity when he realized that he had raised a significant following of radicals around the U.S. and Canada who were enthralled with his vision for Technocracy and didn't care whether Columbia University was involved or not. Neither did they care that Scott was personally bankrupt and an incompetent business manager. They wanted change, even radical change, now!

During the latter part of 1933, with Scott still imposing on M. King Hubbert for living arrangements, they made their move. Hubbert was a brilliant and well-educated geophysicist who was willing to work with Scott and provided a continuing semblance of credibility to Scott's radicalism. Under Scott's direction, Hubbert's scientific skills and knowledge of engineering could further educate him and provide a solid base from which to travel the country stumping for Technocracy. As they conspired to carry Technocracy further, Scott and Hubbert compiled articles of incorporation in late 1933 and subsequently filed them in early 1934 in New York to create a membership organization called Technocracy, Inc.

Society was ripe for Technocracy during the depths of the Great Depression. It certainly appeared that capitalism was dead. Joblessness, deflation, hunger, anger at politicians and capitalists, and other social stresses had people begging for an explanation as to what went wrong and what could be done to fix it. Technocracy, Inc. had both: Capitalism had died a natural death, and a new Technocracy-oriented society would save them. The engineers, scientists and technicians who would operate this Technocratic Utopia would eliminate all waste and corruption, people would only have to work 20 hours per week, and every person would have a job! Abundance would be everywhere. The only price for this was that they had to get rid of the politicians and the political institutions and let the technocrats run things instead. Nobody protested because most already wanted to throw the politicians out, whom they had already blamed for the Depression.

This sentiment was reinforced in a book by Harry A. Porter

---

22   *New York Times*, March 5, 1933.

released in later 1932 titled *Roosevelt and Technocracy*, where he assured that

Just as the Reformation established Religious Freedom, just as the Declaration of Independence brought about our Political Freedom, Technocracy promises Economic Freedom.[23]

Porter's plan included abandoning the gold standard, suspending the stock exchanges and nationalizing railroads and public utilities. Freedom notwithstanding, Porter then called for President-elect Franklin D. Roosevelt to be sworn in as Dictator rather than President so that he could overturn the existing economic system in favor of Technocracy:

Drastic as these changes from the present order of things may be, they will serve their purpose if only to pave the way for the Economic Revolution – and Technocracy.[24]

Roosevelt didn't take Porter up on declaring himself dictator, but he did abolish the gold standard, confiscated all the citizens' gold, and nationalized certain industries. Otherwise, the egocentric Roosevelt was happy enough to implement many of Technocracy's other ideas, but there was no way he was going to hand the country over to Technocracy's technical cadre.

Technocracy, Inc.

Depression notwithstanding, Howard Scott presented a utopian dream that technology held the key to relieve man from the drudgery of labor. Other critics might think that he merely used that promise to deceive more people into becoming members of his almost cult-like following. After all, a free lunch sounds mighty pleasing to someone out of work and with a family to feed. Second, he knew perfectly well how to leverage the public's increasing anger against politicians, bankers and industrialists to his own advantage. Finally, there was the smoke-and-mirror aspect of the incomplete and faulty science that Scott used to convince people that Technocracy could actually work to everyone's benefit. Such a phenomenon was reminiscent of the "magic elixir"

23   Harry A. Porter, *Roosevelt and Technocracy*, (Wetzel Publishing Company,1932) Foreward iii.
24   ibid., p.63

medicinal cure-alls sold during the 1800s that promised to cure any and all diseases that one could possibly have.

With the memory of the Great War still fresh in the minds of many, the beginning of World War II on September 1, 1939 was earth-shaking. Germany's invasion of Poland all but guaranteed to involve all of Europe. Japan and China were already at war with each other, adding to the risk of an all-out World War. Thus, the momentum and impact of Technocracy, Inc. sharply waned into the 1940s, and it never regained its former attraction again. However, during those intervening years, between 1933 and 1939, the march of Technocracy, Inc. left an indelible mark on history. Unfortunately, historians recorded very little of this era because of the previous Hearst editorial moratorium on the word "Technocracy".

Immediately upon incorporation of Technocracy, Inc. in 1934, Scott and Hubbert recognized that they needed to create a manifesto that would clearly communicate their vision to the public. Working feverishly to meet the public's demand for more information, they completed and published the 280 page *Technocracy Study Course*[25] that same year. It established a detailed framework for Technocracy in terms of energy production, distribution and usage. Under Scott's close supervision, it was actually Hubbert who penned most of the pages. As far as Scott was concerned, this was the first full expression of what he really had in mind for Technocracy; previously, only bits and pieces had been revealed here and there in speeches and newspaper articles. The public demanded more, and independent of Scott's organizational efforts, many study groups had spontaneously popped up around the nation and in Canada. The word Technocracy was on the lips of literally hundreds of thousands of people. Scott knew that he had a limited amount of time to convert these groups into the membership rolls of Technocracy, Inc. To more fully understand what Scott and Hubbert had to offer, we must look carefully at the *Technocracy Study Course.*

Technocracy Study Course

This treatise was specifically designed as a study course to ful-

---

25   Note: The *Technocracy Study Course* is readily available on the Internet in a scanned format.

fill the needs of individual groups that were meeting in homes, halls, churches and granges across the U.S. and Canada. Without top-down guidance, different groups were headed in different directions. The big question is, what was the ideology that Scott and Hubbert intended to implant?

The Preface of the Study Course details some basic elements of the organization itself:

Technocracy, Inc. is a non-profit membership organization incorporated under the laws of the State of New York. It is a Continental Organization. It is not a financial racket or a political party.

Technocracy, Inc. operates only on the North American Continent through the structure of its own Continental Headquarters, Area Controls, Regional Divisions, Sections and Organizers as a self-disciplined self-controlled organization....

Technocracy declares that this Continent has a rendezvous with Destiny; that this Continent must decide between Abundance and Chaos within the next few years. Technocracy realizes that this decision must be made by a mass movement of North Americans trained and self-disciplined, capable of operating a technological mechanism of production and distribution on the Continent when the present Price System becomes impotent to operate....

Technocracy offers the specifications and the blueprints of Continental physical operations for the production of abundance for every citizen.[26]

Here we see, first, an organizational structure with an intensive hierarchy that roughly resembles a para-military organization: Headquarters, Controls, Divisions, Sections, etc. Second, it is interesting to note that they had to assure readers that Technocracy, Inc. was "not a financial racket or political party"; apparently they had been accused of both. Third, the Study Course is a blueprint for the future. As such, a blueprint normally contains diagrams of various elevations and details such as are necessary for the complete and forthwith construction of a building or structure. Thus,

---

26   Scott and Hubbard, *Technocracy Study Course*, (Technocracy, Inc., 1934), p. vii.

we should treat the *Technocracy Study Course* with due respect that its purpose is very clear; Scott and Hubbert intended to build a new society that did not currently exist.

In the Preface, a glimpse into the scope of Technocracy is seen:

Technocracy is dealing with social phenomena in the widest sense of the word; *this includes not only actions of human beings, but also everything which directly or indirectly affects their actions.* **Consequently, the studies of Technocracy embrace practically the whole field of science and industry.** *Biology, climate, natural resources, and industrial equipment all enter into the social picture.*[27] [Emphasis added]

There is no doubt that Technocracy, Inc. intended to be an agent of change for a new social structure, although there was nothing that qualified either Scott or Hubbert to play the role of sociologists. That did not hinder them in the slightest. Simply put, they believed that the actions of human beings, both direct and indirect, were the root cause of societal problems and that they were directly related to biology, climate and natural resources. The absence of enlightened scientific management would doom mankind to certain destruction. It is not coincidental that the most visible and manipulative modern agents of change - Sustainable Development, Agenda 21, global warming, the U.N.'s green economy and the modern ecology movement, etc. - all hold to the same underlying assumptions.

Scott's version of Technocracy was intensely focused on energy. Whether human or mechanical, all work involves the expenditure of energy. Humans and beasts of burden eat food, and machines consume electricity, gas, oil, etc. This emphasis on energy was most certainly fine-tuned by the presence of M. King Hubbert who was a well-educated and aspiring geophysicist trained in energy-related science. In 1955, Hubbert went on to create his "Peak Oil Theory", commonly known as Hubbert's Peak, that stated that known reserves of oil would peak and go into decline as demand and consumption increased to an unsustainable level. It is also not coincidental that Hubbert is often revered as a "founding fa-

---

27   Ibid., p. x.

ther" of the modern environmental and Sustainable Development movements.

According to Scott and Hubbert, the distribution of energy resources and the goods they produce must be monitored and measured in order for their system to work. Every engineer knows that you cannot control what you cannot monitor and measure. Both Scott and Hubbert were keenly aware that constant monitoring and precise measuring would enable them to control society with scientific precision.

It is not surprising then that the first five out of seven requirements for Technocracy were:

- *Register on a continuous 24 hour-per-day basis the total net conversion of energy.*

- *By means of the registration of energy converted and consumed, make possible a balanced load.*

- *Provide a continuous inventory of all production and consumption.*

- *Provide a specific registration of the type, kind, etc., of all goods and services, where produced and where used.*

- *Provide specific registration of the consumption of each individual, plus a record and description of the individual.*[28]

In 1934, such technology did not exist. Time was on the Technocrat's side, however, because this technology does exist today, and it is being rapidly implemented to do exactly what Scott and Hubbert specified, namely, to exhaustively monitor, measure and control every facet of individual activity and every ampere of energy delivered and consumed in the life of such individual. The end result of centralized control of all society was clearly spelled out on page 240:

The end-products attained by a high-energy social mechanism on the North American Continent will be:

(a) A high physical standard of living, (b) a high standard of public health, (ç) a minimum of unnecessary labor, (d) a minimum of wastage of non-replaceable resources, (e) an edu-

---

28   Ibid., p. 232.

*cational system to train the entire younger generation indiscriminately as regards all considerations other than inherent ability - **a Continental system of human conditioning.***

***The achievement of these ends will result from a centralized control** with a social organization built along functional lines...*[29] [Emphasis added]

A word must be said about the above mention of the North American continent. Both Scott and Hubbert viewed the entire continent, from Mexico to Canada, as the logical minimum unit for Technocracy. They never specified how such a merger might take place. If Roosevelt had become dictator as proposed by Porter[30], perhaps he might have led a military campaign to conquer our two closest neighbors. Whatever the case, it was presumptuous from the start to assume that Canada and Mexico would willingly participate in Technocracy's utopian scheme, giving up their respective political systems simply because a group of radical engineers suggested it. What is particularly disturbing is Scott's and Hubbert's total disregard for the nation-state and national sovereignty; they would have wiped away both with the stroke of a pen. It is not coincidental that today's call for a New World Order is predicated on the same assumed necessity of eradicating national sovereignty and the structure of the nation-state.

The *Technocracy Study Course* also called for money to be replaced by Energy Certificates which would be issued to all citizens at the start of each new energy accounting period. These certificates could be spent for goods and services during the defined period but would expire just as a new allotment for the next period would be sent. Thus, the accumulation of private wealth would not be possible. Neither Scott nor Hubbert viewed private property or accumulated wealth as allowable in a Technocracy. After all, it was capitalism that caused all the trouble in the first place, and the accumulation of wealth due to ownership of private property was the primary culprit. In a Technocracy, then, all property, resources and the means of production would be held in a public trust for the benefit of all. They reasoned that since all needs for work, leisure and health were to be so abundantly

---

29   Ibid., p. 240.
30   Porter, *Roosevelt and Technocracy*, (Wetzel Publishing Company, 1932).

met, people would willingly trade private property for the utopian dream.

By 1937, the topic of Technocracy had been discussed, analyzed, argued over, rehashed and regurgitated. This was an inevitable outcome given the complex implications of trading one economic system for another. People's fears were ignited by the prospect of such change, and so there was never an end to heated interchanges. By this time, however, Technocracy, Inc. finally produced a concise definition that adequately revealed what it was really all about:

> Technocracy is the **science of social engineering**, the scientific operation of the entire social mechanism to produce and distribute goods and services to the entire population of this continent. For the first time in human history it will be done as a scientific, technical, engineering problem.[31] [Emphasis added]

William Knight

It is not certain how William Knight was originally introduced to Howard Scott, but it was likely through the Technical Alliance that was created by Veblen and Scott in 1919. Scott thought highly enough of Knight to appoint him to be Director of Operations of Technocracy, Inc.

Knight was attributed to have been an associate of the famous electrical engineer and radical socialist, Charles Steinmetz, who is largely credited for his theory and development of alternating current that helped to enable the industrial revolution. Steinmetz was born in Germany but was forced to flee because of his radical essays on socialism, making his way to Greenwich Village in time to join ideological forces with Thorstein Veblen, Howard Scott and the other members of the Technical Alliance in 1919.

Steinmetz was definitely a radical player and decidedly pro-communist. According to one historian, Steinmetz

> ...saw electrification as the chief agency of Socialism and on Lenin's seizure of power he offered to assist "in the technical sphere and particularly in the matter of electrification in a

---

31   "What Is Technocracy?", *The Technocrat*, Vol. 3, No. 4, 1938.

practical way, and with advice." Lenin replied regretting that
he could not take advantage of his offer but enclosing his picture, which Steinmetz promptly placed in a place of honor in
his laboratory.[32]

If Knight were present at meetings of the Technical Alliance,
it would have been Steinmetz, Veblen and Scott who shaped his
views of Technocracy. Even though there were differences of
opinion on the implementation of Technocracy, Knight apparently remained a loyal underling for the rest of his life, in spite
of Technocracy's decline in popularity after the 1930s. However,
there is more to Knight's involvement, as one historian notes,

*Scott placed a man named William Knight in charge of politi-
cal organization. Knight was an aeronautical engineer who
had been employed by various American subsidiaries of the
German aircraft industry.* Knight was clearly a Hitler supporter, and steered Technocracy, Inc. toward the Nazi model. *Scott began to wear a double breasted black suit, gray
shirt and blue neck tie. The Technocracy, Inc. rank and file, in
turn, donned gray uniforms and adopted fascist style salutes
of greeting. They also deployed fleets of metallic gray automobiles and rigid marches and formations. Knight was convinced that for Technocracy to move forward it would have
to recognize that it was a revolutionary movement. Despite
Scott's embrace of his new authoritarian image, however,
Knight was frustrated at Scott's lack of charisma and the de-
cisiveness needed in a modern "Leader."*[33] [Emphasis added]

Original photographs of Technocracy, Inc.'s meetings and activities confirm the rigidly enforced dress code, and while sympathizers may have thought it to be clever, it was very discon-
certing to non-Technocrats. Making a visual connection between
Technocrats and the rise of Hitler in Nazi Germany was not difficult for most Americans.

Knight lobbied Scott to turn Technocracy, Inc. into a revolution,
but Scott refused believing that the certain collapse of capitalism

---

32   Routledge and Paul, *The Rise of the Technocrats: A Social History*, (W.H.G.
Armytage, 1965,1965,) p. 238.
33   Patrick Glenn Zander, *Right modern technology, nation, and Britain's extreme right in
the interwar period (1919--1940)*, (Proquest UMI , 2009), p. 83.

would automatically launch Technocracy into power. In any case, Scott hated politicians and the political system and viewed a "political revolution" as just another expression of politics. Historian William Aiken had this to say about Knight:

> He thought Scott the "greatest prophet since Jesus Christ" but was also certain that "he will never lead a revolution except in Greenwich Village." In Knight's view "Howard is not made out of the stuff of a Lenin, a Mussolini or a Hitler. We must have men who know what a revolution means and how to bring it about."[34]

History does not record much more about Knight, but we can be thankful that his strategy did not prevail and that he remained a loyal follower of Scott, not otherwise attempting an end-run around him to promote open revolution. Technocracy might well have succeeded if Scott had adopted Knight's political theory for action.

In any case, American democracy was found to be unwilling to entertain Technocracy, and it was soundly repudiated for all of these reasons:

- National sovereignty and the Constitutional form of government were not dispensable.

- Nobody was willing to give up private property or the possibility of accumulating private wealth.

- The apparent similarities between Technocracy, Inc. and Nazi fascism were abhorrent to most Americans.

- The grandiose promises of Technocracy were seen as so much "free lunch", and toward the end of the Great Depression, everybody knew from experience that there was no such thing.

Nevertheless, major portions of the Technocracy platform quietly made their way into Roosevelt's New Deal[35] and as World War II progressed, the American public quickly forgot about Technocracy, Inc. and Howard Scott. During WW II from 1940-1943, Technocracy, Inc. was banned in Canada due to accusations of subversive activity. As M. King Hubbert's career advanced with

---

34   Aiken, p. 111.
35   Armytage, p. 240.

major oil companies, he found it in his own interest to formally disassociate himself from Technocracy although he never renounced its principles. William Knight followed his "messiah" until his death. The current offices of Technocracy, Inc. are located in the remote town of Ferndale, Washington state, where many remaining historical documents are stored.

At Columbia University, however, the radical tenets of Technocracy continued in the halls of academia. Columbia has always prided itself for academic interaction among professors, departments and disciplines, and interact they did. Some 40 years later in 1973, Technocracy was destined to reemerge at Columbia under a new name, a new sponsorship and an expanded strategy to dominate the world rather than just the North American continent.

Technocracy and the Third Reich

In both ideology and practice, Technocracy found better soil in Nazi Germany than it did in the United States. At the time, the word "Technocracy" was not yet anathema to the nation's press. For instance in 1933, the New York Times correctly tied together Technocracy and Nazi leaders:

*A strong but non-imperialistic Germany rising to the heights of prosperity through the **proper application of technocracy** was pictured to the German masses in the usual weekend barrage of speeches by Nazi leaders today.*[36] [Emphasis added]

It has been noted that Technocracy in America did not succeed due to a lack of a social strategy with which to implement itself. This was not the case in Germany where Technocracy had grown at the same pace and for the same reasons as in the U.S. The German industrial machine was well acquainted with Taylorism and the application of Scientific Management. Engineering, science and research were highly esteemed as a gateway to future prosperity and strength. Germany felt the pain of the Great Depression to a worse degree than the U.S. because it had never fully recovered from the dislocations and consequences of World War One. Thus,

---

36   "Hitler Demands Troops Lead Reich," *The New York Times*, August 21, 1933.

Germany was driven to excel in all areas of advancement. Its technocratic movement that had started in the 1920s was fully asserting itself by the time Hitler ascended to power.

Dr. Gottfried Feder, secretary to the Minister of the Economy, echoed Technocratic thinking in a 1933 speech before the National Socialists of Danzig:

The liberalistic-capitalistic age long ago exhausted the possibility of consuming production made possible by great technical developments. Thereupon man became the slave of the machine. National socialism, on the other hand, realizes that mighty technical tasks and possibilities have remained which can be solved only by the planned mobilization of technique for the battle against unemployment... the wealth of every people is measured by its capacity to organize its resources.[37]

An earlier *New York Times* article documented some similarities and differences between the German and American Technocracy movements:

Germany has her own technocratic movement in the Technokratische Union with headquarters in Berlin. Although it has taken its name from its American counterpart, it is not an offshoot of the latter but an indigenous growth. Nevertheless, German technocracy, which has just taken organized form, agrees with the American brand on all but two major points.[38]

First, the Germans didn't buy into Scott's system of energy credits, which they termed "electric dollars". Second, they stressed humanism as the religion of technocracy, whereas Scott wanted nothing to do with any kind of religion. However, the points of agreement are revealing: "Like their American economic kin, they are against capitalism, against the profit system and against the gold standard."[39] These commonalities gave reason for more-than-casual communications between Scott and his German counterparts:

The German technocratic union is in touch with Howard

---

[37]   Ibid.
[38]   "Germans Modify Our Technocracy," *The New York Times*, January 22, 1933.
[39]   Ibid.

Scott in New York and dreams of creating an international technocratic organization, which, indeed, its leaders deem indispensable for realizing the technocratic ideal.[40]

Although there was no internal record of Scott's conversations with German technocrats, it is clear that they existed. However, since the Germans were proud inventors and rabid nationalists, extensive effort was expended to position themselves as the sole arbiters of rational Technocracy, even though they worked in the mostly irrational system of National Socialism. The German version needed to be sold to its citizens as "made-in-Germany". The facts undermined the reality of the matter. Three years of the German journal of Technocracy, *Technokratie*, was surveyed and found to contain a heavy concentration of translated reprints from Technocracy journals in America.[41] As a submerged movement, Technocracy lived on in Germany, but as a public movement, it was summarily axed by the German government in 1935:

The journal Technokratie and with it the German Technocratic Society came to a sudden end in 1935, ironically just when opportunities for technocrats within the Nationalist State began to improve. The Third Reich had room for individual technocrats, but not for a technocratic movement.[42]

Thus, as in America, when the *movement* of Technocracy collided with the existing political structure, it was rejected. In the United States, it was Roosevelt and his New Deal, and in Germany it was Hitler and Nazi Socialism. Political rejection had no impact on Technocracy because technocrats believed that their vision of the future was all but guaranteed, regardless of political resistance. If Technocracy could be likened to a submarine, it simply closed the hatch and submerged in order to continue its mission unseen and undetected. Of the former members of the formal movement, there is no record of any repudiation of their technocratic ideology, methodologies or practices; they simply continued on as before, communicating in private but without a meeting hall.

---

40   Ibid.
41   Monika Renneberg and Mark Walker, *Scientists, engineers and National Socialism, Science, Technology and National Socialism* (Cambridge University Press, 1994), p.5.
42   Ibid.

Renneberg and Walker's detailed study on *Technocracy and National Socialism* concluded with this blunt statement:

Technocracy, like technology, is fundamentally ambivalent and proved compatible with the most extreme aspects of German Fascism. Without technocracy, the most barbaric, irrational and backward-looking policies of the Third Reich, including, "euthanasia", involuntary sterilization, the brutal repression of the Socialist movement, ruthless imperialism, ideological warfare on the Eastern front, genocide and efforts to create a "master race" would have been impossible.[43]

After Germany's defeat in WWII, many of the direct perpetrators of "crimes against humanity" were brought to justice during the famous Nuremberg trials. The Technocrats, however, as *indirect enablers* were not seen as ones who should be held accountable for anything, and indeed, they became an important part of the war reparations process and were carted off to other Western nations to resume their scientific and engineering duties in the service of other governments.

Indeed, American technocrats and sympathizers within the U.S. Government were quick to rescue and provide cover for their German counterparts. A top-secret program called Operation Paperclip commenced in 1944 that sought to bring top Nazi scientists to America under secret military contracts while whitewashing their past and high-ranking connections with Nazi Socialism. Annie Jacobson notes in her recent 575-page book on *Operation Paperclip,*

The program had a benign public face and a classified body of secrets and lies. "I'm mad on technology," Adolf Hitler told his inner circle at a dinner party in 1942, and in the aftermath of the German surrender more than sixteen hundred of Hitler's technologists would become America's own.[44]

These were the same technologists who eagerly gave Hitler almost total victory over all of Europe!

The famous rocket scientist Wernher von Braun, for instance, was a prominent member of the Nazi party and also a member

---

43   Ibid., p. 11.
44   Annie Jacobsen, *Operation Paperclip*, (Little Brown & Co., 2014).

of Hitler's SS. Under Hitler's command, he ran an underground slave labor facility where his rockets were being built. After his relocation (along with other members of his engineering team) to the U.S. via Operation Paperclip, von Braun went on to design the rockets that put America's spaceship on the moon, but not before becoming a naturalized citizen in 1955.

In another example, the inventor of the ear thermometer, Dr. Theodor H. Benzinger, worked at the Naval Medical Research Institute from 1947 to 1970. He ultimately held 40 patents on his inventions. When Benzinger passed in 1999 at the age of 94, he was eulogized in glowing terms by the *New York Times*, but not one word was mentioned about the work he performed on concentration camp prisoners in Nazi Germany during WWII.

In a more transparent setting, devoid of Operation Paperclip cloaking, both men would have likely stood trial at Nuremberg with the rest of their war criminal associates. Instead, the European brand of Technocracy quietly melded back into its American counterpart and continued on as if nothing had happened.

Rebirth

Whatever Technocracy represented in the 1930s and earlier, it was cleverly regurgitated in **Zbigniew Brzezinski's** book *Between Two Ages: America's Role in the Technetronic Era*. This book was never a "best seller" on any literary list, but it was the book that caught the eye and admiration of **David Rockefeller**. The Rockefeller dynasty, and David in particular, had always had a difficult time maintaining good public relations with the American public. Collectively, the Rockefellers represented the global-minded Eastern Establishment that was bent on selling American sovereignty to international interests. Simply put, Rockefeller needed a young blood academic like Brzezinski in order to justify his own globalist dreams.

The fact that Brzezinski was a professor at Columbia University opens up a necessary side note regarding the connection between the Rockefeller family and Columbia. In 1928, John D. Rockefeller, Jr. leased the ground to develop the future Rockefeller Center in New York City - from Columbia University. In fact, Rockefeller took on a 27 year lease with three 21-year options to renew, for a total of 87 years lease. The lease was cut short in 1985 after 52 years when Columbia agreed to sell the 11.7 acres of land under the Rockefeller Center to the Rockefeller Group for a tidy all-cash sum of $400 million. It was a record price for any single parcel ever sold in New York City. To put this windfall into perspective, the total value of Columbia's existing endowment at the time was reported to be only $683 million. When adding to that sum 52 years of lease payments, reported to be $11.1 million per year in 1973 onward, the Rockefeller clan can be seen as a major benefactor of Columbia University, if not *the* major benefactor in the 20ᵗʰ century.

But Rockefeller family involvement with Columbia predated the Rockefeller Center leasing arrangement by at least several years. In 1919, John D. Rockefeller financed the building of Teachers College Columbia University with a $1 million one-time gift, which was noted at the time as being the largest gift ever made to an institution for training teachers.[45]

Understanding these connections may explain why Rockefeller turned to Columbia when he picked Brzezinski to be his principal ideologue for the next 40 plus years. It is inconceivable that both were unaware of the history of Technocracy at Columbia during the 1930s. In his book, *Between Two Ages*, Brzezinski expanded upon the original Technocracy that was originally limited to the North American continent, to one of a global nature but with virtually identical ends:

[The technetronic era] involves the gradual appearance of a more controlled and directed society. Such a society would be dominated by an elite whose claim to political power would rest on allegedly superior scientific know-how. Unhindered by the restraints of traditional liberal values, this elite would not hesitate to achieve its political ends by using the latest modern techniques for influencing public behavior and keeping society under close surveillance and control.[46]

Brzezinski gave a succinct background that led up to his

---

45   "Rockefeller Gifts Total $530,853,632", *New York Times*, May 24, 1937.
46   Zbigniew Brzezinski, *Between Two Ages: America's Role in the Technetronic Era*, (Viking Press, 1970), p 97.

Technetronic Era. He wrote that mankind had moved through three great stages of evolution and was in the middle of the fourth and final stage. The first stage he described as "religious", combining a heavenly "universalism provided by the acceptance of the idea that man's destiny is essentially in God's hands" with an earthly "narrowness derived from massive ignorance, illiteracy, and a vision confined to the immediate environment."[47]

The second stage was nationalism, stressing Christian equality before the law, which "marked another giant step in the progressive redefinition of man's nature and place in our world." The third stage was Marxism, which, said Brzezinski, "represents a further vital and creative stage in the maturing of man's universal vision." The fourth and final stage was Brzezinski's Technetronic Era, or the "ideal of rational humanism on a global scale - the result of American-Communist evolutionary transformations."[48]

In considering our current structure of governance, Brzezinski stated,

Tension is unavoidable as man strives to assimilate the new into the framework of the old. For a time the established framework resiliently integrates the new by adapting it in a more familiar shape. But at some point the old framework becomes overloaded. The newer input can no longer be redefined into traditional forms, and eventually it asserts itself with compelling force. Today, though, the old framework of international politics - with their spheres of influence, military alliances between nation-states, the fiction of sovereignty, doctrinal conflicts arising from nineteenth century crises - is clearly no longer compatible with reality.[49]

One of the most important "frameworks" in the world, and especially to Americans, is the Constitution of the United States. It was this document that outlined and enabled the most prosperous nation in the history of the world. Was our sovereignty really "fiction"? Was the American vision no longer compatible with reality? Brzezinski further stated,

The approaching two-hundredth anniversary of the Declara-

---

47   Ibid.
48   Ibid., p. 246.
49   Ibid.

tion of Independence could justify the call for a national constitutional convention to reexamine the nation's formal institutional framework. Either 1976 or 1989 - the two-hundredth anniversary of the Constitution - could serve as a suitable target date culminating a national dialogue on the relevance of existing arrangements.... Realism, however, forces us to recognize that the necessary political innovation will not come from direct constitutional reform, desirable as that would be. The needed change is more likely to develop incrementally and less overtly...in keeping with the American tradition of blurring distinctions between public and private institutions.[50]

In Brzezinski's Technetronic Era then, the "nation-state as a fundamental unit of man's organized life has ceased to be the principal creative force: International banks and multinational corporations are acting and planning in terms that are far in advance of the political concepts of the nation-state."[51]

Brzezinski's philosophy clearly pointed forward to **Richard Gardner**'s *Hard Road to World Order* that appeared in Foreign Affairs in 1974, where Gardner stated,

In short, the "house of world order" would have to be built from the bottom up rather than from the top down. It will look like a great "booming, buzzing confusion", to use William James' famous description of reality, but an end run around national sovereignty, eroding it piece by piece, will accomplish much more than the old-fashioned frontal assault.[52]

That former approach which had produced few successes during the 1950s and 1960s was being traded for a velvet sledgehammer. It would make little noise but would still drive the spikes of globalization deep into the heart of nations around the world, including the United States. Indeed, the Trilateral Commission, jointly established by Brzezinski and Rockefeller, was the chosen vehicle that finally got the necessary traction to actually *create* their New International Economic Order.

In over 40 years since the founding of the Trilateral Commission,

---

50   Ibid.

51   Ibid.

52   Richard Gardner, "The Hard Road to World Order", *Foreign Affairs*, (1974), p. 558.

the historical record clearly testifies to its success. The applied doctrines of Agenda 21, Sustainable Development and the energy Smart Grid that have resulted from Trilateral interactions testify to their ideological grounding in historic Technocracy.

CHAPTER 3

THE TRILATERAL COMMISSION

President Reagan ultimately came to understand Trilateral's value and invited the entire membership to a reception at the White House in April 1984 - David Rockefeller, Memoirs, 2002[52]

First Signs of Concern

M y interest in the Trilateral Commission started soon after the presidential election of **Jimmy Carter**[53] and **Walter Mondale**. As a young financial analyst and writer, I carefully followed Carter's initial round of appointees to the top positions in his cabinet and other important posts. After all, Carter had made a big campaign pitch about being an "establishment outsider" with few contacts within the Beltway. Who would he bring to the table? As the list of appointees piled up, I noticed that several were members in the Trilateral Commission, whatever that was, and my curiosity was immediately peaked. After digging up and sifting through a list of Trilateral Commission members, and seeing over a dozen Trilateral appointees, it became immediately obvious that some sort of coup was underway, but what?

It was about this time that Antony C. Sutton entered my life. We both were attending one of the first major gold conferences in New Orleans where he had been invited to speak about his new book, *The War on Gold*. The hotel was probably too small for the size of the conference because every area was packed with people, including the in-hotel coffee shop where we had to eat breakfast. By the time I arrived at the restaurant, there were no empty tables to be found. The host told me that if I wanted to eat, he would have to seat me anywhere he could find an open seat at a table. Reluctantly, I followed him to a small booth where a complete stranger was already halfway through his meal.

---

52   David Rockefeller, *Memoirs* (Random House, 2002), p.418.
53   Note: For clarification, Trilateral Commission member names are in bold.

I had no idea who this person was and probably didn't care too much because I was very hungry and anxious to get off to the first presentation. When we introduced ourselves with small talk, I was immediately taken by his British accent and genteel mannerisms and found him quite easy to talk to. Within a few minutes I learned that he was an economics professor and research fellow who had just been forced out of The Hoover Institution for War, Peace and Revolution at Stanford University. He was clearly shaken because academia was his life and Stanford was his publisher; after all, they had already published his monumental and internationally acclaimed series on the transfer of technology from the West to the East. I later learned that when Sutton was on a research "hunt", he never left a single stone unturned. In fact, his co-scholars at Hoover jokingly called him the "Hoover vacuum cleaner" because of his voracious appetite for details.

When Sutton told me that he was forced out of Hoover by **David Packard**, the president of Stanford, I immediately remembered seeing his (Packard's) name on the membership list of the Trilateral Commission. Packard was also founder and chairman of Hewlett-Packard. Apparently, Sutton's professional research had begun to focus on this group of people, many of whom he had researched in other study projects. Like me, he also began to wonder why they were popping up all over the Carter Administration. In any case, Packard apparently decided to shut down the "vacuum cleaner" before he got any further in his research.

When both of us realized that we were tracking the same group of elitists, even if from different backgrounds, our conversation immediately became intense. Both of us finished breakfast and were still talking until others let us know we had the table to ourselves long enough, but not before we shook hands on the very pressing need to collaborate on getting out the story of the Trilateral Commission. Within weeks we started a monthly newsletter, *Trilateral Observer*, in order to release the initial results of our research as quickly and smoothly as possible. After two years, we used this material to compile and publish two books, *Trilaterals Over Washington, Volumes I* and *II*. As more people read our material, we began to get requests for radio and television interviews. Before Carter's term was completed, we had appeared on well over 350 radio programs all over the country.

The crowning media event was my appearance on the Larry King Show in Washington, DC, where he was a late-night host for the largest radio network in the nation, Mutual Broadcasting. In fact, I sat across the table from **Charles Heck,** who was the Executive Director of the Trilateral Commission at the time. What was supposed to be a one-hour point-counterpoint debate with Heck stretched into a three-hour marathon. To Larry King's astonishment, the switchboards were lit up and the callers were angrily attacking Mr. Heck as he shared what the Commission was attempting to do. Since most callers didn't have their facts straight, I was able to gently correct them and lay out the actual record, with direct quotes from Trilaterals themselves and their Trilateral publications. Although I ended up defending Heck from being misrepresented, my factual material made him look all the worse and the next round of callers were even more angry. When the show ended, Larry King thanked us and shook his head, genuinely astounded, and exclaimed, "I have never seen anything like this in my life."

The next day, I received a frantic call from B. Dalton Booksellers saying that they were getting calls from all over the country requesting *Trilaterals Over Washington* and could I please express a couple of review copies to them so that they could assemble their first stocking order. Well, I sent the books, but they never called back and an order never materialized; in fact, upon calling several B. Dalton stores across the country, Sutton and I heard repeatedly that the book was out of print and the publisher was out of business. Really?

Yes, we had been blacklisted by one of the largest book selling chains in the nation! Upon further investigation, we discovered a close connection to a member of the Trilateral Commission sitting on the board of directors of B. Dalton's parent company, Dayton Hudson, which is now Target. We also never heard another peep out of Larry King or Mutual Broadcasting Radio.

Trilateral Basics

The idea to create the Trilateral Commission was first informally presented to people at the elitist Bilderberg group meeting in Europe in 1972, by **David Rockefeller** and **Zbigniew Brzezinski**. They had flown there together for just that purpose, and because they were encouraged by so many of their elitist brethren, they returned to the U.S. and formed the Commission in 1973.

According to each issue of the official Trilateral Commission quarterly magazine *Trialogue,*

> *The Trilateral Commission was formed in 1973 by private citizens of Western Europe, Japan and North America to foster closer cooperation among these three regions on common problems. It seeks to improve public understanding of such problems, to support proposals for handling them jointly, and to nurture habits and practices of working together among these regions.*[54]

Further, *Trialogue* and other official writings made clear their stated goal of creating a "New International Economic Order". President **George H.W. Bush** later talked openly about creating a "New World Order", which has since become a synonymous phrase.

Rockefeller was chairman of the ultra-powerful Chase Manhattan Bank, a director of many major multinational corporations and "endowment funds" and had long been a central figure in the Council on Foreign Relations (CFR). Brzezinski, a brilliant strategist for one-world idealism, was a professor at Columbia University and the author of several books that have served as "policy guidelines" for the Trilateral Commission. Brzezinski served as the Commission's first executive director from its inception in 1973 until late 1976 when he was appointed by President **Jimmy Carter** as Assistant to the President for National Security Affairs.

The initial Commission membership consisted of approximately three hundred people, with roughly one hundred each from Europe, Japan and North America. Membership was also roughly

---

54   *Trialogue*, Trilateral Commission (1973).

divided among academics, politicians and corporate magnates; these included international bankers, leaders of prominent labor unions and corporate directors of media giants.

The word "commission" was puzzling since it is usually associated with instrumentalities set up by governments. It seemed out of place for a private group unless we could determine that it really was an arm of a government, an unseen government, different from the visible government in Washington. The inclusion of European and Japanese members indicated a global government rather than a national government. We hoped that the concept of a sub-rosa world government was just wishful thinking on the part of the Trilateral Commissioners. The facts, however, lined up quite pessimistically.

It is important to note that Brzezinski and Rockefeller did not initially seek advice from the Council on Foreign Relations but rather from the global Bilderberg group. If the Council on Foreign Relations could be said to be a spawning ground for many of the concepts of one-world idealism, then the Trilateral Commission was the "task force" assembled to assault the beachhead. Already the Commission had placed its members in the top posts the U.S. had to offer.

President **James Earl Carter**, the Georgia peanut farmer turned politician who promised, "I will never lie to you," was chosen to join the Commission by Brzezinski in 1973. It was Brzezinski, in fact, who first identified Carter as presidential timber, and subsequently educated him in economics, foreign policy, and the ins-and-outs of world politics. Upon Carter's election, his first appointment placed Brzezinski as assistant to the president for national security matters. More commonly, he was called the head of the National Security Council because he answered only to the president; some rightly said Brzezinski held the second most powerful position in the U.S.

Carter's running mate, **Walter Mondale**, was also a member of the Commission.

On January 7, 1977 *Time Magazine*, whose editor-in-chief, **Hedley Donovan** was a powerful Trilateral, named President Carter "Man of the Year". The sixteen-page article in that issue not only failed to mention Carter's connection with the Trilateral Commission but also stated the following:

> As he searched for Cabinet appointees, Carter seemed at times hesitant and frustrated disconcertingly out of character. His lack of ties to Washington and the Party Establishment - qualities that helped raise him to the White House - carry potential dangers. He does not know the Federal Government or the pressures it creates. He does not really know the politicians whom he will need to help him run the country.[55]

Was this portrait of Carter as a political innocent simply inaccurate or was it deliberately misleading? By December 25, 1976, two weeks before the *Time* article appeared, Carter had already chosen his cabinet. Three of his cabinet members, **Cyrus Vance**, **Michael Blumenthal**, and **Harold Brown,** were Trilateral Commissioners and the other non-Commission members were not unsympathetic to Commission objectives and operations. In total, Carter appointed no fewer than twenty Trilateral Commissioners to top government posts, including:

- **Zbigniew Brzezinski** - National Security Advisor
- **Cyrus Vance** - Secretary of State
- **Harold Brown** - Secretary of Defense
- **W. Michael Blumenthal** - Secretary of the Treasury
- **Warren Christopher** - Deputy Secretary of State
- **Lucy Wilson Benson** - Under Secretary of State for Security Affairs
- **Richard Cooper** - Under Secretary of State for Economic Affairs
- **Richard Holbrooke** - Under Secretary of State for East Asian and Pacific Affairs
- **Sol Linowitz** - co-negotiator on the Panama Canal Treaty
- **Gerald Smith** - Ambassador-at-Large for Nuclear Power Negotiations
- **Elliott Richardson** - Delegate to the Law of the Sea Conference

---

55   "Jimmy Carter: Man of the Year", *Time Magazine*, January 7, 1977.

- **Richard Gardner** - Ambassador to Italy
- **Anthony Solomon** - Under Secretary of the Treasury for Monetary Affairs
- **Paul Warnke** - Director, Arms Control and Disarmament Agency
- **Robert R. Bowie** - Deputy Director of Intelligence For National Estimates
- **C. Fred Bergsten** - Under Secretary of Treasury
- **James Schlesinger** - Secretary of Energy
- **Elliot Richardson** - Delegate to Law of the Sea
- **Leonard Woodcock** - Chief envoy to China
- **Andrew Young** - Ambassador to the United Nations

When you include Carter and Mondale, these Commission members represented almost one-third of the entire membership from the United States roster.

Was there even the slightest evidence to indicate anything other than collusion? Hardly! **Zbigniew Brzezinski** spelled out the qualifications of a 1976 presidential winner in 1973:

The Democratic candidate in 1976 will have to emphasize work, the family, religion and, increasingly, patriotism....The new conservatism will clearly not go back to laissez faire. It will be a philosophical conservatism. It will be a kind of conservative statism or managerism. There will be conservative values but a reliance on a great deal of co-determination between state and the corporations.[56]

On May 23, 1976 journalist Leslie H. Gelb wrote in the not-so-conservative *New York Times*, "[Brzezinski] was the first guy in the Community to pay attention to Carter, to take him seriously. He spent time with Carter, talked to him, sent him books and articles, educated him."[57] **Richard Gardner** (also of Columbia University) joined into the "educational" task, and as Gelb noted, between the two of them they had Carter virtually to themselves. Gelb continued: "While the Community as a whole was looking elsewhere, to Senators Kennedy and Mondale...it paid off. Brzezinski, with

---

56   Sutton & Wood, *Trilaterals Over Washington* (August, 1979), p. 7.
57   Leslie Gelb, "Jimmy Carter", *New York Times*, May 23, 1976.

Gardner, was now the leading man on Carter's foreign policy task force."[58]

Although **Richard Gardner** was of considerable academic influence, it should be clear that Brzezinski was the "guiding light" of foreign policy in the Carter administration. Along with Commissioner Vance and a host of other Commissioners in the State Department, Brzezinski had more than continued the policies of befriending our enemies and alienating our friends. Since early 1977 we had witnessed a massive push to attain "normalized" relations with Communist China, Cuba, the USSR, Eastern European nations, Angola, etc. Conversely, we had withdrawn at least some support from Nationalist China, South Africa, Zimbabwe (formerly Rhodesia), etc. It was not just a trend: It was an epidemic.

Needed: A More Just and Equitable World Order

The Trilateral Commission held their annual plenary meeting in Tokyo, Japan, in January 1977. Carter and Brzezinski obviously could not attend as they were still in the process of reorganizing the White House. They did, however, address personal letters to the meeting, which were reprinted in *Trialogue*, the official magazine of the Commission:

It gives me special pleasure to send greetings to all of you gathering for the Trilateral Commission meeting in Tokyo. I have warm memories of our meeting in Tokyo some eighteen months ago, and am sorry I cannot be with you now.

My active service on the Commission since its inception in 1973 has been a splendid experience for me, and it provided me with excellent opportunities to come to know leaders in our three regions.

As I emphasized in my campaign, a strong partnership among us is of the greatest importance. We share economic, political and security concerns that make it logical we should seek ever-increasing cooperation and understanding. And this cooperation is essential not only for our three regions, but in the global search for a more just and equitable world

---

58   ibid.

order. I hope to see you on the occasion of your next meeting in Washington, and I look forward to receiving reports on your work in Tokyo.

Jimmy Carter[59]

Brzezinski's letter, in a similar vein, follows:

The Trilateral Commission has meant a great deal to me over the last few years. It has been the stimulus for intellectual creativity and a source of personal satisfaction. I have formed close ties with new friends and colleagues in all three regions, ties which I value highly and which I am sure will continue.

I remain convinced that, on the larger architectural issues of today, collaboration among our regions is of the utmost necessity. This collaboration must be dedicated to the fashioning of a more just and equitable world order. This will require a prolonged process, but I think we can look forward with confidence and take some pride in the contribution which the Commission is making.

Zbigniew Brzezinski[60]

The key phrase in both letters was "more just and equitable world order". Did this emphasis indicate that something was wrong with our present world order, that is, with national structures? Yes, according to Brzezinski, and since the present "framework" was inadequate to handle world problems, it must be done away with and supplanted with a system of global governance.

In September 1974, Brzezinski was asked in an interview by the Brazilian newspaper *Veja*, "How would you define this New World Order?" Brzezinski answered:

When I speak of the present international system I am referring to relations in specific fields, most of all among the Atlantic countries: commercial, military, mutual security relations, involving the international monetary fund, NATO etc. We need to change the international system for a global system in which new, active and creative forces recently developed - should be integrated. This system needs to include

59   "Looking Back ¦And Forward," *Trialogue*, (Trilateral Commission, 1976)
60   ibid.

*Japan, Brazil, the oil producing countries, and even the USSR,
to the extent which the Soviet Union is willing to participate
in a global system.*[61]

When asked if Congress would have an expanded or diminished role in the new system, Brzezinski declared, "the reality of
our times is that a modern society such as the U.S. needs a central
coordinating and renovating organ which cannot be made up of
six hundred people."[62]

Understanding the philosophy of the Trilateral Commission
was and is the only way to reconcile the myriad of apparent con-
tradictions in the information filtered through the national press.
For instance, how was it that the Marxist regime in Angola derived the great bulk of its foreign exchange from the offshore oil
operations of Gulf Oil Corporation? Why did Andrew Young insist
that "Communism has never been a threat to Blacks in Africa"?
Why did the U.S. funnel billions in technological aid to the Soviet
Union and Communist China? Why did the U.S. apparently help
its enemies while chastising its friends?

A similar and perplexing question is asked by millions of
Americans today: Why do we spend trillions on the "War on
Terror" around the world and yet ignore the Mexican/U.S. bor-
der and the tens of thousands of illegal aliens who freely enter
the U.S. each and every month? These "illegals" include not only
Mexicans, but many other nationalities from Central and South
America and from Mideast countries.

These questions, and hundreds of others like them, cannot be
explained in any other way: The U.S. Executive Branch was not an-
ti-Marxist or anti-Communist; it has tread on the stepping stones
of Marxism as it marched toward Brzezinski's Technetronic Era.
In other words, those ideals which led to the heinous abuses of
Hitler, Lenin, Stalin, and Mussolini were now being accepted as
necessary inevitability by our elected and appointed leaders.

This hardly suggests the Great American Dream. It is very
doubtful that Americans would agree with Brzezinski or the
Trilateral Commission. It is the American public who is paying

---

61   *Veja Magazine*, (Brazil, 1974).
62   ibid.

the price, suffering the consequences, but not understanding the true nature of the situation.

This nature, however, was not unknown or unknowable. It was never secret, per se. Senator Barry Goldwater (R-AZ) issued a clear and precise warning in his 1979 book, *With No Apologies*:

> The Trilateral Commission is international and is intended to be the vehicle for multinational consolidation of the commercial and banking interests by seizing control of the political government of the United States. The Trilateral Commission represents a skillful, coordinated effort to seize control and consolidate the four centers of power - political, monetary, intellectual and ecclesiastical.[63]

Follow the Money, Follow the Power

What was the economic nature of the driving force within the Trilateral Commission? It was the giant multinational corporations - those with Trilateral representation - which consistently benefited from Trilateral policy and actions. Polished academics such as Brzezinski, Gardner, Allison, McCracken, Henry Owen etc., served only to give "philosophical" justification to the exploitation of the world.

Don't underestimate their power or the distance they had already come by 1976. Their economic base was already established. Giants like Coca-Cola, IBM, CBS, Caterpillar Tractor, Bank of America, Chase Manhattan Bank, Deere & Company, Exxon, and others virtually dwarf whatever remains of American businesses. The market value of IBM's stock alone, for instance, was greater than the value of all the stocks on the American Stock Exchange. Chase Manhattan Bank had some fifty thousand branches or correspondent banks throughout the world. What reached our eyes and ears was highly regulated by CBS, the *New York Times*, *Time Magazine*, etc.

The most important thing of all is to remember that the political coup de grâce preceded the economic coup de grâce. The domination of the Executive Branch of the U.S. government pro-

---

63   Barry Goldwater, *With No Apologies*, (Morrow, 1979), p. 280.

vided all the necessary political leverage needed to skew U.S. and global economic policies to their own benefit.

By 1977, the Trilateral Commission had notably become expert at using crises to manage countries toward the New World Order; yet, they found menacing backlashes from those very crises that they tried to manipulate.

In the end, the biggest crisis of all was that of the American way of life. Americans never counted on such powerful and influential groups working against the Constitution and freedom, either inadvertently or purposefully, and even now, the principles that helped to build this great country are all but reduced to the sound of meaningless babbling.

Trilateral Entrenchment: 1980-2007

It would have been damaging enough if the Trilateral domination of the Carter administration was merely a one-time anomaly, but it was not!

Subsequent presidential elections brought **George H.W. Bush** (under Reagan), **William Jefferson Clinton**, **Albert Gore** and **Richard Cheney** (under G. W. Bush) to power.

Thus, every Administration since Carter has had top-level Trilateral Commission representation through the President or Vice-president, or both! It is important to note that Trilateral hegemony has transcended political parties; they have dominated - and continue to dominate - both the Republican and Democrat parties with equal aplomb.

In addition, the Administration before Carter was very friendly and useful to Trilateral doctrine as well; President Gerald Ford took the reins after President Richard Nixon resigned and then appointed Nelson Rockefeller as his Vice President. Neither Ford nor Rockefeller were members of the Trilateral Commission, but Nelson was **David Rockefeller**'s brother and that says enough. According to Nelson Rockefeller's memoirs, he originally introduced then-governor **Jimmy Carter** to David and Brzezinski.

How has the Trilateral Commission orchestrated their goal of creating a New International Economic Order? Most notably, they seated their own members at the top of the institutions of global trade, global banking and foreign policy.

For instance, the World Bank is one of the most critical mechanisms in the engine of globalization.[64] Since the founding of the Trilateral Commission in 1973, there have been only seven World Bank presidents, all of whom were appointed by the President. Of these eight, six were pulled from the ranks of the Trilateral Commission!

Robert McNamara (1968-1981)

A.W. Clausen (1981-1986)

Barber Conable (1986-1991)

Lewis Preston (1991-1995)

James Wolfenson (1995-2005)

Paul Wolfowitz (2005-2007)

Robert Zoellick (2007-2012)

Jim Yong Kim (2012-Present)

Another good evidence of domination is the position of U.S. Trade Representative (USTR), which is critically involved in negotiating the many international trade treaties and agreements that have been necessary to create the New International Economic Order. Since 1977, there have been twelve USTRs appointed by the President. Nine have been members of the Trilateral Commission!

Robert S. Strauss (1977-1979)

Reubin O'D. Askew (1979-1981)

William E. Brock III (1981-1985)

Clayton K. Yeutter (1985-1989)

Carla A. Hills (1989-1993)

Mickey Kantor (1993-1997)

Charlene Barshefsky (1997-2001)

Robert Zoellick (2001-2005)

---

64   Patrick Wood, "Global Banking: The World Bank", *The August Forecast & Review.*

Rob Portman (2005-2006)

Susan Schwab (2006-2009)

Ron Kirk (2009-2013)

Michael Froman (2013-Present)

This is not to say that Clayton Yeuter, Rob Portman and Ron Kirk were not friendly to Trilateral goals because they clearly were, and each had significant involvement with other Trilateral members in the past.

The Secretary of State cabinet position has seen its share of Trilaterals as well: **Henry Kissinger** (Nixon, Ford), **Cyrus Vance** (Carter), **Alexander Haig** (Reagan), **George Shultz** (Reagan), **Lawrence Eagleburger** (G.H.W. Bush), **Warren Christopher** (Clinton) and **Madeleine Albright** (Clinton) There were some Acting Secretaries of State that are also noteworthy: **Philip Habib** (Carter), **Michael Armacost** (G.H.W. Bush), **Arnold Kantor** (Clinton), **Richard Cooper** (Clinton). Hillary Clinton (Obama) was not a Trilateral, but her husband, **William Clinton**, was.

Lastly, it should be noted that the Federal Reserve has likewise been dominated by Trilaterals: **Arthur Burns** (1970-1978), **Paul Volker** (1979-1987), **Alan Greenspan** (1987-2006). While the Federal Reserve is a privately-owned corporation, the President "chooses" the Chairman to a perpetual appointment. The more recent heads of the Federal Reserve, Ben Bernanke and Janet Yelen, are not members of the Trilateral Commission, but they clearly followed the same globalist policies as their predecessors.

The point raised here is that Trilateral domination over the U.S. Executive Branch has not only continued but has been strengthened from 1976 to the present. The pattern has been deliberate and persistent: Appoint members of the Trilateral Commission to critical positions of power so that they can carry out Trilateral policies.

The question is and has always been, do these policies originate in consensus meetings of the Trilateral Commission where two-thirds of the members are not U.S. citizens? The answer is all too obvious.

Trilateral-friendly defenders attempt to sweep criticism aside by suggesting that membership in the Trilateral Commission is incidental and that it only demonstrates the otherwise high quality of appointees. Are we to believe that in a country of 317 million people only these 100 or so are qualified to hold such critical positions? Again, the answer is all too obvious.

Where Does the Council on Foreign Relations Fit?

While virtually all Trilateral Commission members from North America have also been members of the CFR, the reverse is certainly not true. It is natural to over-criticize the CFR because most of its members seem to fill the balance of government positions not already filled by Trilaterals.

The power structure of the Council is seen in the makeup of its board of directors: No less than 44 percent (12 out of 27) are members of the Commission! If director participation reflected only the general membership of the CFR, then only 3-4 percent of the board would be Trilaterals.[65]

Further, the president of the CFR is **Richard N. Haass**, a very prominent Trilateral member who also served as Director of Policy Planning for the U.S. Department of State from 2001-2003.

Trilateral influence can easily be seen in policy papers produced by the CFR in support of Trilateral goals.

For instance, the 2005 CFR task force report on the *Future of North America* was perhaps the major Trilateral policy statement on the intended creation of the North American Union. Vice-chair of the task force was Dr. Robert A. Pastor who emerged as the "Father of the North American Union" and was directly involved in Trilateral operations since the 1970s. While the CFR claimed that the task force was "independent", careful inspection of those appointed reveal that three Trilaterals were carefully chosen to oversee the Trilateral position, one each from Mexico, Canada and the United States: **Luis Rubio**, **Wendy K. Dobson** and **Carla A. Hills**, respectively.[66] Hills has been widely hailed as the principal

---

65   Board of Directors, *Council on Foreign Relations*, http://www.cfr.org/about/people/board_of_directors.html.

66   "Building a North American Community", *Council on Foreign Relations*, (2005).

architect of the North American Free Trade Agreement (NAFTA) that was negotiated under President **George H.W. Bush** in 1992.

The bottom line is that the Council on Foreign Relations, thoroughly dominated by Trilaterals, serves the interests of the Trilateral Commission and not the other way around!

Trilateral Globalization in Europe

The content of this chapter thus far suggests ties between the Trilateral Commission and the United States. This is not intended to mean that Trilaterals are not active in other countries as well. Recalling the early years of the Commission, **David Rockefeller** wrote in 1998,

> *Back in the early Seventies, the hope for a more united EUROPE was already full-blown - thanks in many ways to the individual energies previously spent by so many of the Trilateral Commission's earliest members.*[67] *[Capitals in original]*

Thus, since 1973 and in parallel with their U.S. hegemony, the European members of the Trilateral Commission were busy creating the European Union (EU). In fact, the EU's Constitution was authored by Commission member **Valery Giscard d'Estaing** in 2002-2003 when he was President of the Convention on the Future of Europe.

The steps that led to the creation of the European Union are unsurprisingly similar to the steps being taken to create the North American Union today. As with the EU, lies, deceit and confusion are the principal tools used to keep an unsuspecting citizenry in the dark while they forge ahead without mandate, accountability or oversight.

Case Study: NAFTA Explained

It is necessary to have a practical understanding of the methods used by the Trilateral Commission to achieve their New International Economic Order. To this end, our discussion must digress to the topic of trade treaties, agreements and regulations, and exactly how they have been used against us. As boring as that

---

67   David Rockefeller, *In the Beginning: The Trilateral Commission at 25*, (Trilateral Commission, 1998), p.11.

may sound, it actually provides all the elements of a made-for-TV drama: Collusion, secrecy, manipulation and deceit. One must use detective-like skills to grasp the modus operandi. As you discover how the game works, you will understand every current and future plot as well. You will also understand why nine out twelve U.S. Trade Representatives, who lead the trade negotiations, have all been members of the Trilateral Commission.

In Article 1, Section 8 of the U.S. Constitution, authority is granted to Congress "To regulate commerce with foreign nations." An effective end-run around this insurmountable obstacle would be to convince Congress to voluntarily turn over this power to the President. With such authority in hand, the President could freely negotiate treaties and other trade agreements with foreign nations and then simply present them to Congress for a straight up or down vote requiring only a simple 51 percent majority instead of 66 percent, with no amendments possible. This again points out elite disdain for a Congress that is elected to be representative "of the people, by the people and for the people."

The first so-called "Fast Track" legislation (officially known as Trade Promotion Authority) was passed by Congress in 1974, just one year after the founding of the Trilateral Commission. It was the same year that Nelson Rockefeller was confirmed as Vice President under President Gerald Ford, neither of whom were elected by the U.S. Public; Ford had become President after the resignation of Richard Nixon. As Vice-President, Nelson Rockefeller was, according to the Constitution, seated as the president of the U.S. Senate.

According to *Public Citizen*, the bottom line of Fast Track is that

...the White House signs and enters into trade deals before Congress ever votes on them. Fast Track also sets the parameters for congressional debate on any trade measure the President submits, requiring a vote within a certain time with no amendments and only 20 hours of debate.[68]

When an agreement is about to be given to Congress, high-powered lobbyists and political hammer-heads are called in to manipulate congressional hold-outs into voting for the legisla-

---

68   "Fast Track Talking Points", *Global Trade Watch*, Public Citizen (http://www.citizen. org/hot_issues/print_issue.cfm?ID=141).

tion. With only 20 hours of debate allowed, there is little opportunity for public involvement.

The Council of the Americas, founded by **David Rockefeller** (Nelson Rockefeller's brother) in 1965, played an instrumental part in the passage of this 1974 legislation. According to Rockefeller himself,

The Council of the Americas played an integral role in the ultimately successful effort to secure TPA (Trade Promotion Authority)... the Council lobbied hard for the legislation. Although the vote in the House was extremely close (215 ayes to 214 nays), the Senate passed TPA more easily.[69]

With Nelson Rockefeller presiding as President of the Senate, it is little wonder that it passed there with ease. Nevertheless, Congress clearly understood the risk of giving up this power to the President, as evidenced by the fact that they put an automatic expiration date on it. Since the expiration of the original Fast Track, there has been a very contentious trail of Fast Track renewal efforts. In 1996, President Clinton utterly failed to re-secure Fast Track after a bitter debate in Congress. After another contentious struggle in 2001/2002, President Bush was able to renew Fast Track for himself in the Trade Act of 2002, just in time to negotiate the Central American Free Trade Agreement (CAFTA) and insure its passage in 2005.

It is startling to realize that since 1974, Fast Track has been used in a small minority of trade agreements. Under the Clinton presidency, for instance, some 300 separate trade agreements were negotiated and passed normally by Congress, but only two of them were submitted under Fast Track: NAFTA and the GATT Uruguay Round. In fact, from 1974 to 1992, there were only three instances of Fast Track in action: GATT Tokyo Round, U.S.-Israel Free Trade Agreement and the Canada-U.S. Free Trade Agreement. Thus, NAFTA was only the fourth invocation of Fast Track up until that time.

Soon after NAFTA, Clinton used Fast Track authority to submit the Uruguay Round Agreements Act, which was passed by the Senate on December 1, 1994 and signed into law on December

---

69   David Rockefeller, *Memoirs*, (Random House, 2011), p. 438.

8. This sweeping treaty provided for the creation of the World Trade Organization which has been instrumental in reforming international trade. Subsequent annual WTO meetings typically made headlines not because of their disastrous trade policies but because of the violent street protests staged by activists from all over the world.

The selective use of Fast Track legislation suggests a very narrow agenda. These trade bamboozles didn't stand a ghost of a chance to be passed without it, and the global elite knew it. Fast Track was created as a very specific legislative tool to accomplish a very specific executive task -- namely, to "fast track" the creation of the "New International Economic Order" envisioned by the Trilateral Commission in 1973!

Article Six of the U.S. Constitution states that "all Treaties made, or which shall be made, under the Authority of the United States, shall be the supreme Law of the Land and the Judges in every State shall be bound thereby, any Thing in the Constitution or Laws of any State to the contrary notwithstanding." Because international treaties supersede national law, Fast Track has allowed an enormous restructuring of U.S. law without resorting to a Constitutional Convention. It is a clear example of the "end run around national sovereignty" that **Richard Gardne**r had called for in 1974. In this case, it was the counter-move to the failed "frontal assault" by **Henry Kissinger** and **Zbigniew Brzezinski** as early as 1972 when they called for a Constitutional Convention to change the very fabric of our nation. Those suggestions were overwhelmingly rejected by the American public as outrageous and dangerous. In the end, Fast Track achieved that and more.

North American Free Trade Agreement

NAFTA was negotiated under the executive leadership of Republican President **George H.W. Bush**. **Carla Hills** is widely credited as being the principal architect and negotiator of NAFTA. Both Bush and Hills were members of the Trilateral Commission!

With Bush's first presidential term drawing to a close and Bush desiring political credit for NAFTA, an "initialing" ceremony of NAFTA was staged (so Bush could take credit for NAFTA) in October, 1992. Although very official looking, most Americans did not understand the difference between initialing and signing; at the time, Fast Track was not implemented and Bush did not have the authority to actually sign such a trade agreement.

Bush subsequently lost a publicly contentious presidential race to Democrat **William Jefferson Clinton**, but they were hardly polar opposites on the issue of Free Trade and NAFTA. The reason? Clinton was also a seasoned member of the Trilateral Commission. Immediately after inauguration, Clinton became the champion of NAFTA and orchestrated its passage with a massive Executive Branch effort.

Prior to the 1992 election, however, there was a fly in the Trilateral ointment, namely, presidential candidate and billionaire Ross Perot, founder and chairman of Electronic Data Systems (EDS). Perot was politically independent, vehemently anti-NAFTA and chose to make it a major campaign issue in 1991. In the end, the global elite would have to spend huge sums of money to overcome the negative publicity that Perot gave to NAFTA.

At the time, some political analysts believed that Perot, being a billionaire, was somehow put up to this task by the same elitists who were pushing NAFTA. Presumably, it would accumulate all the anti-globalists in one tidy group, thus allowing the elitists to determine who their true enemies really were. It is a moot point today whether he was sincere or not, but it did have that outcome, and Perot became a lightning rod for the whole issue of free trade.

Perot hit the nail squarely on the head in one of his nationally televised campaign speeches:

*If you're paying $12, $13, $14 an hour for factory workers and you can move your factory south of the border, pay a dollar an hour for labor, hire young -- let's assume you've been in business for a long time and you've got a mature workforce - pay a dollar an hour for your labor, have no health care - that's the most expensive single element in making a car - have no environmental controls, no pollution controls, and no retirement, and you didn't care about anything but making money, **there will be a giant sucking sound going south**....*[70] [Emphasis added]

70   Ross Perot, "Excerpts From Presidential Debates", (1992).

Perot's message struck a nerve with millions of Americans, but it was unfortunately cut short when he entered into public campaign debates with fellow candidate **Albert Gore**. Simply put, Gore ate Perot's lunch, not so much on the issues themselves, but on having superior debating skills. As organized as Perot was, he was no match for a politically and globally seasoned politician like **Al Gore**. To counter the public relations damage done by Perot, all the stops were pulled out as the NAFTA vote drew near. As proxy for the global elite, the President unleashed the biggest and most expensive spin machine the country had ever seen.

Former Chrysler chairman Lee Iacocca was enlisted for a multi-million dollar nationwide ad campaign that praised the benefits of NAFTA. The mantra, carried consistently throughout the many spin events: "Exports. Better Jobs. Better Wages." all of which have turned out to be empty promises.

Bill Clinton invited three former presidents to the White House to stand with him in praise and affirmation of NAFTA. This was the first time in U.S. history that four presidents had ever appeared together. Of the four, three were members of the Trilateral Commission: **Bill Clinton**, **Jimmy Carter** and **George H.W. Bush**. Gerald Ford was not a Commissioner, but was nevertheless a confirmed globalist insider. After Ford's accession to the presidency in 1974, he promptly nominated Nelson Rockefeller (**David Rockefeller**'s oldest brother) to fill the Vice Presidency that Ford had just vacated.

The academic community was enlisted when, according to *Harper's Magazine* publisher John MacArthur,

...there was a pro-NAFTA petition, organized and written by MIT's Rudiger Dornbusch, addressed to President Clinton and signed by all twelve living Nobel laureates in economics, and exercised in academic logrolling that was expertly converted by Bill Daley and the A-Team into PR gold on the front page of The New York Times on September 14. 'Dear Mr. President,' wrote the 283 signatories...[71]

Lastly, prominent Trilateral Commission members themselves took to the press to promote NAFTA. For instance, on May 13,

---

71   John MacArthur, *The Selling of Free Trade*, (Univ. of Cal. Press, 2001) p. 228.

1993, Commissioners **Henry Kissinger** and **Cyrus Vance** wrote a joint op-ed that stated,

> *[NAFTA] would be the most constructive measure the United States would have undertaken in our hemisphere in this century.*[72]

Two months later, Kissinger went further:

> *It will represent the most creative step toward a new world order taken by any group of countries since the end of the Cold War, and the first step toward an even larger vision of a free-trade zone for the entire Western Hemisphere. **[NAFTA] is not a conventional trade agreement, but the architecture of a new international system.**[73]* [Emphasis added]

It is hardly fanciful to think that Kissinger's hype sounds quite similar to the Trilateral Commission's original goal of creating a New International Economic Order.

On January 1, 1994, NAFTA became law. Under Fast Track procedures, the house had passed it by 234-200 (132 Republicans and 102 Democrats voting in favor), and the U.S. Senate passed it by 61-38.

That Giant Sucking Sound Going South

To understand the potential impact of the North American Union, one must understand the impact of NAFTA.

NAFTA promised greater exports, better jobs and better wages. Since 1994, just the opposite has occurred. The U.S. trade deficit soared, approaching $1 trillion dollars per year; the U.S. has lost some 1.5 million jobs, and real wages in both the U.S. and Mexico have fallen significantly.

Patrick Buchanan offered a simple example of NAFTA's deleterious effect on the U.S. economy:

> *When NAFTA passed in 1993, we imported some 225,000 cars and trucks from Mexico, but exported about 500,000 vehicles to the world. In 2005, our exports to the world were still a shade under 500,000 vehicles, but our auto and truck imports from Mexico had tripled to 700,000 vehicles.*

---

72   Henry Kissinger and Cyrus Vance, Op Ed, *Washington Post*, May 13, 1993.
73   Henry Kissinger, Op-Ed. *Los Angeles Times*, July 18, 1993.

As McMillion writes, Mexico now exports more cars and trucks to the United States than the United States exports to the whole world. A fine end, is it not, to the United States as "Auto Capital of the World"?

What happened? Post-NAFTA, the Big Three just picked up a huge slice of our auto industry and moved it, and the jobs, to Mexico.[74]

Of course, this only represents the auto industry, but the same effect has been seen in many other industries as well. Buchanan correctly noted that NAFTA was never just a trade deal. Rather, it was an "enabling act - to enable U.S. corporations to dump their American workers and move their factories to Mexico." Indeed, this is the very spirit of all outsourcing of U.S. jobs and manufacturing facilities to overseas locations.

Respected economist Alan Tonelson, author of *The Race to the Bottom*, notes the smoke and mirrors that cloud what has really happened with exports:

Most U.S. exports to Mexico before, during and since the (1994) peso crisis have been producer goods - in particular, parts and components sent by U.S. multinationals to their Mexican factories for assembly or for further processing. The vast majority of these, moreover, are reexported, and most get shipped right back to the United States for final sale. In fact, by most estimates, the United States buys 80 to 90 percent of all of Mexico's exports.[75]

Tonelson concludes that "the vast majority of American workers have experienced declining living standards, not just a handful of losers."

Mexican economist and scholar Miguel Pickard sums up Mexico's supposed benefits from NAFTA:

Much praise has been heard for the few 'winners' that NAFTA has created, but little mention is made of the fact that the Mexican people are the deal's big 'losers.' Mexicans now face

---

74   Patrick Buchanan, "The Fruits of NAFTA", *The Conservative Voice*, March 10, 2006.

75   Alan Tonelson, *The Race to the Bottom*, (Westview Press, 2002) p. 89.

*greater unemployment, poverty, and inequality than before
the agreement began in 1994.*[76]

In short, NAFTA has not been a friend to the citizenry of the
United States or Mexico. Still, this was the backdrop against which
the North American Union (NAU) is being acted out. The globalization players and their promises have remained pretty much
the same, both just as disingenuous as ever.

Prelude to the North American Union

Remember that a core element of Technocracy, Inc. in the
1930s was the continental integration of Mexico, the United
States, Canada, Central America and portions of South America to
include Columbia and Venezuela. Howard Scott never addressed
the issue of how to integrate these nations, but a solution was
proposed with the creation of NAFTA. Soon after it was passed in
1994, Dr. Robert A. Pastor began to push for a "deep integration"
which NAFTA could not provide by itself. His dream was summed
up in his book, *Toward a North American Union*, published in
2001. Unfortunately for Pastor, the book was released just a few
days prior to the 9/11 terrorist attacks in New York and thus received little attention from any sector.

However, Pastor had the right connections. He was invited to
appear before the plenary session of the Trilateral Commission
held in Ontario, Canada on November 1-2, 2002, to deliver a paper drawing directly on his book. His paper, *A Modest Proposal To
the Trilateral Commission*, made several recommendations:

- *...the three governments should establish a North American Commission (NAC) to define an agenda for Summit
  meetings by the three leaders and to monitor the implementation of the decisions and plans.*

- *A second institution should emerge from combining
  two bilateral legislative groups into a North American
  Parliamentary Group.*

- *The third institution should be a Permanent Court on
  Trade and Investment.*

- *The three leaders should establish a North American*

---

76   Miguel Pickard, "Trinational Elites Map North American Future in 'NAFTA Plus'",
(http://www.irc-online.com).

> Development Fund, whose priority would be to connect
> the U.S.-Mexican border region to central and southern
> Mexico.
> * The North American Commission should develop an in-
>   tegrated continental plan for transportation and infra-
>   structure.
> * ...negotiate a Customs Union and a Common External
>   Tariff.
> * Our three governments should sponsor Centers for North
>   American Studies in each of our countries to help the
>   people of all three understand the problems and the po-
>   tential of North America and begin to think of themselves
>   as North Americans.[77]

Pastor's choice of the words "Modest Proposal" were almost comical considering that he intended to reorganize the entire North American continent.

Nevertheless, the Trilateral Commission was completely on board. Subsequently, it was Pastor who emerged as the U.S. vice-chairman of the CFR task force that was announced on October 15, 2004:

> The Council has launched an independent task force on the
> future of North America to examine regional integration
> since the implementation of the North American Free Trade
> Agreement ten years ago.... The task force will review five
> spheres of policy in which greater cooperation may be need-
> ed. They are: deepening economic integration; reducing the
> development gap; harmonizing regulatory policy; enhancing
> security; and devising better institutions to manage conflicts
> that inevitably arise from integration and exploit opportuni-
> ties for collaboration.[78]

Independent task force, indeed! A total of twenty-three members were chosen from the three countries. Each country was represented by a member of the Trilateral Commission: **Carla**

---

77   Dr. Robert A. Pastor, "A Modest Proposal To the Trilateral Commission", Trilateral Commission , 2002.

78   "Council Joins Leading Canadians and Mexicans to Launch Independent Task Force on the Future of America", (http://www.cfr.org/world/council-joins-leading-canadians-mexicans-launch-independent-task-force-future-north-america/p7454), October 15, 2004.

A. Hills (U.S.), **Luis Rubio** (Mexico) and **Wendy K. Dobson** (Canada). Robert Pastor served as the U.S. vice-chairman. This CFR task force was unique in that it focused on economic and political policies for all three countries, not just the U.S. The Task Force stated purpose was to

> *...identify inadequacies in the current arrangements and suggest opportunities for deeper cooperation on areas of common interest. Unlike other Council-sponsored task forces, which focus primarily on U.S. policy, this initiative includes participants from Canada and Mexico, as well as the United States, and will make policy recommendations for all three countries.*[79]

Richard Haass, chairman of the CFR and long-time member of the Trilateral Commission, pointedly made the link between NAFTA and integration of Mexico, Canada and the U.S.:

> *Ten years after NAFTA, it is obvious that the security and economic futures of Canada, Mexico, and the United States are intimately bound. But there is precious little thinking available as to where the three countries need to be in another ten years and how to get there. I am excited about the potential of this task force to help fill this void.*[80]

Haass' statement "there is precious little thinking available" underscores a repeatedly used elitist technique. That is, first decide what you want to do, and second, assign a flock of academics to justify your intended actions. This is the crux of academic funding by NGOs such as the Rockefeller Foundation, Ford Foundation, Carnegie-Mellon, etc. After the justification process is complete, the same elites that suggested it in the first place allow themselves to be drawn in as if they had no other logical choice but to play along with the "sound thinking" of the experts.

The task force met three times, once in each country. When the process was completed, it issued its results in May, 2005, in a paper titled *Building a North American Community* and subtitled *Report of the Independent Task Force on the Future of North America*. Even the sub-title suggests that the "future of North America" is a fait accompli decided behind closed doors.

79   ibid.
80   ibid.

Some of the recommendations of the task force were:

- Adopt a common external tariff
- Adopt a North American Approach to Regulation
- Establish a common security perimeter by 2010
- Establish a North American investment fund for infrastructure and human capital
- Establish a permanent tribunal for North American dispute resolution
- An annual North American Summit meeting that would bring the heads-of-state together for the sake of public display of confidence
- Establish minister-led working groups that will be required to report back within 90 days, and to meet regularly
- Create a North American Advisory Council
- Create a North American Inter-Parliamentary Group.[81]

Sound familiar? It should. Many of the recommendations are verbatim from Pastor's "modest" presentation to the Trilateral Commission mentioned above, or from his earlier book, *Toward a North American Union*.

Shortly after the task force report was issued, the heads of all three countries did indeed meet together for a summit in Waco, Texas on March 23, 2005. The specific result of the summit was the creation of the Security and Prosperity Partnership of North America (SPP). The joint press release stated,

We, the elected leaders of Canada, Mexico, and the United States, have met in Texas to announce the establishment of the Security and Prosperity Partnership of North America.

We will establish working parties led by our ministers and secretaries that will consult with stakeholders in our respective countries. These working parties will respond to the priorities of our people and our businesses, and will set specific, measurable, and achievable goals. They will outline concrete steps that our governments can take to meet these goals, and

---

81   "Building a North American Community", Council on Foreign Relations, 2005.

set dates that will ensure the continuous achievement of results.

Within 90 days, ministers will present their initial report after which, the working parties will submit six-monthly reports. Because the Partnership will be an ongoing process of cooperation, new items will be added to the work agenda by mutual agreement as circumstances warrant.[82]

Once again, we saw Pastor's North American Union ideology being continued, but this time as an outcome of a summit meeting of three heads-of-states. The question must be raised, "Who was really in charge of this process?"

Indeed, the three premiers returned to their respective countries and started their "working parties" to "consult with stakeholders". In the U.S., the "specific, measurable, and achievable goals" were only seen indirectly by the creation of a government website billed as "Security and Prosperity Partnership of North America". The stakeholders are not mentioned by name, but it was clear that they were generally representatives of business interests of members of the Trilateral Commission!

The second annual summit meeting took place on March 30-31, 2006, in Cancun, Mexico among Bush, Fox and Canadian prime minister Stephen Harper. The Security and Prosperity Partnership agenda was summed up in a statement from Mexican president Vicente Fox:

We touched upon fundamental items in that meeting. First of all, we carried out an evaluation meeting. Then we got information about the development of programs. And then we gave the necessary instructions for the works that should be carried out in the next period of work... We are not renegotiating what has been successful or open in the Free Trade Agreement. It's going beyond the agreement, both for prosperity and security.[83]

---

82   "North American Leaders Unveil Security and Prosperity Partnership, International Information Programs", U.S. Govt. Website.
83   Vincente Fox, "Concluding Press Conference at Cancun Summit", March 31, 2006.

Regulations instead of Treaties

It may not have occurred to the reader that the two SPP summits resulted in no signed agreements. This is not accidental nor a failure of the summit process. The so-called "deeper integration" of the three countries is being accomplished through a series of regulations and executive decrees that avoid citizen watchdogs and legislative oversight.[84]

In the U.S., the 2005 Cancun summit spawned some 20 different working groups that would deal with issues from immigration to security to harmonization of regulations, all under the auspices of the Security and Prosperity Partnership. The SPP in the U.S. was officially placed under the Department of Commerce, headed by Secretary Carlos M. Gutierrez, but other Executive Branch agencies also had SPP components that reported to Commerce.

After two years of massive effort by investigative journalists, the names of the SPP working group members were never discovered, nor was the result of their work. Furthermore, Congressional oversight of the SPP process was completely absent.

The director of SPP, Geri Word, was contacted to ask why a cloud of secrecy was hanging over SPP. According to investigative journalist Jerome Corsi, Word replied, "We did not want to get the contact people of the working groups distracted by calls from the public."[85]

This paternalistic attitude is a typical elitist mentality. Their work - whatever they have dreamed up on their own - is too important to be distracted by the likes of pesky citizens or their elected legislators.

This elite change of tactics must not be understated: Regulations and Executive Orders have replaced Congressional legislation and public debate. There is no pretense of either. This is another Gardner-style "end-run around national sovereignty, eroding it piece by piece."

Apparently, the Trilateral-dominated Bush administration believed that it had accumulated sufficient power to ram the NAU

---

84   Pickard, p. 1
85   Jerome Corsi, "Bush sneaking North American super-state without oversight?", *WorldNetDaily*, June 12, 2006.

down the throat of the American People, whether they protested or not.

Robert A. Pastor: A Trilateral Commission Operative

As mentioned earlier, Pastor was hailed as the father of the North American Union, having written more papers about it, delivered more testimonies before Congress, and headed up task forces to study it, than any other single U.S. academic figure. He was a tireless architect and advocate of the NAU. Although he might seem to have been a fresh, new name in the globalization business, Pastor has a long history with Trilateral Commission members and the global elite.

He is the same Robert Pastor who was the executive director of the 1974 CFR task force (funded by the Rockefeller and Ford Foundations) called the Commission on U.S.-Latin American Relations - aka the Linowitz Commission. The Linowitz Commission, chaired by an original Trilateral Commissioner, **Sol Linowitz**, was singularly credited with the giveaway of the Panama Canal in 1976 under the Carter presidency. All of the Linowitz Commission members were members of the Trilateral Commission save one, Albert Fishlow; other members were **W. Michael Blumenthal, Samuel Huntington, Peter G. Peterson, Elliot Richardson** and **David Rockefeller**.

One of Carter's first actions as President in 1977 was to appoint **Zbigniew Brzezinski** to the post of National Security Advisor. In turn, one of Brzezinski's first acts was to appoint his protégé, Dr. Robert A. Pastor, as director of the Office of Latin American and Caribbean Affairs. Pastor then became the Trilateral Commission's point-man to lobby for the Canal giveaway.

To actually negotiate the Carter-Torrijos Treaty, Carter sent none other than **Sol Linowitz** to Panama as temporary ambassador. The 6-month temporary appointment avoided the requirement for Senate confirmation. Thus, the very same people who created the policy became responsible for executing it.

The Trilateral Commission's role in the Carter Administration has been confirmed by Pastor himself in his 1992 paper *The Carter Administration and Latin America: A Test of Principle*:

In converting its predisposition into a policy, the new administration had the benefit of the research done by two private commissions. Carter, Vance, and Brzezinski were members of the Trilateral Commission, which provided a conceptual framework for collaboration among the industrialized countries in approaching the full gamut of international issues. With regard to setting an agenda and an approach to Latin America, the most important source of influence on the Carter administration was the Commission on U.S.-Latin American Relations, chaired by Sol M. Linowitz.[86]

As to the final Linowitz Commission reports on Latin America, most of which were authored by Pastor himself, he states,

The reports helped the administration define a new relationship with Latin America, and 27 of the 28 specific recommendations in the second report became U.S. policy.[87]

The Security and Prosperity Partnership was quietly terminated in August 2009 when its website was updated to say "The Security and Prosperity Partnership of North America (SPP) is no longer an active initiative. There will not be any updates to this site."[88]

Pastor's deep involvement with Trilateral Commission members and policies is irrefutable. In 1996, when Trilateral Commissioner **Bill Clinton** nominated Pastor as Ambassador to Panama, his confirmation was forcefully knocked down by Senator Jesse Helms (R-NC) who held a deep grudge against Pastor for his central role in the giveaway of the Panama Canal in 1976.

Conclusion

It is clear that the Executive Branch of the U.S. was literally hijacked in 1976 by members of the Trilateral Commission, upon the election of President **Jimmy Carter** and Vice-President **Walter Mondale**. This near-absolute domination, especially in

---

86   Dr. Robert A. Pastor, "The Carter Administration and Latin America: A Test of Principle", *The Carter Center*, July 1992, p. 9.

87   ibid. p. 10.

88   "The SPP is dead. Let's keep it that way", September 24, 2009, (http://rabble.ca/news/2009/09/spp-dead-lets-keep-it-way).

the areas of trade, banking, economics and foreign policy, has continued unchallenged and unabated to the present.

Windfall profits have accrued to interests associated with the Trilateral Commission, but the effect of their "New International Economic Order" on the U.S. has been nothing less than devastating.

The philosophical underpinnings of the Trilateral Commission have the appearance of being pro-Marxist and pro-Socialist, but only as a stepping stone leading to Brzezinski's Technetronic, or Technocratic, society. They are solidly set against the concept of the nation-state and in particular, the Constitution of the United States. Thus, national sovereignty must be diminished and then abolished altogether in order to make way for the New International Economic Order that will be governed by an unelected global elite with their self-created legal framework.

If you are having a negative reaction against Trilateral-style globalization, you are not alone. A 2007 *Financial Times/Harris* poll revealed that less than 20 percent of people in six industrialized countries (including the U.S.) believe that globalization is good for their country while over 50 percent are outright negative towards it.[89] While citizens around the world are feeling the pain of globalization, few understand why it is happening and hence, they have no effective strategy to resist it.

The American public has never, ever conceived that such forces would align themselves so successfully against freedom and liberty. Yet, the evidence is clear; steerage of America has long since fallen into the hands of an actively hostile enemy that intends to remove all vestiges of the very things that made us the greatest nation in the history of mankind.

---

89   FT/Harris poll on Globalization, (http://www.FT.com).

CHAPTER 4

TRANSFORMING ECONOMICS

Technocracy proposed a completely different economic system that had never been implemented in the history of the world. It was to be a system run by scientists and engineers who would make decisions based on their application of the Scientific Method to control both social and economic matters. Price-based economics, with its proven laws of supply and demand, would be replaced with an energy-based system controlled by the distribution and consumption of energy. Consumers would be forced to abandon traditional money in return for energy credits that would be spent to acquire goods and services that are artificially priced based on the energy consumed in bringing those goods and services to the marketplace. People would work at assigned jobs deemed to be best suited for their education, skills, intelligence and temperament. Thus, the Technocracy would therefore minimize the use of raw materials by assuring maximum efficiency, minimum waste, and reasonable amounts of end-user consumption. Who would decide what is reasonable for your personal consumption? They would. Each person would receive according to his need, as long as his need was within bounds allowed by the technocratic regulators.

The elements of this new economic system can thus be seen very clearly in the *Technocracy Study Course*:

- *Register on a continuous 24 hour-per-day basis the total net conversion of energy.*
- *By means of the registration of energy converted and consumed, make possible a balanced load.*
- *Provide a continuous inventory of all production and consumption.*
- *Provide a specific registration of the type, kind, etc., of all goods and services, where produced and where used.*
- *Provide specific registration of the consumption of each*

individual, plus a record and description of the individual.[90]

The second item above intended to "make possible a balanced load," and this is the heart of the system. Incessant monitoring of every action within the system makes possible the calculations necessary for a state of balance, or equilibrium. This would require continuous adjustment of both output and consumption, with the limiting factor being resource usage.

If it seems to you that such an economic model is completely Orwellian in nature, it is because that is exactly the case. It would micromanage every last detail of your life according to the formulas and algorithms created by the enlightened scientists and engineers.

The apparent lunacy of Technocracy becomes more clear as you dig deeper into it. How is it then, that we find the United Nations as the primary driver for Technocracy in all the nations of the world? This is a pressing question that will be answered in short order, but not before a little further explanation to lay the groundwork.

The United Nations has had a uniform strategy across all of its many units to foster the creation of a so-called "green economy". A partial definition of what this means is found in a statement by the United Nations Governing Council of the U.N. Environmental Programme (UNEP):

> *A green economy implies the decoupling of resource use and environmental impacts from economic growth... These investments, both public and private, provide the mechanism for the reconfiguration of businesses, infrastructure and institutions, and for the adoption of sustainable consumption and production processes.*[91]

Sustainable consumption? Reconfiguring businesses, infrastructure and institutions? What do these words mean? This is not merely a reshuffle of the existing order but a total replacement with a completely new economic system, one that has never before been seen or used in the history of the world. This is un-

---

90   Hubbert and Scott, p. 232.
91   Governing Council of the UN Environmental Programme (UNEP), "Green Economy",
(United Nations, 2009), p. 2.

derscored by UNEP when it further states, *"our dominant [cur-rent] economic model may thus be termed a 'brown economy.'"* To UNEP, there is a consistent sense of urgency to kill off the existing brown economy in favor of a green economy.

Brown is bad. Green is good. Brown represents the failed past. Green represents the bright future.

However, to grasp what it means to decouple resource use and environmental impacts from economic growth, the focus must be on the word *decoupling*. The International Resource Panel (IRP), another unit of UNEP, gives a clear definition:

> *While 'decoupling' can be applied in many fields, from alge-bra to electronics, the IRP applies the concept to sustainable development in two dimensions. Resource decoupling means reducing the rate of the use of resources per unit of economic activity. Impact decoupling means maintaining economic output while reducing the negative environmental impact of any economic activities that are undertaken. Relative decou-pling of resources or impacts means that the growth rate of the resources used or environmental impacts is lower than the economic growth rate, so that resource productivity is rising. Absolute reductions of resource use are a consequence of decoupling when the growth rate of resource productivity exceeds the growth rate of the economy.*[92]

Note that decoupling has no meaning outside of the UN's con-cept of sustainable development.

UNEP actually maintains a dedicated web site titled Green Economy where prominently labeled subsections are seen: Climate Change, Ecosystem Management, Environmental Governance and Resource Efficiency. Their initiative, Partnership for Action on Green Economy (PAGE), states that it is,

> *...a response to the outcome document of the United Nations Conference on Sustainable Development (Rio+20), entitled The Future We Want, which recognizes the green economy as a vehicle for sustainable development and poverty eradi-cation.*[93]

---

92   Fischer-Kowalski, Swilling, et.al, "Decoupling: Natural Resource Use and Environ-mental Impacts From Economic Growth", (International Resource Panel, 2011), p. 5.
93   See http://www.unep.org/greeneconomy/page

Who is the "we" in *The Future We Want*? Well, since none of this was ever put to a public vote in any country in the world, it is obvious that it refers only to themselves.

Nevertheless, we can see that the green economy is *"a vehicle for sustainable development and poverty eradication."* It is also clear that the green economy concept is an outcome of the U.N. Conference on Sustainable Development (Rio+20, held in Rio de Janeiro on June 20-22, 2012). The U.N.'s first Rio conference held in 1992 created the original and definitive document for sustainable development called *Agenda 21*. The Rio+20 conference was held to further Agenda 21 and Sustainable Development on a global basis.

The above mentioned PAGE document further states that there are four main U.N. agencies that are focused in unison on creating the green economy:

- United Nations Environment Programme (UNEP)
- International Labour Organization (ILO)
- United Nations Industrial Development Organization (UNIDO)
- United Nations Institute for Training and Research (UNITAR)

Together, PAGE will

build enabling conditions in participating countries by shifting investment and policies towards the creation of a new generation of assets, such as clean technologies, resource efficient infrastructure, well-functioning ecosystems, green skilled labour and good governance.[94]

Note that it is the U.N. who asserts that *they* will shift investment and policies in order to achieve their desired outcomes of efficiency and governance. In direct Technocracy lingo, *governance* refers to management of society by engineering experts who alone can create a "resource efficient infrastructure".

In this short treatment of the green economy, I have purposely tread lightly to show that it is wrapped up in a network of global agendas that is squarely focused on the original tenet of Technocracy, namely, *Sustainable Development*. No doubt a

---

94   Ibid.

technocrat reading this book will cry "foul!" at this assertion. While it is true that the literal term of "Sustainable Development" was not coined by the original Technocrats, most would be jealous that someone else beat them to it. The fact of the matter is that Sustainable Development is conceptually identical to Technocracy's "balanced load".

The foundational document for Technocracy, Inc. was the book *Technocracy Study Course*, written primarily by co-founder M. King Hubbert. In it he stated,

Although it [the earth] is not an isolated system the changes in the configuration of matter on the earth, such as the erosion of soil, the making of mountains, the burning of coal and oil, and the mining of metals are all typical and characteristic examples of irreversible processes, involving in each case an increase of entropy.[95]

As a scientist, Hubbert tried to explain (or justify) his argument in terms of physics and the law of thermodynamics, which is the study of energy conversion between heat and mechanical work. Entropy is a concept within thermodynamics that represents the amount of energy in a system that is no longer available for doing mechanical work. Entropy thus increases as matter and energy in the system degrade toward the ultimate state of inert uniformity. In layman's terms, entropy means once you use it, you lose it for good. Furthermore, the end state of entropy is "inert uniformity" where nothing takes place.

The Technocrat's avoidance of *social entropy* is to increase the efficiency of society by the careful allocation of available energy and measuring subsequent output in order to find a state of "equilibrium", or balance. Hubbert's focus on entropy is further evidenced by Technocracy, Inc.'s logo, the well-known Yin Yang symbol that depicts balance.

According to Hubbert's thinking then, if man uses up all the available energy and/or destroys the ecology in the process, it cannot be repeated or restored ever again and *man will cease to exist.* Hubbert believed that mankind faces extinction unless efficiency and sustainable resource practices are maximized and

---

95   Hubbert & Scott, p. 49.

that such efficiencies and practices can only be imposed by un-elected and unaccountable scientists, engineers and technicians.

In short, the heartbeat of Technocracy *is* Sustainable Development. It calls for an engineered society where the needs of mankind are in perfect balance with the resources of nature. Furthermore, this necessitates the "decoupling of resource use and environmental impacts from economic growth" as stated above. In other words, the driver is resource availability rather than economic growth.

The introduction of the PAGE brochure reiterates this idea: "A green economy is one that results in improved human well-being and social equity, while significantly reducing environmental risks and ecological scarcities".[96]

The bottom line is that the U.N. agenda for a green economy is nothing more than warmed-over Technocracy from the 1930s.

Technocracy's utopian siren call in the 1930s promised the same human well-being, social equity and abundance beyond measure. Technocrats failed to deliver on their promises and were generally rejected by society by the end of the 1930s.

It is necessary to review exactly how the United Nations arose in the first place, if for no other reason than to tie these policies to the same global elite as represented by the Trilateral Commission. Notably, the Commission was co-founded by and initially financed by **David Rockefeller**, who was at the time chairman of Chase Manhattan Bank. The Rockefeller family also played a prominent role in the history of the United Nations, for which I will defer to the words of U.N. Secretary General Ban Ki-moon in 2012 com-memorating the Rockefeller Foundation's "global philanthropy" and the establishment of the League of Nations Library:

> *I am honoured to be here on this eighty-fifth anniversary of the historic donation of John D. Rockefeller Jr. to the League of Nations Library. At the time, Mr. Rockefeller said he made the gift based on the conviction that "peace must finally be built on the foundation of well-informed public opinion." This powerful statement rings true today.*
>
> *It is fitting that we are naming this room after him. I thank*

---

96   Ibid.

the family for donating the portrait of John D. Rockefeller that was displayed at the Rockefeller Foundation for 65 years. In offering this generous gift, David Rockefeller said he hoped it would serve as a reminder of his father's generosity – but more importantly his conviction that strong international organizations can help create a just, equitable and peaceful world.

The Rockefeller family has lived up to this conviction, providing immense support for the League of Nations and the United Nations over the years. The original donation to this library was particularly significant. Even today, the interest provides approximately $150,000 every biennium to this wonderful library. That makes it possible to care for its many priceless historical treasures, including a signed copy of the Treaty of Versailles and the Covenant of the League of Nations.

This Library also safeguards more recent history, including the Universal Declaration of Human Rights, with original letters from Eleanor Roosevelt and René Cassin. I applaud the mission of this library to serve international understanding. I am deeply grateful to all the staff. You make an enormous contribution through your help for researchers and citizens who are interested in the United Nations' history and work. I personally want to thank the Rockefeller family for my own office — and the entire United Nations campus on the East Side of Manhattan.

When Rockefeller's donation of the land was announced in the General Assembly in 1945, the Hall was filled with loud applause. The United States Ambassador cheered Mr. Rockefeller's "magnificent benevolence". I am deeply grateful to the esteemed members of the Rockefeller family and the Rockefeller Foundation for continuing the noble tradition of supporting international organizations devoted to peace. As recently as this past June, at the Rio+20 summit on sustainable development, the Rockefeller Foundation and the United Nations Global Compact launched a new framework for action to help meet social and environmental needs.[97]

---

97   UN Secretary-General, "Marking Historic Donation to the League of Nations Library-Hails Rockefeller Foundation's 'Global Philanthropy'", September 2, 2012.

"Magnificent benevolence", indeed. The United Nations head-quarters was built in 1949 on 17 acres of prime real estate - donated by John D. Rockefeller, Jr. - in New York City on First Avenue between East 46th and East 48th Streets. It is not hard to see the tight financial relationship between the U.N. and Rockefeller interests that started so many decades ago. It is only slightly more obscure to see what the Rockefellers have received in return for their benevolent support.

In many ways, ideology can be compared to a virus. History is riddled with failed ideas that were forgotten as soon as they were uttered; many virus mutations terminated before they ever had a chance to infect other victims. What is necessary for a virus to spread is contagion, or a medium by which it can be transmitted. In order for Technocracy to make a resurgence on the world stage, it also required a contagion by which entire societies and social systems could be successfully infected. This medium is the United Nations, and the Rockefeller consortium used it with great effectiveness to deceive the nations into believing that Sustainable Development (e.g., Technocracy's "balance") could solve all of the world's problems and bring peace, prosperity and social justice to everyone. Indeed, the mass of global humanity is embracing the promises of technocratic utopianism as if there is no other possibility for the salvation of mankind.

As a writer with an economist perspective, it is very disappointing that economists of the academic world are completely ignoring the impacts and outcomes of the U.N.'s so-called green economy. If it were an argument in a vacuum, I would not be concerned in the slightest. But this is actually happening today where academia actually is leading the charge. No one is even questioning the outcomes of their utopian studies, much less repudiating them.

Agenda 21 and Sustainable Development

Agenda 21 is Technocracy's plan for the 21st century. The agent of implementation is Sustainable Development. The driver is the United Nations. The perpetrators are members of the Trilateral Commission and their globalist cronies. The victims are all the peoples of the world.

As you will see, it is no understatement that the policies of Agenda 21 and Sustainable Development are already fully injected into the fabric of economic, political and social life everywhere. While the "what" is certainly important, the "who" is even more critical to understand. Where did Agenda 21 come from? Was it spontaneous? Was it created by legions of global wannabes at the U.N.?

In 1992, the United Nations Conference on Environment and Development (UNCED) sponsored the Earth Summit that met in Rio de Janeiro, Brazil. It was attended by representatives from 172 governments with 116 being heads-of-state, who labored for 12 intense days to produce several non-legally binding documents. First, there was the 300-page *Agenda 21* document that was essentially the blueprint for implementation of Sustainable Development and all of its surrounds under the aegis of "green" and "smart". Second, there was the *Rio Declaration on Environment and Development*, commonly known as the *Rio Declaration*, that set forth 27 principles that would guide implementation of Sustainable Development. Third, there was the *Authoritative Statement of Principles for a Global Consensus on the Management, Conservation and Sustainable Development of All Types of Forests*, a set of recommendations for the sustainable management of forestry.

The Rio Declaration also produced three legally binding agreements that were opened for signature by participating nations. First, there was the *Convention on Biological Diversity* that covered ecosystems, species and genetic resources, and that ultimately produced the massive 1,140-page *Global Biodiversity Assessment* document. Second, there was the *United Nations Framework Convention on Climate Change* (UNFCCC) that led to the so-called Kyoto Protocol in 1997; the purpose of UNFCCC was to address climate change and reduce greenhouse gas emissions. Third, there was the *United Nations Convention to Combat Desertification* (UNCCD) that addressed Sustainable Development in countries that experience serious drought or increase in desert areas.

During the Rio conference, the then-Secretary General of the U.N., Boutros-Ghali, also called for the creation of the *Earth*

Charter which was later completed and published on June 29, 2000. The preamble to the *Earth Charter* states,

> *We stand at a critical moment in Earth's history, a time when humanity must choose its future. As the world becomes increasingly interdependent and fragile, the future at once holds great peril and great promise. To move forward we must recognize that in the midst of a magnificent diversity of cultures and life forms we are one human family and one Earth community with a common destiny. We must join together to bring forth a sustainable global society founded on respect for nature, universal human rights, economic justice, and a culture of peace. Towards this end, it is imperative that we, the peoples of Earth, declare our responsibility to one another, to the greater community of life, and to future generations.*[98]

It is not coincidental that the principal author of the *Earth Charter* was Stephen C. Rockefeller, the son of the former Vice President Nelson Rockefeller and nephew of **David Rockefeller**. Stephen Rockefeller has been a key player in the Rockefeller family by serving as a trustee of the Rockefeller Brothers Fund and as a director of the Rockefeller Philanthropy Advisors. Stephen has never been a member of the Trilateral Commission, but he was a founder of the interfaith movement and has been active for decades to infuse globalization into religion all over the world.

At any rate, the Rio Declaration was a busy and productive event, kicking off the biggest salvo of globalist mumbo-jumbo the world has ever seen at one time. As you might expect by now, there is more to the story. Indeed, Rio did not materialize out of nowhere, but rather was carefully planned and orchestrated for years in advance.

According to an important U.N. document published in 2010 and titled *Sustainable Development: From Brundtland to Rio 2012*,

> *In 1983, the UN convened the WCED [World Commission on Environment and Development], chaired by Norwegian Prime Minister Gro Harlem Brundtland. Comprised of representatives from both developed and developing countries, the*

---

98   Earth Charter, UNESCO, (http://www.unesco.org/education/tlsf/mods/theme_a/ img/02_earthcharter.pdf).

Commission was created to address growing concern over the "accelerating deterioration of the human environment and natural resources and the consequences of that deterioration for economic and social development." Four years later, the group produced the landmark publication Our Common Future (or the Brundtland report) that provided a stark diagnosis of the state of the environment. The report popularized the most commonly used definition of sustainable development: "Development that meets the needs of current generations without compromising the ability of future generations to meet their own needs."[99]

In the very next paragraph, the U.N. ties the knot between the Rio Declaration and the so-called Brundtland Commission:

The Brundtland report provided the momentum for the landmark 1992 Rio Summit that laid the foundations for the global institutionalization of sustainable development... Agenda 21 included 40 separate chapters, setting out actions in regard to the social and economic dimensions of sustainable development, conservation and management of natural resources, the role of major groups, and means of implementation.[100]

Thus, the Brundtland Commission can be directly credited with two important things: memorializing the phrase "Sustainable Development" and laying the groundwork for the 1992 Rio conference that produced *all* of the above-mentioned documents, agreements and memorandums.

There were admittedly other U.N. activities dating as far back as 1972 that provided some fuel to the fire that was ignited by the Brundtland Commission, but this Commission is and has been widely understood to be the quintessential creator of Agenda 21 and modern Sustainable Development.

The Chair of the Brundtland Commission was none other than Trilateral Commission member **Gro Harlem Brundtland**. She has been universally acclaimed as being the main driver behind the Commission and the principal architect and editor of its con-

99   "Sustainable Development: From Brundtland to Rio 2012", *United Nations Headquarters*, 2010.
100   Ibid.

cluding report, *Our Common Future*. Formerly the Prime Minister of Norway, Brundtland was Harvard educated and a long-time activist for environmental causes.

If this were likened to a football game, the United Nations might have held the ball in place, but it was Brundtland who performed the initial kickoff.

It is an interesting side-note that Brundtland is currently co-chair of a global organization known as The Elders, whose website states, "The Elders is founded on the idea that we now live in a 'global village', an increasingly interconnected, interdependent world."[101] Other elders include Trilateral Commission members **Jimmy Carter**, **Mary Robinson** and **Ernesto Zedillo**. Of course, The Elders are self-appointed but nevertheless view themselves as the real elders of the global village known to them as planet earth.

After the Earth Summit was completed, the Trilateral Commission's influence was hardly over. President **George H. Bush** had personally attended the Summit in Rio, and while he rejected some parts of the signing ceremonies, he did sign the *Framework Convention on Climate Change*. Soon-to-be President **William Jefferson Clinton** blasted Bush for his inept leadership and stated, "I would be signing every one of those documents--proudly."[102]

After his election, President Clinton wasted no time in starting the implementation of Agenda 21. On March 3, 1993, just one month before the official Agenda 21 book was released, Clinton hastily announced a program called the National Performance Review (NPR) and appointed Vice President **Al Gore** as its first director. On September 11, 1993, Clinton finalized the NPR by signing Executive Order 12862. In 1998, the truer colors of NPR were revealed when it was renamed the National Partnership for Reinventing Government.

Why the need to reinvent our government? In short, implementing Agenda 21 and Sustainable Development would require a different form of government that was out of the view of the

---

101   See www.TheElders.org.

102   "EARTH SUMMIT : Clinton Blasts Bush for U.S. 'Holdout' in Rio", *Los Angeles Times*, June 13, 1992.

public and lawmakers alike. Agenda 21 would be implemented across America through a system of regional governance entities called Councils of Governments, or COGS. At the local level, these COGS quietly apply these un-American policies while generally keeping the public in the dark. Section 4 of the U.S. Constitution states, "The United States shall guarantee to every State in this Union a Republican Form of Government." Regional governance by unelected and unaccountable COGS is the polar opposite of a Republican Form of Government.

On April 23, 1993, the official *Agenda 21* 300 page, 40-chapter book was published, and it was widely heralded by the rest of the world. In the U.S., it was mostly a non-event. There is little doubt that if the *Agenda 21* book had been circulated in the U.S. as an official policy document, there would have been a significant backlash, if not outright rebellion. Clinton instead opted for an "end-run around national sovereignty" by signing Executive Order 12852 on June 29, 1993 that created the President's Council on Sustainable Development (PCSD). Vice President **Al Gore** wrote about Clinton's intent:

Its goal, he declared, was to find ways "to bring people together to meet the needs of the present without jeopardizing the future."[103]

This direct quote from **Bill Clinton** rings back to **Gro Brundtland's** definition of Sustainable Development found in *Our Common Future*:

*Sustainable development is development that **meets the needs of the present without compromising the ability of future generations** to meet their own needs.* [Emphasis added]

Although there would be no record of it, my guess is that somewhere in the 1980s, the Trilateral Commission (or some prominent members thereof) met to purposely hammer out a clever marketing slogan that would sell their Technocracy to the world. It has definitely made the rounds. You will frequently find this exact phrase in general planning documents for local cities, towns and counties all across America!

103 President's Council on Sustainable Development, Sustainable America: A New Consensus (Washington, DC: U.S. Government Printing Office, February 1996), p. 2.

By 1998, the PCSD produced its own book, *Sustainable America*, that personalized Agenda 21 policies for the U.S. According to one report,

> *The **crown jewel of the PCSD's work** is the national action strategy articulated in the report, Sustainable America. The report spells out a specific set of national goals, backs these with a broad set of policy recommendations, and details specific actions necessary to support their implementation. Finally, the report also includes a tentative set of indicators to measure the country's progress toward achieving the goals proposed. The PCSD's co-chairs and the task forces kept their eyes on the prize: **articulating a road map for the U.S.**[104]* [Emphasis added]

Roadmap, indeed. The only problem is that the rest of America was never told what was going on right under their nose.

In regional and local implementation scenarios, it became known as *Local Agenda 21*, or simply, LA21. However, don't think the American public wasn't catching on and throwing up a roadblock; and don't think that the PCSD didn't feel the heat. J. Gary Lawrence, an advisor to the PCSD, gave a telling speech in June 1998 in England, titled *The Future of Local Agenda 21 in the New Millennium* and let the proverbial cat out of the bag:

> *Participating in a UN advocated planning process would very likely bring out many of the conspiracy-fixated groups and individuals in our society such as the National Rifle Association, citizen militias and some members of Congress. **This segment of our society who fear "one-world government" and a UN invasion of the United States through which our individual freedom would be stripped away would actively work to defeat any elected official who joined "the conspiracy" by undertaking LA21. So, we call our processes something else, such as comprehensive planning, growth management or smart growth.**[105]* [Emphasis added]

104   Crescencia Maurer, *The U.S. President's Council on Sustainable Development: A Case Study*, September 1998.
105   J.Gary Lawrence, "The Future of Local Agenda 21 in the New Millennium", *The Millemium Papers Issue 2*, 1998, p. 5.

If you have ever wondered why local officials don't know what you are talking about when you mention Agenda 21 or LA21, now you know why. The language was changed. Instead, ask them what they know about comprehensive planning, growth management or smart growth and you will have a lengthy conversation! As Lawrence concluded his talk, he hinted at the sea of change directly ahead in 1999 and beyond: "The next step is organizational transformation so that LA21 is not a process but a state of being." Today, his goal has largely been met with 717 regional government entities across 50 states, all continuously implementing Agenda 21 and Sustainable Development policies.

Some readers may still be wondering exactly how Sustainable Development is related to Technocracy. The answer is contained in the word "development" which in all cases refers to *economic* development. The U.N.'s so-called "green economy" is synonymous with Sustainable Development, which is prescribed by Agenda 21, which is derived from the Technocracy-based economic model. Virtually every local planning document created in the last ten years will have economic development language embedded in it; frequently used terms include public-private partnerships, smart growth, comprehensive planning, urban renewal, collaborative planning, land use planning and so on. In every instance, you must remember that the green economy is not the same as America's traditional capitalist economy. The green economy changes the rules of the game and produces new winners and losers. Those who haven't recognized this changing economic landscape will most often find themselves on the outside looking in wondering what happened to the world they once understood.

What is Sustainable Economy?

What does the green economy mean in practical terms? To answer this question we must turn to the official documents of Sustainable Development:

1. *Agenda 21: Programme of Action For Sustainable Development.* (A21) This 294 page, 40-chapter book, published in 1993, is the original specification for Agenda 21 that was decided at the Earth Summit in Rio in June 1992.

2. *Global Biodiversity Assessment* (GBA). This 1140-page doc-
    ument was published by the United Nations Environment
    Programme in 1995 and greatly expands many sections
    of the Agenda 21 document.

The following will give a short summary of a few areas that are
clearly addressed in the A21 and GBA documents.

Education

Education was seen as foundational to promote Sustainable
Development dogma. In order to promote global transformation,
global education standards were needed. Agenda 21 addressed
this in Chapter 36:

> *Education is critical for promoting sustainable development
> and improving the capacity of the people to address environ-
> mental and development issues... [members agree to] achieve
> environmental and development awareness in all sectors
> of society on a world-wide scale as soon as possible... non-
> governmental organizations can make an important con-
> tribution in designing and implementing educational pro-
> grammes.*[106]

The Bill and Melinda Gates Foundation, for instance, is such
a Non-Governmental Organization (NGO) that made an "important contribution" by funding the development of Common Core
State Standards (CCSS) for education in 2008 - to the tune of $239
million! Gates turned to another NGO, the National Governors
Association (NGA), to spread Common Core State Standards
throughout America. The NGA's website claims that Common
Core is a "state-led effort", but nothing could be further from the
truth; it was a top-down implementation of a global program,
forced down the throat of unsuspecting state educators and parents.

Free Trade

Agenda 21's treatment of Free Trade and Protectionism quickly give away the people who created it, namely, members of the
Trilateral Commission and their globalist friends. It is therefore
not surprising that A21 states that all nations should

---

106   Agenda 21, p.265.

*Halt and reverse protectionism in order to bring about fur-
ther liberalization and expansion of world trade... facilitate
the integration of all countries into the world economy and
the international trading system... implement previous commitments to hold and reverse protectionism and further expand market access.*[107]

Such promotion by Trilateral members started well before
1992, however. In 1976, Trilateral Commission member **Carla A.
Hills** chaired the U.S. delegation to the U.N. Conference on Human
Settlements (Habitat I). Her report stated,

*To achieve universal progress in the quality of life, a fair and
balanced structure of the economic relations between states
has to be promoted. It is therefore essential to implement
urgently the **New International Economic Order**, based
on the Declaration and Programme of Action approved by
the General Assembly in its sixth special session, and on the
Charter of Economic Rights and Duties of the States.*[108]

Thus, Hills set the tone for the outcome of the Habitat I conference, namely, to stimulate the urgent implementation of the
"New International Economic Order", a phrase and concept that
was found nowhere else except in Trilateral Commission literature and talking points.

Agriculture

The *Global Biodiversity Assessment* calls for a reduction of agricultural acreage, restrictions on unsustainable activities, and a
return of existing land to native habitat condition:

*And while agriculture has benefitted enormously from bio-
diversity, its success has contributed increasingly to the loss
of biodiversity. Land use for human food production now oc-
cupies over one-third of the world's land area - in 1991 crop-
land covered 11% of the world's land area, and permanent
pasture 26% - and is the leading cause of habitat conversion
on a global basis.*[109]

---

107   Agenda 21, p. 21
108   "U.N. Conference on Human Settlements", *Habitat I*, 1976, p. 6, Item 14.
109   Vernon Heywood, ed, *Global Biodiversity Assessment*, (Cambridge University Press
1996), p. 943.

Agriculture makes a relatively small contribution to overall economic activity in America as measured by the Gross Domestic Product, but it represents a large part of personal expenditures and is necessary for the sustaining of life. Nevertheless, pressure has been increasingly placed on American farmers and ranchers to curtail their production activities, to the extent that tens of thousands have been driven out of business over the last 25 years.

Dams and Reservoirs

Policies and calls for the destruction and removal of dams began during the Clinton Administration under Secretary of the Interior **Bruce Babbitt**, who was also a member of the Trilateral Commission along with Clinton and Gore. In 2012 Babbitt wrote, "dam removal has evolved from a novelty to an accepted means of river restoration."[110] The GBA was instrumental in moving the destruction of dams from Babbitt's novelty to what it is today:

> ...dam construction is the most obvious human intervention leading to the loss of wetland habitats... Rivers are also being influenced through human activities in their catchments, which are being influenced by embankments, draining deforestation, urbanization and industry. The remaining free-flowing large river systems are relatively small and nearly all situated in the far north.[111]

There are approximately 65,000 dams in the United States, and some 22,000 have been targeted for removal. There is nothing logical about dam removal. Hydroelectric power is the cheapest and most efficient source of energy available where it is possible. Economic activity surrounding lakes and reservoirs includes marinas, campgrounds, restaurants, housing developments, recreation facilities, etc., all of which would be wiped out if the water disappears.

Property Rights

Private property is eschewed, calling for government control of rights and resources that will be "licensed" in certain situa-

---

110   Bruce Babbitt, "The Dawn of Dam Removal", Patagonia, 2012.
111   *GBA, p. 755*

tions:

> Property rights can still be allocated to environmental public goods, but in this case they should be restricted to usufructual or user rights. Harvesting quotas, emission permits and development rights... are all examples of such rights.[112]

The word "usufruct" is derived from Roman law and means "the legal right of using and enjoying the fruits or profits of something belonging to another." Since Rome claimed ownership to everything, people had to apply for "rights" which they would never be able to own outright. Such rights can be revoked by the owner at any time.

In 1976, Trilateral Commission member **Carla A. Hills** said the following about land and property rights:

> Land, because of its unique nature and the crucial role it plays in human settlements, cannot be treated as an ordinary asset, controlled by individuals and subject to the pressures and inefficiencies of the market. Private land ownership is also a principal instrument of accumulation and concentration of wealth and therefore contributes to social injustice; if unchecked, it may become a major obstacle in the planning and implementation of development schemes. Social justice, urban renewal and development, the provision of decent dwellings and healthy conditions for the people can only be achieved if land is used in the interests of society as a whole.[113]

The consistent use of the word "usufruct" in documents such as the GBA serve to explain why the Federal government is rushing to lock up as much as 50 percent of all the available land in the United States. For those property owners who will not sell, their property rights are then diminished to the point where their property has no remaining value in the market.

Population Control

It is stating the obvious that all economic activity ultimately depends on people as consumers. People buy things for survival and for pleasure. Increasing population has afforded economic

---

112   GBA, Sec. 12.7.5.
113   Ibid.

growth in America since the day it was founded in 1776. Agenda 21 and GBA declare that in order to put resources back into balance with current human consumption, there will have to be a significant shrinkage in population:

A reasonable estimate for an industrialized world society at the present North American material standard of living would be one billion. At the more frugal European standard of living, 2-3 billion would be possible.[114]

There are approximately 7.2 billion people on the planet today. While the GBA does not suggest ways to get rid of 5-6 billion people outright, it does suggest that we must lower our standard of living to the point of being in balance with what they think the environment can supply to us. In 1804, global population was one billion people. Extrapolating consumption per capita back to that level would almost satisfy the GBA's criteria. Of course, that would be an economic disaster because 95% of all commercial enterprises would be put out of business, and those that remain would be shrunken beyond recognition.

Information management

As documented in the *Technocracy Study Course* in 1934, three of the original requirements were:

- *Provide a continuous inventory of all production and consumption*
- *Provide a specific registration of the type, kind, etc., of all goods and services, where produced and where used*
- *Provide specific registration of the consumption of each individual, plus a record and description of the individual.*[115]

It is not surprising to see this exact Technocracy-inspired terminology turn up in the A21 document:

Expand or promote databases on production and consumption and develop methodologies for analyzing them... Assess the relationship between production and consumption, environment, technological adaption and innovation, economic

---

114   BGA, 11.2.3.2.
115   Hubbert & Scott, p. 232.

growth and development, and demographic factors... Identify balanced patterns of consumption worldwide.[116]

Other things that have been deemed unsustainable by A21 and the GBA include things like power line construction, harvesting timber, hunting, dams and reservoirs, automobiles, fencing off pasture, private land ownership, grazing of livestock, livestock, electric appliances, rural living, paved roads, railroads, and a plethora of others. Any activity to expand activities in these areas will now be met with fierce resistance, while activity to curtail them will be praised as sustainable.

Sustainable Development is a Trojan horse that looks good on the outside but is filled with highly toxic and militant policies on the inside. It promises a utopian dream that it cannot possibly deliver. There is no economic growth if living standards and consumption patterns regress back into the 1800s, or if population is curtailed. There is no economic satisfaction if people cannot easily enjoy and transfer real property or accumulate wealth and savings. There is no personal satisfaction if people are constantly under a microscope for analysis of their sustainable activity, or the lack of it.

---

116   Agenda 21, p. 32.

CHAPTER 5

TRANSFORMING GOVERNMENT

Society is built on three legs: economics, politics and religion. These three must be mutually compatible or the society will not last long, and the dust bin of history has plenty of examples of societies that failed when division set in. During the transition from Capitalism to Technocracy, today's modern society appears to be dysfunctional and irrational. The underlying reality is that as the societal model morphs into Technocracy, nothing is clear to those who try to understand the world using traditional and outdated concepts. The reader has already discovered how radically different the "green" economy is compared to traditional price-based economic theory. Now we must explore how management of society will be conducted by Technocrats, and how that differs from traditional political concepts of a government which is, in the famous words of Abraham Lincoln at the Gettysburg Address, "of the people, by the people and for the people".

In America, government has traditionally been based on geographical boundaries. A city has "city limits", a county has a "county line" and a state has borders. Within those geographical limits, the citizens exercise political autonomy to create whatever kind of life they want to enjoy, and each grouping of citizens must determine how to best run its own infrastructure, education, health care, social services, etc.

Technocracy turns this concept on its head by dissolving sovereign borders while calling for a system of governance based on *Functional Sequence* that removes a segment of responsibility from the lower political entity and awards it to a higher level. To an engineer like M. King Hubbert (co-founder of Technocracy, Inc. in 1934), this was a perfectly natural and "efficient" way of viewing the Technate, or the individual unit of Technocracy that contained citizens. According to Hubbert then,

The basic unit of this organization is the Functional

Sequence. A Functional Sequence is one of the larger industrial or social units, the various parts of which are related one to the other in a direct functional sequence.

*Thus among the major Industrial Sequences we have transportation **(rail-roads, waterways, airways, highways and pipe lines); communication (mail, telephone, telegraph, radio and television); agriculture (farming, ranching, dairying, etc.)**; and the major industrial units such as **textiles, iron and steel**, etc.*

*Among the Service Sequences are **education** (this would embrace the complete training of the younger generation), and **public health (medicine, dentistry, public hygiene, and all hospitals and pharmaceutical plants as well as institutions for defectives)**.*[113] [Emphasis added]

Furthermore, Hubbert envisioned the appointed head of each Functional Sequence as belonging to a continental board of directors which itself would be headed by a Continental Director. For each of these "functions", there would be no democratic discussion or vote because the engineering expert-in-charge knows best how to run things by applying logic and efficiency. Furthermore, even though local control is promised for a myriad of other issues, these Functional Sequences would be merely provided as services to the individual Technates.

It is not a stretch to correlate Hubbert's vision to modern implementation of Functional Sequences such as health care (Obamacare), control over water (Army Corps of Engineers), land (Councils of Governments), agricultural practices (Bureau of Land Management), education (Common Core), energy (Department of Energy, Smart Grid), transportation (Metropolitan Planning Organizations), emergency management (FEMA) and so on. Not long ago, all of these functions were under local or personal control within the context of traditional geographic boundaries such as cities, towns, counties and states. A town, for instance, had a locally-elected school board that set education policy for itself. Emergency management was managed by a fire board or city council. Land use was determined by an elected zoning board.

---

113   Hubbert and Scott, p. 218.

Hubbert's above reference to "institutions for defectives" is disturbing and shows evidence of his strong views on eugenics as a necessary Functional Sequence. Apparently, the inefficiencies of defectives and their high cost of maintenance are not to be tolerated in a system that strives for perfect efficiency. In California, where Technocracy, Inc. found its largest support, eugenics was in its heyday during the 1930s where over 20,000 men, women and children were deemed defective and were subsequently sterilized by force. This is a dark history of California, by the way, but I can personally attest to the reality of it. This writer was adopted at birth by a woman who had been forcibly sterilized because her older brother was deemed to be genetically "retarded". A few years later, it was determined that her brother was not retarded at all, but had been deprived of oxygen at birth, thus producing brain damage. An investigative article written in 2012 by *CNN Health* stated,

> *Thirty-two states had eugenics programs, but California was in a league of its own... In California, the eugenics movement was led by figures such as David Starr Jordan, president of Stanford University, and Harry Chandler, publisher of the Los Angeles Times.... California's movement was so effective that in the 1930s, members of the Nazi party asked California eugenicists for advice on how to run their own sterilization program. "Germany used California's program as its chief example that this was a working, successful policy," Cogdell said. "They modeled their law on California's law."[114]*

Shamefully for California, its eugenics and forced sterilization program continued to operate until 1963. On a national and global scale, eugenics is still alive and well, most often associated with the population control policies put forth by Agenda 21.

As mentioned earlier in this book, President **Bill Clinton** signed Executive Order 12862 on September 11, 1993 that formalized the National Performance Review (NPR) which was headed up by **Al Gore**. NPR was later more accurately renamed the National Partnership for Reinventing Government. The intellectual work that brought Clinton and Gore to take action was a book titled *Reinventing Government* by Osborne and Gaebler. The

---

114   "California's dark legacy of forced sterilizations", *CNN Health*, March 15, 2002

book was published on February 1, 1993 and reviewed as follows on May 1, 1993:

> *In Reinventing Government, David Osborne and Ted Gaebler attempt to chart a course between big government and laissez faire. They want nothing to do with "ideology". Rather,* **Osborne and Gaebler are technocrats in search of pragmatic answers.** *"Reinventing Government," they write, "addresses how governments work, not what governments do." Thus, from the standpoint of what governments do, the book is a proverbial grab bag of policy prescriptions, some good, some bad.*[115] [Emphasis added]

Yes, you read that right: They were *"technocrats in search of pragmatic answers."* Osborne and Gaebler were completely in tune with historic Technocracy by focusing on "how governments work, not what governments do". In fact, Technocrats have *never* cared about political ideology, but rather only about the best and most efficient solutions to any problem that could be described in engineering terms. Thus, historic Technocracy gave them convenient license to tackle the Functional Sequences of government in ways not previously seen. Historians have already credited Osborne and Gaebler as being the singular inspiration behind Clinton's Partnership on Reinventing Government, but the fact that they were technocrats gives a different perspective on the matter. Indeed, they set the course for reinventing government along the lines of Functional Sequences that would support and incentivize the reinvented economic system of Technocracy, also described as the "green economy" of Sustainable Development.

Vice President **Al Gore** chose David Osborne to be his senior advisor in running the National Performance Review, and he subsequently became the principal author of the NPR report that *Time Magazine* allegedly called "the most readable federal document in memory".

Clinton's program was so impressive that by 1999, it was picked up by the United Nations as a global program under the auspices of the U.N. Public Administration Programme (UNPAP). In a docu-

---

115   Franklin Harris, Jr., "Reinventing Government", Freeman, May 1 1993.

ment titled *The Global Forum on Reinventing Government*, UNPAP describes what happened as follows:

> *The Global Forum was first organized by the Government of the United States in 1999. Since then, it has emerged as one of the most significant global events to address government reinvention. Subsequent forums have been organized by the Governments of Brazil, Italy, Morocco, Mexico, and the Republic of Korea, respectively. During the 6th Global Forum held in Seoul in May 2005, the United Nations Under-Secretary-General invited participants to the 7th Global Forum to be held at the UN Headquarters.*[116]

This further confirms the global push toward Technocracy because governments throughout the world must be similarly transformed if they are to be compatible with an energy-based economic system run by technocrats and not by elected officials.

Essentially, the goal of reinventing government was to convert from a bureaucratic to a business model of governance. When Clinton first announced his initiative in March 1993, he stated, "Our goal is to make the entire federal government less expensive and more efficient, and to change the culture of our national bureaucracy away from complacency and entitlement toward initiative and empowerment."[117] The first three - cutting expenses, improving efficiency, encouraging initiative - can be seen as the typical mantra of Technocracy, but "empowerment" needs some explanation.

In a corporate sense, empowerment refers to a results-oriented culture where authority to decide how to complete a given outcome is pushed down the chain of command to the lowest level of management. When senior managers declare a certain strategy for their organization, that strategy is broadcast to the organization with instructions to "get it done" by whatever means they can employ. Whatever the mission is, there might be different ways to act locally in different settings to achieve the common outcome.

---

116   UN Public Administration Programme, The Global Forum on Reinventing Government, (http://unpan1.un.org/intradoc/groups/public/documents/un/unpan026997. pdf).
117   Breul and Kamensky, "Federal Government Reform: Lessons from Clinton's 'Reinventing Government' and Bush's 'Management Agenda' Initiatives", *Public Administration Review Vol. 68, No. 6* , (Nov. - Dec., 2008), pp. 1009-1026.

This is radically different from a bureaucratic structure that operates within a structure of laws imposed by elected national, state or local legislative bodies. It must be remembered that the United States was founded as a Republic based on the Rule of Law. Government servants were to uphold and implement the law and were not allowed to act outside of those legal bounds no matter what the setting. Entire government organizations as well as all of their employees were bound by the same laws, to be interpreted in the same way in every issue and practice.

The newly reinvented system of governance puts its emphasis on implementing regulations rather than on enforcing laws. If legal obstacles are encountered, the organization is empowered to take whatever pragmatic approach they can devise to skirt the law in favor of the regulation. If empowerment means pragmatism, which it does, then it fits perfectly with the other Technocratic goals that Clinton expressed. The theoretical result of emphasizing regulations over laws is a lawless government and could have been recognized as such in 1993.

How does this work in practice? Modern examples are all around us, but none better than the breakdown of our southern border with Mexico. Section 4 of Article IV of the U.S. Constitution states,

The United States shall guarantee to every State in this Union a Republican Form of Government, and shall protect each of them against Invasion; and on Application of the Legislature, or of the Executive (when the Legislature cannot be convened), against domestic Violence.

In addition, there are many specific laws that state exactly how the border is to be set up, who is allowed to enter, and under what terms and conditions. The Executive Branch, on the other hand, chooses not to enforce the law but rather enforces its own regulations even when they are contrary to the law. In 2012, President Obama directed the Department of Homeland Security to implement a new non-deportation policy expressed in the form of regulations. This quickly prompted a lawsuit by Immigration Customs and Enforcement (ICE) agents to block the policies because it forced them to break the law *and* the Constitution:

The lawsuit, filed in federal court in the Northern District of Texas, argues that the administration policies fail to pass muster on three grounds: They infringe on Congress' right to set immigration policy, they force ICE agents to disregard the 1996 law, and the Homeland Security Department didn't follow the federal Administrative Procedure Act, which requires agencies to write regulations and put them out for public comment before taking big steps.[118]

In another matter on July 28, 2014, all Republican members of the Texas House and Senate signed a letter to President Obama asking him to enforce existing law on immigration. U.S. Representative Lamar Smith (R-TX) stated, "The President has it in his power right now, if he were to enforce current immigration laws, to stop this surge coming across the border."[119]

To say that the U.S. Border with Mexico is becoming a lawless wasteland is an understatement. Illegal entrants flood all sections of the border, knowing the odds of being detained are virtually nil. Many even walk through border checkpoints with impunity, knowing that border agents will not stop them. Required medical screening and criminal background checks are not performed, and stated destinations are not verified.

Border security may be an extreme example of an "empowered" government, but it reveals the attitude and practice of Technocrats who feel that their system of regulations and outcomes are more important than standing laws, sitting Congressional representatives and the Constitution. Someone may argue that things like this happened prior to Clinton's initiative to reinvent government, to which I would answer, "Yes, there were instances of very bad government behavior in the past, but now it has become the norm." In the end, the Executive and Legislative Branches of our government will be nose-to-nose in a battle of will to see who gets to call the shots.

The old saying that "Possession is nine-tenths of the law" is false, but it serves to make this point: The President is CEO over 2.2 million Federal workers and has autonomous control over

118   "Immigration agents sue to stop Obama's non-deportation policy", *Washington Times*, August 23, 2012.
119   "Texas GOP Congressmen to Obama: Enforce Existing Immigration Law", *WOAI News Radio*, July 28, 2014.

how the annual budget is allocated and spent. Congress has 635 members. Who is going to win when push comes to shove? We already know the answer to this question, as the Executive Branch already treats Congress with complete disregard and impunity, enforcing laws it wants to enforce while ignoring laws it does not want to enforce. Even more alarming is the almost total disregard for the U.S. Constitution.

In the end, reinventing government is about creating and implementing a system of management control found in major global corporations. Just like in the corporate world, there is no room for disobedience or dissent. Compliance, conformity and loyalty to the corporate mission statement are all that matters. Unlike people, corporations don't have a soul; they exist solely to make a profit for their stockholders. But the government doesn't have stockholders, does it? Let's examine that question more closely.

The Alliance for Redesigning Government (ARG) is a non-profit (NGO) that was founded to create a learning network for change agents in government at all levels for the express purpose of reinventing government. IBM partnered with the ARG to provide the technology for a comprehensive distance-learning system that would distribute volumes of information to every corner of the nation. Financial supporters at the top of the list included Anderson Consulting, AT&T, General Electric, Goldman Sachs and Co., IBM, NYNEX, and Xerox. Philanthropic donations poured in from ARCO Foundation, Aspen Institute, Carnegie Corporation, Annie E. Casey Foundation, Ford Foundation, John D. and Catherine T. MacArthur Foundation, the Pew Charitable Trusts, and the Rockefeller Foundation, among others. The Board of Advisors included Trilateral Commission members Sen. **William Roth** (R-Delaware) and **John Sweeney**, president of the AFL-CIO.

The Alliance then formally introduced the Public-Private Partnerships as a tool-of-choice for economic development. According to its own literature,

Partnerships between government agencies and private for-profit and non-profit organizations have proven to be an effective tool for planning and implementing programs. Public-private partnerships have been working effectively

for many years. Susan and Norma Fainstein in their research of "Public-Private Partnerships for Urban (Re) Development in the United States" note that the original federal urban renewal legislation in 1949 provided for locally operated redevelopment authorities (public agencies) to **acquire land using powers of eminent domain and then to sell the land at a reduced price to private corporations for development.** [Ed. Note: this is the scheme]

As economic growth has slowed and government resources have become more limited, public-private partnerships have formed to undertake projects that had previously been funded by the federal government. The Fainsteins' research indicates that during the years when Ronald Reagan was president, the federal government began a policy of decentralization and deregulation. Funding for many categorical entitlement urban development and social service programs was eliminated and block grants were provided to states and localities to be used at their discretion. **At that time, the Fainsteins' report, the use of public-private partnerships changed in nature.** *[Ed. Note: This is how the scheme is implemented]* **Private for-profit and not-for profit corporations began to negotiate partnerships undertaking economic development and affordable housing rehabilitation and construction projects in exchange for tax incentives, subsidies, or future profits.**[120] [Emphasis added]

Does the government have stockholders? Absolutely! Global corporations and banks, NGOs and globalist foundations. Furthermore, they expect a return on their investments, namely, privatized "sweetheart" deals that lock out competitors. In many cases, this gives the "private" party a monopoly over the services offered. Citizens are only seen as consumers.

Prior to the 1993 Clinton/Gore initiative, the goal of government was to serve the people. Now the goal is not to serve the people but rather to serve its stockholders. Previously, the goal was to facilitate a price-based, free-market economic system.

---

120 "Government Partnerships", Alliance for Reinventing Government web site, 2000.

Now the goal is to facilitate an energy-based green economy predicated on Sustainable Development and Agenda 21 policies.

The bottom line is that our Federal government, as represented by the Executive Branch and all of its agencies, no longer represents the citizens of the nation, and *that* is why Congress and the Constitution have been effectively neutered. Lastly, we see the clear trail of Trilateral Commission members from start to finish.

Transforming Education

This topic could enjoy its own chapter heading, but the discussion is placed here because education is controlled by the government and has been transformed by it along with all the other Functional and Service Sequences discussed above.

The 1930s *Technocracy Study Course* had much to say about education, and it pointedly explains why modern technocrats have undertaken the systemization of education in America under such programs as *No Child Left Behind* and more recently, *Common Core*. While we explored the concept of Functional Sequences earlier in this chapter, more needs to be said about Service Sequences such as education and health care which were seen as closely aligned with each other for the sake of running a perfectly efficient society. That Technocracy proposed complete control over education is seen in statements like,

> Among the Service Sequences are education (**this would embrace the complete training of the younger generation**), and public health (medicine, dentistry, public hygiene, and all hospitals and pharmaceutical plants as well as institutions for defectives).[121] [Emphasis added]

The idea of "complete" points to social conditioning from birth to the point of entering the workforce and beyond in the form of adult education. Just as today's public health is a cradle-to-grave Service Sequence, so also is education, for the Technocrats saw the mental state of the learner as a function of his conditioning. Thus, educational conditioning and health care became inseparable disciplines which could serve society only together in a per-

---

121   Hubbert & Scott, p. 218.

manently symbiotic fashion. The joint record-keeping design is seen in statements like this:

> There is, likewise, **a complete record on all hospitals, on the educational system,** amusements, and others on the more purely social services. This information makes it possible to know exactly what to do at all times in order to maintain the operation of the social mechanism at the highest possible load factor and efficiency.[122]

There is no room for human individuality in Technocracy where the only goal is to "maintain the operation of the social mechanism at the highest possible load factor and efficiency." However, humans are not merely machines, and neither is society. They are not to be valued only by what they produce or how efficiently they produce it. And yet, Technocracy persisted in the *outcome-based* mentality where all of society (and people therein) would be measured, analyzed, correlated, corrected and conditioned from cradle to grave. I have purposely used the term "outcome-based" to emphasize where this modern term used in educational circles came from. Outcome-based society demands an outcome-based educational system. However, it is not really education at all. It is a conditioning no different than training a dog or other animal to repeat a task based on some predetermined stimulus. Inherent ability beyond performing the task is superfluous. Technocracy, Inc. could not have been more clear on this:

> The **end products attained** by a high-energy social mechanism on the North American Continent will be
>
> (a) a high physical standard of living, (b) a high standard of public health, (c) a minimum of unnecessary labor, (d) a minimum of wastage of non-replaceable resources, (e) **an educational system to train the entire younger generation indiscriminately as regards all considerations other than inherent ability—a Continental system of human conditioning.**[123] [Emphasis added]

Fast-forward again to 1992 and the Agenda 21 document that

---

122   Ibid., p. 232.
123   Ibid.

also deals extensively with education in Chapter 36. It starts out by stating:

> *Education, raising of public awareness and training are linked to virtually all areas in Agenda 21, and even more closely to the ones on meeting basic needs, capacity-building, data and information, science, and the role of major groups.*[124]

It then follows up with the initial subject title, *Reorienting education towards sustainable development*, which mirrors the earlier document:

> *Education, including formal education, public awareness and training should be recognized as a process **by which human beings and societies can reach their fullest potential.** Education is **critical for promoting sustainable development** and improving the capacity of the people to address environment and development issues. While basic education provides the underpinning for any environmental and development education, the latter needs to be incorporated as an essential part of learning... It is also **critical for achieving environmental and ethical awareness, values and attitudes, skills and behavior** consistent with sustainable development and for effective public participation in decision-making. To be effective, environment and development education should deal with the dynamics of both the physical/biological and socio-economic environment and human (which **may include spiritual**) development, should be integrated in all disciplines, and should employ formal and non-formal methods and effective means of communication.*[125]

This was a grand scheme of Agenda 21, but one for which it had no direct means of developing or implementing; it merely pointed out that reforming education is critical to the implementation of Agenda 21 in its entirety. Later in Chapter 36, the solution is suggested:

> *Countries, assisted by **international organizations, nongovernmental organizations** and **other sectors**, could strengthen or establish national or regional centres of ex-*

124   Daniel Sitarz ed., *Agenda 21: The Earth Summit strategy to save our planet*, United Nations Conference on Environment & Development, (Earth Press, 1993), Chap. 36, p. 320.
125   Ibid.

cellence in interdisciplinary research and education in environmental and developmental sciences, law and the management of specific environmental problems.[126] [Emphasis added]

Thus, when single nations are unable to reform education by themselves, the task should be turned over to international organizations (e.g., the United Nations) and non-governmental organizations (NGOs). This is precisely what happened when the Bill and Melinda Gates Foundation decided to fund the creation of the Common Core State Standards that would be implemented throughout the states and into every grade in every school in America. The resulting set of standards was jointly copyrighted by two private organizations, as stated on the CoreStandards.org web site:

Please be advised that any publication or public display must include the following notice: "© Copyright 2010 **National Governors Association Center** *for Best Practices and* **Council of Chief State School Officers.** *All rights reserved."*[127] [Emphasis added]

On February 17, 2009, President Obama signed into law the *American Recovery and Reinvestment Act of 2009 (ARRA),* which was the major economic stimulus bill designed to pull the economy out of a near-collapsed condition. Initially funded to the tune of $787 billion, $4.35 billion was allotted for a competitive education grant program called "Race to the Top". For states that qualified, and all did, funds were poured out like water to the financially-stressed states. Of course, strings were attached, but at the time they accepted the funds, the states were not told exactly what they those strings were. There were hints:

- *Adopting standards and assessments that prepare students to succeed in college and the workplace and to compete in the global economy;*
- *Building data systems that measure student growth and success, and inform teachers and principals about how they can improve instruction.*[128]

---

126   Ibid., p. 323.
127   Common Core copyright notice (http://www.corestandards.org).
128   "Race to the Top", Executive Summary, (Department of Education, 2014), (http://www2.

In fact, the states unwittingly signed on to accept the entirety of Common Core State Standards that were still under development by private organizations, funded by private donations. When the publishing date arrived, it was the National Governors Association and the Council of Chief State School Officers who trotted out this Trojan horse and simultaneously let down the stairway in 46 states. As word began to trickle out to parents what had happened, a groundswell of resistance suddenly appeared and continues to the present. Some states have subsequently passed legislation to ban Common Core altogether. Many parents pulled their kids out of government schools in favor of home schooling but are still in a dilemma: the SAT tests necessary for college entrance have already been redesigned to test for Common Core material.

Not surprisingly, the Common Core curriculum is focused squarely on Sustainable Development and Biodiversity issues with an over-the-top layer of sexual content. What was formerly classed as education is now transformed into indoctrination and conditioning, or training. This is an important distinction to grasp: Humans receive education but animals receive training. But to the technocrat mindset, humans are only animals and thus should be trained as well.

In any case, adopting standards and building data systems are the top priorities that the states signed on for. As mentioned above, Technocracy coupled education with healthcare. It is also not surprising that Obamacare and Common Core are tightly coupled in the area of data collection. Common Core requires massive data collection of up to 400 data points per student, whereas the Affordable Care Act (ACA or "Obamacare") requires comprehensive and ongoing data collection without limitation. But is there any direct relationship between Common Core and Obamacare? Yes!

Under Subtitle B, Section 4101 of the Affordable Care Act, a grant program was authorized for the establishment of school-based health centers (SBHC).

> *PROGRAM.—The Secretary of Health and Human Services (in this subsection referred to as the "Secretary") shall establish*

ed.gov/programs/racetothetop/index.html).

a program to award grants to eligible entities to support the operation of school-based health centers.[129]

Essentially, this is a merging of the school with the health care system, and the ACA clearly explains the details for delivery of health services, but more importantly, the integration of data collection:

Sec. 399Z-1 (A). PHYSICAL. - **Comprehensive health assessments**, *diagnosis, and treatment of minor, acute, and chronic medical conditions, and referrals to, and follow-up for, specialty care and oral health services*

Sec. 399Z-1 (B). MENTAL HEALTH. - **Mental health and substance use disorder assessments**, *crisis intervention, counseling, treatment, and referral to a continuum of services including emergency psychiatric care, community support programs, in-patient care, and outpatient programs.*[130]
[Emphasis added]

The term "assessment" refers to comprehensive collection of data and if anyone would doubt that, this phrase will remove all doubt: "the SBHC will comply with Federal, State, and local laws concerning patient privacy and student records."[131]

All data collected from K-1 through K-12 will be associated with the student for life, and since it is collected during "assessments" by largely unqualified personnel, the student will be forever tainted by the collector's opinions. This is not only wrongheaded, but it is patently dangerous for the individual as well as society as a whole; there are no provisions to correct or appeal data wrongly entered or data based on bad opinions.

I have publicly stated many times that Obamacare is not about healthcare but about collecting data. The same is true of Common Core. It is not about education but rather about collecting data. Now that these two branches of Service Functions have been fused together, yet another key criteria of original Technocracy has been fully met. The machine that will train the future work force now has the perfect monitoring and control system in place that will enable it to function.

---

129   Affordable Care Act, 2009, p. 1135.
130   Ibid., p. 1137.
131   Ibid., p. 1138.

CHAPTER 6

TRANSFORMING RELIGION

It has already been stated that society rests on three identical pillars: Economics, Politics and Religion. To the extent that they are compatible with each other, a society will prosper. Likewise, society will falter to the extent of disharmony or outright removal of one or more pillars. In America, all three areas are under attack at the same time. It is therefore no wonder that society is straining at the seams, or that it seems so different today compared to 40 years ago.

- Our existing price-based economic system is being reinvented with new and untested "green" economic theories that decouple resource use from economic growth.
- Our political system of Constitutional Rule of Law is being replaced by a system of autocratic regulations, created and enforced by unelected and unaccountable Technocrats.
- Our moral system of Judeo-Christian ethics has been consistently excluded from government, with a seemingly impenetrable barrier placed between church and state and is being replaced with a humanistic religion based on Scientism.

Having a Constitution that was originally based on principles of Biblical Christianity, it is therefore no wonder that respect for the Constitution has slipped in direct proportion to respect of Christianity. John Adams, a signer of the Declaration of Independence and the second President of the U.S., declared,

We have no government armed with power capable of contending with human passions unbridled by morality and religion. . . . Our constitution was made only for a moral and religious people. It is wholly inadequate to the government of any other.[132]

132   John Adams, *The Works of John Adams, Second President of the United States,* Charles Francis Adams, editor (Boston: Little, Brown, and Co. 1854), Vol. IX, p. 229, October 11, 1798

Since America has already moved on from any sense of an absolute morality and scoffs at a religion that would dare to put constraints on aberrant behavior, the Constitution truly is an inadequate document for the 21st century.

The sum of this is that the architects of Technocracy knew full well that every pillar of society must be reinvented lest their utopian dream quickly falter and fail. We have already examined the economic and political and must now turn to religion to see how it will all fit together.

As discussed in the first chapter of this book, Scientism is an extension of Positivism, which is based on a mixture of pseudo-science and empirical science. It states that science alone, with its self-selected priesthood of engineers and scientists, is the only source of truth about the nature of man, the physical world and universal reality. By definition it rejects the existence of God and all notions of divine truth as are found in the Bible. Since Scientism generally undergirds Technocracy, we must see how it also supports post-modern religion and practices.

Scientism has much in common with Humanism in that it is exclusively man-centered. In other words, it is all about what man can achieve through his own knowledge and skills. This is not to be confused with empirical science where the Scientific Method can be used to create repeatable experiments. Scientism associates itself with empirical science in order to gain credibility, but it uses pseudo-science to trick adherents into believing something that is false. The Oxford Dictionary defines *pseudo-science* as "A collection of beliefs or practices mistakenly regarded as being based on scientific method." Some of these beliefs and practices may appear as pure magic to the uninitiated, but they are nevertheless promoted as being "based in science" and are therefore infallible and immutable.

What sets a philosophy apart from a cult is whether or not a priesthood is necessary to interpret. Anyone can learn about and discuss the philosophies of ancient Greece for instance, and in that sense they are attainable by all. However, when knowledge is so obfuscated that it requires an interpreter or an oracle to explain it to common people, a priesthood is born and a cult is formed around it. To understand what the "god" of science has to say today, you must inquire of the "priest" of science, and you must decide to take his "teachings" by faith, even if there is empirical evidence to the contrary.

Henri de Saint-Simon (1760-1825) was already noted to be the early father of modern Technocracy. He believed that a scientific elite would ultimately rule over all facets of societal affairs. However, Saint-Simon also had an outspoken position on religion, as expressed in his 1825 work, *New Christianity*. After upbraiding both Catholics and Protestants for gross heresies against what he viewed as the "divine principle", his consistent demand was that

The main aim which you should urge men to work for is the improvement of the moral and physical condition of the most numerous class; and you should create a form of social organization suitable for the encouragement of this work, and to ensure that it has priority over all other undertakings, however important they may seem.[133]

Thus, the social organization designed to relieve poverty and war was the first and only important goal of religion. It was a great "brotherhood of man" that would save the world and a call for churches to become, in essence, community organizers. In the next paragraph, Saint-Simon revealed more compelling details:

*Now that the size of the planet is known, you should make the **scientists, artists, and industrialists** draw up a general plan of enterprises designed to make the domain of the human race as productive and agreeable as possible in every way.*[134] [Emphasis added]

This may be the first call to use churches to drive technocrats for the common purpose of remaking society from a holistic perspective, and completely focused on man. By the turn of the century, a more formal doctrine of Humanism had been developed, and it was represented by the American Ethical Union whose legal arm was the American Civil Liberties Union (ACLU). At the peak of Technocracy fever in 1933, "Humanist Manifesto I" was published and read in part,

---

133   Henri Saint-Simon, *The New Christianity*, (1825).
134   Ibid.

Science and economic change have disrupted the old beliefs. Religions the world over are under the necessity of coming to terms with new conditions created by a vastly increased knowledge and experience... Today man's larger understanding of the universe, his scientific achievements, and deeper appreciation of brotherhood, have created a situation which requires a new statement of the means and purposes of religion. Such a vital, fearless, and frank religion capable of furnishing adequate social goals and personal satisfactions may appear to many people as a complete break with the past.[135]

This was not an anomaly. Forty years later in 1973, "Humanist Manifesto II" was published and continued the same line of thinking:

The next century can be and should be the humanistic century. Dramatic scientific, technological, and ever-accelerating social and political changes crowd our awareness.... Using technology wisely, we can control our environment, conquer poverty, markedly reduce disease, extend our life-span, significantly modify our behavior, **alter the course of human evolution** *and cultural development, unlock vast new powers, and provide humankind with unparalleled opportunity for achieving an abundant and meaningful life.*[136] [Emphasis added]

In both Manifestos, one can see the early influence of Saint-Simon's brotherhood of man ruled by a technological elite. In the second instance, attention must be given to the phrase, "alter the course of human evolution" because it introduces for the first time the concept of Transhumanism which will be explored shortly in the chapter *Transforming Humanity*.

By the time "Humanist Manifesto III" was published in 2003, the focus was sharpened but not changed:

Knowledge of the world is derived by observation, experimentation, and rational analysis. Humanists find that science is the best method for determining this knowledge as well as for solving problems and developing beneficial technologies....

---

135   Humanist Manifesto I, *The New Humanist*, Vol. VI, No.3, 1933.
136   Humanist Manifesto II. *The Humanist*, Vol. XXXIII, No. 5.6, 1973.

*Working to benefit society maximizes individual happiness...
we support a just distribution of nature's resources and the
fruits of human effort so that as many as possible can enjoy
a good life.*[137]

By now, you should see the dovetailing of purpose between
Humanism and Technocracy: Scientific Method, Sustainable
Development, reallocation of nature's resources, and the utopian
goal of everyone enjoying the good life. This merging of purpose
didn't happen by accident, and to understand it further, a look at
the Aspen Institute for Humanistic Studies is in order.

Humanism today has been "taught" throughout the business
world by the Aspen Institute for Humanistic Studies, particularly to the multinational corporation community. The major financiers of Aspen also are the major financiers of Trilateralism,
and as of 1980, no fewer than seven members of the Trilateral
Commission were serving on the board of directors.

Aspen Institute was founded in 1949 by Professor Giuseppe
Borgese, Chancellor Robert M. Hutchins (both of University of
Chicago) and Walter Paepcke, a Chicago businessman. In 1957,
Robert O. Anderson became chairman and was its guiding
force until 1969. (Anderson became a member of the Trilateral
Commission upon its founding in 1973.) In 1969, chairmanship
switched to Joseph E. Slater, a member of the Council on Foreign
Relations and formerly of the Ford Foundation. In 1989, the
Aspen Institute for Humanistic Studies shortened its name to the
Aspen Institute, perhaps to somewhat mask its ongoing focus on
humanism.

The two leading foundations contributing to Aspen were
Atlantic-Richfield (ARCO) and the Rockefeller Foundation.
Moreover, the largest single institutional shareholder in ARCO
was Chase Manhattan (4.5%) and the largest individual shareholder was **Robert O. Anderson** who was also on the board of
directors of Chase Manhattan Bank. Other backers represented
the Morgan banking interests, indicating that the majority of fi-

---

137   "Humanist Manifesto III", *The Humanist*, 2003 (http://americanhumanist.org/
humanism/Humanist_Manifesto_III).

nancing came from the international banks in New York City, and more specifically, from foundations controlled by Rockefeller and Morgan interests. Another surprise donor was revealed to be the National Endowment for the Arts (taxpayer-funded), which provided almost one-third of Aspen's total financing in 1979.

Today, funding sources continue to include major globalist foundations that are tightly connected to members of the Trilateral Commission, including the Carnegie Foundation, Ford Foundation, William and Flora Hewlett Foundation, David and Lucile Packard Foundation, Alfred P. Sloan Foundation, Rockefeller Brothers Fund and the Rockefeller Foundation. Directors and trustees over the years have included individual Trilateral members such as **John Brademas**, **William T. Coleman, Jr.**, **Umberto Colombo** (Italy), **Robert S. Ingersol**, **Henry Kissinger**, **Paul Volker**, **Robert McNamara**, **Madeleine K. Albright**, **Yotaro Kobayashi** (Japan), **Walter Isaacson**, **Gerald M. Levin**, **Mortimer B. Zuckerman** and others.

The prestigious foreign policy arm of Aspen Institute, the Aspen Strategy Group, lists no fewer than 14 members of the Trilateral Commission, including **Madeleine K. Albright**, **Graham Allison**, **Zoe Baird**, **Richard Cooper**, **John Deutch**, **Dianne Feinstein**, **Richard Haass**, **Joseph Nye**, **Condoleezza Rice**, **Strobe Talbot**, **Fareed Zakaria** and **Robert Zoellick**.

To say that Aspen Institute is a captive audience for Trilateral Commission hegemony is an understatement. To realize that they have taught humanism to tens of thousands of top corporate executives from all over the world is staggering.

In 2005, Aspen's President was Trilateral Commissioner **Walter Isaacson**. His "Letter from the President" stated,

*The original goal of the Aspen Institute, in the words of one of its earliest mission statements, was for American business leaders to lift their sights above the possessions which possess them, to **confront their own nature as human beings**, to regain control over their own humanity by **becoming more self-aware**, more **self-correcting** and hence more **self-fulfilling**.*

...But our core mission remains the same. We seek to fos-
*ter **enlightened leadership and open-minded dialogue.***
***Through seminars, policy programs, conferences** and*
***leadership development** initiatives, the Institute and its*
international partners seek to promote nonpartisan inquiry
and an appreciation for timeless values.

*We help people become more **enlightened** in their work and*
enriched in their lives. Together we can learn one of the keys
to being successful in business, leadership and life: balanc-
ing conflicting values in order to find common ground with
our fellow citizens while remaining true to basic ideals.[138]
[Emphasis added]

Religious buzzwords seen above include self-aware, self-correcting, self-fulfilling, enlightened leadership, open-minded dialogue, timeless values, balancing conflicting values and so on. Some readers might equate such terms to New Age Enlightenment, and that would be correct. In striving for pragmatic solutions, Humanists are inclusive and intensely man-centered rather than tradition-centered. In Aspen's case, whether anyone else knew it or not, its religious humanistic agenda was closely aligned with the Trilateral Commission to implement its New International Economic Order, namely, global Technocracy.

United Religions Initiative (URI)

URI was founded in 1993 by William Swing, Bishop of the Episcopal Church Diocese of California, as an interfaith organization that sought to bind religions of the world into one common organization. The concept of interfaith organizations was nothing new, but few had made much headway in a conflict-ridden world. By contrast, URI grew at a spectacular rate, up to 100% per year. In his book, *False Dawn*, Lee Penn writes,

In 2002, New Age author Neale Donald Walsch said that the
URI is "more global in scope, and more universal in reach"
than other interfaith organizations, adding that "I am not
sure that any other interfaith organization casts that wide
a net."[139]

---

138   Aspen Institute, "Letter From the President", (http://www.aspeninstitute.org).
139   Lee Penn, *False Dawn*, (Sophia Perennis, 2005) p. 43.

The people and organizations who have drawn close to URI are striking: The World Economic Forum, Earth Charter Initiative, Ted Turner, Ford Foundation, Dee Hock (inventor of the VISA credit card, founder and former CEO of VISA International), Maurice Strong (Canadian billionaire and organizer of the U.N.'s 1992 Rio Conference) and Bill Gates among others. Former Secretary of State and ex-Chairman of Bechtel Group **George P. Shultz**, also a member of the Trilateral Commission, is listed as an Honorary Chair of the President's council. The URI is also closely allied with the United Nations. At least two URI summit conferences have been held at Stanford University. Carnegie-Melon University in Pittsburgh hosted the 2000 conference.

In 2000, URI co-sponsored the World Millennium Peace Summit of Religious and Spiritual Leaders held at the United Nations in New York City. The Secretary-General of the meeting was Bawa Jain. After the conference, Jain was interviewed by James Harder of *Insight On The News* as saying,

What we need to engage in is an education factor of the different religious traditions and the different theologies and philosophies and practices. That would give us a better understanding, and then I think [we have to deal with] the claims of absolute truth - we will recognize there is not just one claim of absolute truth, but there is truth in every tradition. That is happening more and more when you have gatherings such as these.[140]

The religions represented at the summit included Hinduism, Buddhism, Zoroastrianism, Confucianism, Ba'hai, Christianity, Indigenous, Judaism, Shinto, Jainism, Sikhism, Islam and Taoism, among others, with a heavy representation of eastern religions. Ted Turner, who gave a keynote address at the Summit, denounced his childhood Christian faith because "it was intolerant because it taught we were the only ones going to heaven."

What does URI have to do with anything other than religion? Well, here we are coming back around to the primary topic of this book, as stated in the URI preamble:

We unite in responsible cooperative action to bring the wis-

---

140   James Harder Radio Show, "U.N. Faithful Eye Global Religion", 2000.

*dom and values of our religions, spiritual expressions and in-digenous traditions to bear on the **economic, environmental, political and social challenges** facing our Earth community.*[141] [Emphasis added]

In their document "Principles of URI," item 10 rings out as if it were taken directly out of the book, *Our Common Future,* that kicked off Agenda 21 at the 1992 Rio Conference:

We act from sound ecological practices to protect and preserve the Earth for both present and future generations.[142]

URI does not have an exclusive arrangement with the global elite to promote interfaith reconciliation based on ecology, Sustainable Development, Agenda 21 or the green economy, but the reader should at least see the common purpose, common funding and common alignment with the same global elite who are intent on reinventing the world for Technocracy.

The Earth Charter Initiative

Although earlier but unsuccessful calls for an Earth Charter were made by various other people, the authoritative call came in 1987 from Trilateral Commission member **Gro Brundtland** of Norway, the principal author of *Our Common Future* that led to the Earth Summit in 1992.

In 1992, Maurice Strong, a Canadian billionaire, was Secretary-General of the United Nations Conference on Environment and Development that sponsored and conducted the Earth Summit in Rio de Janeiro that produced the official Agenda 21 document on Sustainable Development. In his opening statement, he declared,

*It is, therefore, of the highest importance that all Governments commit themselves to translate the decisions they take collectively here to national policies and practices required to give effect to them, **particularly implementation of Agenda 21**.*[143] [Emphasis added]

Mikhail Gorbachev was the last president of the Soviet U.S.S.R. before it broke up in 1992, but he attended Strong's Earth Summit in that same year. Soon thereafter, with encouragement from Rio

---

141   United Religions Initiative, *About Page,* (http://www.uri.org/about_uri).
142   Ibid.
143   Maurice Strong, "Opening Remarks", Earth Summit, 1992.

delegates, he founded Green Cross International "to help ensure a just, sustainable and secure future for all by fostering a value shift and cultivating a new sense of global interdependence and shared responsibility in humanity's relationship with nature."[144]

A common connection between Brundtland, Strong and Gorbachev was the elitist Club of Rome where all three were members and Strong and Gorbachev were directors.

Two years later in 1994, Strong and Gorbachev created The Earth Charter which many viewed as a prototype constitution for the New World Order. Although closely associated with the United Nations, Earth Charter indoctrination is meant to take place through *education and religion*, which is one reason that it was strongly supported by URI. Strong himself stated, "the real goal of the Earth Charter is that it will in fact become like the Ten Commandments."[145] Gorbachev was interviewed in 1996 and said, "Cosmos is my God. Nature is my God."[146] It could not be more clear where they were coming from.

In 1996, after three international consultations on what the Earth Charter might contain, a drafting committee was formed and Steven C. Rockefeller was appointed to lead it. Son of the late Nelson A. Rockefeller and nephew of Trilateral Commission founder **David Rockefeller**, Steven was soon appointed to be the Co-Chair of Earth Charter International Council. He became the principal spokesperson and evangelist for the Earth Charter as it was formally adopted in 2000.

Rockefeller was chosen because of his religious career and education. He received his Master of Divinity from the Union Theological Seminary in New York City and his Ph.D. in the philosophy of religion from Columbia University. He was Professor emeritus of Religion at Middlebury College in Vermont and also served as Dean of the College. His financial connection to the Rockefeller dynasty was evident in his chairmanship of the Rockefeller Brothers Fund where his uncle David is director. Most importantly to this discussion, he was Chairman of the Earth Charter International Drafting Committee.

144 "Mission Statement", Green Cross International, (http://www.gcint.org/our-mission).
145 Speech by Maurice Strong, Earth Charter Initiative (1996).
146 Mikhail Gorbachev, interview on the PBS *Charlie Rose Show*, Oct. 23, 1996.

The full text of the Earth Charter is seen in Appendix III of this book, and it is useful to see that much of the text is a virtual duplication of ideas that sprang from the Earth Summit in 1992 and Agenda 21. However, the spiritual nature of the Earth Charter is clearly seen with statements such as,

- *The emergence of a global civil society is creating new opportunities to build a democratic and humane world. Our environmental, economic, political, social, and spiritual challenges are interconnected, and together we can forge inclusive solutions.*

- *The arts, sciences, religions, educational institutions, media, businesses, nongovernmental organizations, and governments are all called to offer creative leadership.*

- *Affirm faith in the inherent dignity of all human beings and in the intellectual, artistic, ethical, and spiritual potential of humanity.*

- *Recognize and preserve the traditional knowledge and spiritual wisdom in all cultures that contribute to environmental protection and human well-being.*

- *Uphold the right of all, without discrimination, to a natural and social environment supportive of human dignity, bodily health, and spiritual well-being.*

- *Affirm the right of indigenous peoples to their spirituality.*

- *Protect and restore outstanding places of cultural and spiritual significance.*

- *Recognize the importance of moral and spiritual education for sustainable living.*

- *Our environmental, economic, political, social, and spiritual challenges are interconnected, and together we can forge inclusive solutions.* [147]

On September 9, 2001, just two days before the infamy of 9/11, a celebration of the Earth Charter was held in Vermont and attended by Steven Rockefeller. The event revealed an elaborately decorated Ark of Hope, modeled loosely after the Biblical Ark of the Covenant, wherein a hand-written copy of the Earth Charter

147   Op. Cit.

on papyrus was placed inside with other supposedly sacred items. After 9/11, the two hundred pound Ark was ceremoniously carried on foot from Vermont to the United Nations headquarters in New York City where it was placed on display. The two ninety-six inch carrying poles were reportedly made from unicorn horns which would ward off evil. For the first time, the religion of the New World Order possessed a tangible icon to be used as an object of worship.

In 2005, in response to the United Nations declaration of a ten-year period to be the *Decade of Education for Sustainable Development,* the Earth Charter Initiative published the *Earth Charter Guidebook for Teachers.* It was subsequently promoted and distributed to tens of thousands of schools around the world. The guiding philosophy of the teaching tool is stated on the first page: "Affirm faith in the inherent dignity of all human beings and in the intellectual, artistic, ethical, and spiritual potential of human beings."[148] The reader should note that while schools are ready and eager to teach Humanism, they are blocked from teaching anything from the doctrines and ethical values of Biblical Christianity.

In like fashion, the Earth Charter Initiative has contacted tens of thousands of churches around the world, persuading many to endorse and join the Earth Charter. Initiates include the Episcopal Church, Presbyterian Church, United Church of Christ, United Church of Canada, National Council of Churches, World Council of Churches, World YMCA, World Council of Religions Leaders, many Catholic orders, and so on.

In summary, these three examples - Aspen Institute, United Religions Initiative and the Earth Charter - give a clear message that the global elite who are implementing a coordinated system of Technocracy are intensely interested in promoting a system of sustainable religion based on Humanism alongside the economic and governance system and thus completing their strategy for a transformed and sustainable global society. Will it work? It is doubtful, but if it does succeed, the result will be something akin to Aldous Huxley's scientific dictatorship in his 1932 book *Brave New World.*

---

148   Mohit Mukherjee, *An Earth Charter Guidebook for Teachers,* (The Earth Charter Initiative International Secretariat, 2005).

The "Green" World Council of Churches

The World Council of Churches (WCC) represents 349 member denominations, which collectively represent over 560 million members in 110 nations. It has been a leader in the Interfaith movement as long as there has been a movement and was a signatory to the Earth Charter. Most importantly, it is a prime example of the new "green theology" being adopted by churches globally.

A founding member of the WCC is the Ecumenical Patriarchate of Constantinople. Patriarch Bartholomew sent an official message to the Interfaith Summit on Climate Change held during September 2014, co-sponsored by the WCC and organized by the U.N. He stated,

Each believer and each leader, each field and each discipline, each institution and each individual must be touched by the call to change our greedy ways and destructive habits [for the sake of climate justice] ... unless we change the way we live; we cannot hope to avoid ecological damage. This means that – instead of solely depending on governments and experts for answers – each of us must become accountable for our slightest gesture and act in order to reverse the path that we are on, which will of course also include prevailing upon governments and leaders for the creation and application of collective policy and practice.[149]

To say that the ecumenical world has been drawn into the web of Sustainable Development is an understatement. In fact, it is wholeheartedly and unequivocally driving the process at the local level, thanks to the United Nations and its global push for the "green economy" of Technocracy. The U.N knows that its agenda would fail without such massive and grass-roots support of religions around the world, and this conference delivered.

One observer to the conference, the Executive Director of GreenFaith, observed,

In the midst of Climate Week this year, the collection of religious events taking place in New York City around the UN Climate Summit is astounding. From the launch of the inter-

---

149 "To save the earth, all must change their ways,", World Council of Churches Press Release, September 19, 2014.

national multi-faith Our Voices Campaign at the UN Church Center to the Religions for the Earth conference at Union Seminary to the People's Climate March, where thousands of people of faith from over twenty different religious traditions will participate, to the multi-faith service at St. John the Divine to a number of other related faith events -- **there has never been such a large amount of religious-environmental activity in one location in the history of the world.** *This week will mark a watershed in the history of religion.* **It will be the time that people remember as the time when the world's faiths declared themselves, irrevocably, as green faiths.**[150] [Emphasis added]

This unabashed support for Sustainable Development did not develop overnight, but rather after the consistent plodding and conditioning over a period of decades. The result today is the completion of Peter Drucker's beloved three-legged stool model, where politics, economics, and religion intersect with a common agenda to create the utopian global society.

---

150 "For the Good of Our Shared Earth: The World Council of Churches and 'Religions for the Earth, *Huffington Post*, September 10, 2014.

CHAPTER 7

TRANSFORMING LAW

A merica was founded upon a Constitution that established a framework of formal law, where society was to be governed by the Rule of Law and not individual government officials. The law was to be clear to understand and then uniformly applied to every citizen regardless of race, religion, creed or economic achievement. In fact, the phrase "EQUAL JUSTICE UNDER LAW" is engraved on the front of the U.S. Supreme Court building in Washington, D.C.

The globalization process to establish the New International Economic Order, or Green Economy, was simply not possible if it were to be ruled by law and not men. In fact, the advance of global transformation could not have taken place at all amidst the myriad of legal systems that are found within the nation-states of the world unless there was some new supra-national legal theory that was capable of either trumping or subverting those various legal systems. Many corporations, for instance, conduct business in one state where their activities and practices are completely legal; but when they conduct business in another country, those same practices may be declared illegal. Thus, the transformation of law became necessary in order to enable the rise of the Trilateral Commission's New International Economic Order and Technocracy. In the process, this unfortunately crushed the U.S. Constitution and turned the Rule of Law upside-down. Other formerly sovereign nations are in the same boat.

The siren-call of globalization is "self-regulation" of industries and trade. The banking industry in New York wants to be self-regulated. The securities industry wants to be self-regulated. The oil industry wants to be self-regulated. The World Trade Organization (WTO) is an expression of self-regulation. What does self-regulation mean? In essence, it means that national authorities backed by national law should keep their hands in their

own pockets and let these industries take care of their own policies, regulations, laws and policing.

The new legal theory to accomplish this is called "Reflexive
Law". The term was originally coined in 1982 by a German legal
scholar, Gunther Teubner. The *German Law Journal* gives us a basic tutorial on the use of the word *reflexive*:

> *Reflexive describes "an action that is directed back upon it-*
> *self". For the purposes of Systems Theory reflexivity is defined*
> *as the application of a process to itself, e.g. "thinking of think-*
> *ing", "communicating about communication", "teaching how*
> *to teach" etc. In the context of law reflexivity could be "mak-*
> *ing laws on law-making", "adjudicating on adjudication", or*
> *"regulating self-regulation". It is obvious, that the focus of*
> *Reflexive Law in this context is rather on procedural than on*
> *substantive law.*[151]

Systems Theory, a foundational concept of Technocracy, is
based on self-regulating systems that depend on feedback for
self-regulation, such as systems found in weather, ecosystems,
life processes, etc. As it applies to law, the law itself is designed to
be self-correcting as it goes along, using feedback from the object
being regulated.

The Journal then goes on to explain:

> *Another meaning of reflexive is "marked by or capable of*
> *reflection", referring to reflexion in its philosophical mean-*
> *ing of "introspective contemplation or consideration of some*
> *subject matter". Here one can find the normative implications*
> *of Reflexive Law as being connected with a concept of ratio-*
> *nality. However, rationality is not understood as a quality of*
> *norms, but in accordance with Discourse Theory rather as*
> *communicative rationality. In a nutshell, decision-making in*
> *a reflexive legal system shall be marked by thorough delib-*
> *eration or reasoning as well as by reflection on the specific*
> *function and limits of law in modern society.*[152]

Discourse Theory is a postmodern tenet that consensus is
achieved by discourse among the various actors involved in a par-

---

151   Gralf-Peter Calliess, "Lex Mercatoria: A Reflexive Law Guide To An Autonomous
Legal System", *German Law Journal*, 2001).
152   Ibid.

ticular issue. Such discourse can include any form of communication plus any amount of outside information that bears on the subject. Thus, papers, studies, related science, expert witnesses, etc., can be brought to a discourse to influence the discussion and the resulting consensus or outcomes.

Lastly, the Journal adds, "a third meaning of reflexive is 'a relation that exists between an entity and itself', i.e. a concept of self-reference. This leads us to the very basic concept of Autopoiesis." Autopoiesis originally referred to the biological world where a cell, for instance, is capable of reproducing itself. The term was later applied to sociology and then to law by Teubner. From a political and legal point of view, it refers to the gradual rise of order out of chaos.[153] Another European legal scholar expands the topic:

Autopoietic law radicalizes the functionalist's instrumentalization of law as a means of social engineering by leaving the driver's seat empty. Rejecting the idea that law, from any single "outside" point, could determine the outcome of social conflicts, autopoietic law stresses the way in which law is a mere, yet highly particular, form of communication.[154]

This is a very difficult topic to understand. Essentially, Reflexive Law assumes that social norms (determined by discourse) are chaotic when compared to substantive or formal law. By applying System Theory, these norms are discovered and then codified with rules that are formulated to reinforce them on a larger scale. As rules are developed and added to other rules, what appeared chaotic is now supposed to have order and harmony. However, the thought of order from chaos is no better than Darwin's unproven theory that species evolve from less complex to more complex. The legal world today experiences more chaos than ever before.

The problem with Reflexive Law is that it cannot operate in a vacuum, as is suggested, but is at all times subject to those who control it. It is ripe for manipulation. Reflexive Law practitioners can thus direct the discourse, the outcome, and the rule-making, in a very real sense like the old West vigilante concept of the local self-appointed sheriff being "judge, jury and executioner".

---

153 Slavoj Zizek, "Less Than Nothing", (Verso, 2012), p. 467.
154 Zumbansen, "Law after the welfare state: formalism, functionalism and the ironic turn of reflexive law", TranState Working Papers, *University of Bremen*, 2009.

Reflexive Law is often associated with the Latin term, *lex mercatoria*, meaning "merchant law". Historically, merchant law was used by merchants (mostly shipping) during the medieval period to settle disputes, and courtrooms were set up along trade routes to hear cases. Merchants made their own laws and rules according to trade customs and best practices, both of which were constantly changing according to the mood of the trade industry. That Reflexive Law is pointed directly at economic issues is seen in statements like,

> *Recent research owes much to Teubner's concept of reflexive law, a self-governing system or form of regulated self-regulation. From this standpoint, lex mercatoria is a paradigm of the new global law. It consists less of detailed rules than of broad principles, such as good faith. Its boundaries are markets, professional communities or social networks, not territories. Instead of being relatively autonomous from political institutions, it depends heavily on other social fields being especially subject to economic pressures. It is not unified but decentered and non-hierarchical. Stimulated by globalisation, it constantly breaks the hierarchical frame of the national constitution within which private rule-making takes place, resulting in a new heterarchical frame, a characteristic of this new global non-state law.*[155]

The last sentence in particular is highly charged: Reflexive Law breaks down private rule-making by a national constitution and duly-elected representatives, replacing it instead with a "new global non-state law".

Furthermore, *lex mercatoria* specifically applies to environmental law. The economic system of Technocracy is working itself out through what the United Nations has termed the "Green Economy". It is based on Sustainable Development and Agenda 21 policies. Thus, it would be no surprise that Reflexive Law is playing the role of enforcer on a global scale. One environmental law journal states,

> *Rather than trying to regulate a social problem as a whole, reflexive law aims to enlist other social institutions to treat*

---

155   Francis Snyder, "Economic Globalisation and the Law in the 21st Century", *Blackwell Publishers*, (2004).

the issue. Reflexive legal strategies look to influence the pro-
cesses of intermediary institutions, such as government agen-
cies and companies, rather than to regulate social behavior
directly.

Reflexive law attempts to provide solutions to the gridlock
of modem law. Reflexive solutions offload some of the weight
of social regulation from the legal system to other social ac-
tors. This is accomplished by proceduralization. Rather than
detailed pronouncements of acceptable behavior, the law
adopts procedures for regulated entities to follow. The proce-
dures are adopted with a design in mind to encourage think-
ing and behavior in the right direction.[156]

Another environmental law journal is more direct:

At the same time, sustainable development's broad sweep
strains our intellectual grasp of its meaning and outruns the
capacity of our current legal and political systems to chan-
*nel society's activities toward its achievement... **there is no***
doubt that sustainable development needs new para-
digms to transform it from visionary rhetoric to a viable
political goal.[157] *[Emphasis added]*

Apparently, Sustainable Development was merely visionary
rhetoric until Reflexive Law was applied. Here we see Reflexive
Law being used as a direct means to achieve a political goal,
namely, the implementation of Sustainable Development. Did
citizens of the world vote on the merits of imposing Sustainable
Development? Hardly. As noted earlier, Sustainable Development
was conceived by the Brundtland Commission led by Trilateral
Commission member **Gro Brundtland**. Did the citizens of the
world vote on policies created by the United Nations' Agenda 21?
No. They were conceived by the same global elite who had a very
narrow and pre-conceived political agenda that would not be de-
terred by public opinion or dissent.

The Environmental Protection Agency (EPA) was established
by Congress under the National Environmental Policy Act of
1969 (NEPA). At that time, Reflexive Law was not yet a gleam in

---

156   Orts, "Reflexive Environmental Law", *Northwestern Law Review,* (1995), p. 1264.
157   Gaines, "Reflexive Law as a Legal Paradigm For Sustainable Development", *Buffalo Environmental Law Journal,* (2002).

Technocracy's eye. The Act "requires federal agencies to integrate environmental values into their decision making processes by considering the environmental impacts of their proposed actions and reasonable alternatives to those actions."[158]

Most Americans simply shake their heads at the crazy rulings and regulations that are produced by the EPA on a continual basis. They see no rhyme or reason to it, but if they were to read *Technocracy Rising*, they would understand perfectly. By 2002, the EPA was in full stride. The same environmental journal from above makes it perfectly clear:

> *In public law, the requirement that federal agencies prepare an environmental impact statement on proposed actions under the National Environmental Policy Act (hereinafter NEPA) has been clearly defined by the Supreme Court as a strictly procedural requirement.* **This makes NEPA quintessentially reflexive**; *the agency is required to study and think about environmental effects, but* **once the statement has been prepared, the agency is free to choose a decision that is more environmentally harmful than other options.**[159] [Emphasis added]

Indeed, the EPA is "*quintessentially reflexive*". Once it has made up its mind on an issue, it can do whatever it pleases to bring it about - again, judge, jury and executioner all in one package.

If it is not already evident, Reflexive Law is always seen in conjunction with social control, that is, how one thinks and behaves. It seeks a recursive and reiterative path to keep pushing at a problem until there is uniform compliance. Perhaps the only way to explain this is through two concrete examples.

In 2003, Stanford University released a book titled *Greening NAFTA* (NAFTA stands for the North American Free Trade Agreement). A friend had recommended it to me because it contained details about a supplemental treaty to NAFTA called the North American Agreement on Environmental Cooperation (NAAEC). The NAAEC in turn had created the *North American Commission for Environmental Cooperation*, or CEC. As it turns

---

158   EPA Web Site (www.epa.gov).
159   Orts.

out, the CEC was "the first international organization created to address the environmental aspects of economic integration."[160]

As I reviewed the book, my eyes fell on a chapter title toward the back, *Coordinating Land and Water Use in the San Pedro River Basin.* The San Pedro River is in southern Arizona, and it just so happened that I had owned a ranch on that same river when I first got out of college in 1968, and so I knew the area like the back of my hand. My interest was immediately aroused. According to the book, the San Pedro River Basin was the first instance of CEC involvement in the U.S. because it was a small and relatively unimportant area and because the headwaters of the San Pedro River originated in Mexico just south of the U.S. border. *Greening NAFTA* explains,

> *Under Articles 13 and 14 [of NAAEC], the Secretariat can accept and review citizen submissions alleging that one of the three countries is not enforcing its existing environmental laws.*[161]

In the case of the San Pedro River Basin submission (i.e., complaint) it came not from a citizen, but from the radical environmental group based out of Tucson, the Southwest Center for Biological Diversity (SCBD). The SCBD was all worked up that environmental damage was being perpetrated along the river by the landowners, farmers and ranchers who lived there. They had no concrete proof that their allegations were substantive or even accurate at all. It was simply an a priori accusation on their part, but the mere charge was enough to set off a chain of events that changed the San Pedro River Basin forever. Here is where the plot thickens. The authors explain:

> *Article 13 can be characterized as an example of postmodern, "soft" or "reflexive" international law because it seeks to influence public and private behavior without the threat of the enforcement of traditional, sanction-based "hard" law.*[162]

Greening NAFTA now explains exactly what Reflexive Law entails:

> *Reflexive law tries to align systematically legal rules with*

---

160   Markell and Knox, *Greening NAFTA*, (Stanford University Press, 2003), p. 2.
161   Ibid. p. 217.
162   Ibid. p. 218.

norms that the relevant actors will internalize. It builds on the realization that the reasons why people actually obey law ultimately lie outside formal adjudication and the power of the state to enforce rules.[163]

Again, Reflexive Law starts out with desired outcomes created by the unelected and unaccountable actors for which there are no specific laws. Of course, they could have appealed to Congress to create legislation, as would be required by the Constitution, but Congress would never go along with this scheme. At the end of the reflexive process, described below, the actual outcomes depended on how well the stakeholders "internalized" what was proposed. In other words, there was no actual legal process at all, but rather a jawboning process that conned the actors into compliance.

"Information disclosure" was shown to be a principal policy instrument of Reflexive Law. That is, the analysis produced along the lines of Discourse Theory was presented with its "recommended outcomes". Public meetings were then held to build consensus between individual citizens and other "actors". In the case of the San Pedro River Basin study, the CEC enlisted the University of Arizona's Udall Center to hold these public meetings. After all was said and done, there was zero consensus among actual citizens of the area. As the book simply notes, "Public comment was emotionally divided on the reduction of irrigated agriculture."[164] Really? In fact, the farmers and ranchers in the area were beyond livid, but the real purpose of the public meetings had nothing to do with getting their voluntary consensus. Rather, the meetings were designed to publicly abuse them until they submitted.

The *Greening NAFTA* authors are very blunt about this:

This experience reveals two powerful incentives at work: shame and the desire to be virtuous while saving money or increasing profit margins. In a post-Holocaust world, human rights NGOs have effectively used shame to induce compliance with universal human rights norms. Also, voluntary pollution reduction has been achieved when it is internally prof-

---

163   Ibid. p. 231.
164   Ibid. p. 228.

itable for an industry to reduce its discharges or an industry anticipates increased regulatory or public pressure to reduce them from the disclosure, such as through public shaming. Shaming works well with pollution, especially toxic pollution, because it draws on deep, perhaps irrational, fears of expo- sure to the risk of serious illness and an innate abhorrence of bodily injury.[165]

Since when is public shame an instrument of legal disputes? What of the farmers and ranchers in the San Pedro River Basin who refused to be shamed into consensus during the Udall Center public hearings? After all, they had zero input into the CEC's study and subsequent "recommendations", nor were they consulted prior to the Southwest Center for Biological Diversity's original complaint. In actuality, they were simply offered other incentives that they were helpless to refuse or refute:

Two concrete incentives that have successfully induced land- owner cooperation under the U.S. Endangered Species Act are fear of a worse regulatory outcome and immunity from liability for changed conditions.[166]

In the end, the farmers and ranchers succumbed to the Reflexive Law process when the regulatory bullies showed up with threats of what would happen to them if they did not buckle under to the CEC's demands. These "actors" included the Bureau of Land Management, manager of the San Pedro Riparian National Conservation Area (SPRNCA) and the U.S. Department of the Army. Accompanying them were several NGOs, including the Nature Conservancy and the Southwest Center for Biological Diversity. The federal threat was "We will bankrupt you with reg- ulations." The NGO threat was "We will bankrupt you with law- suits."

This is "Reflexive Law", and it is 100 percent antithetical to the American Republic, the Rule of Law, the U.S. Constitution and the entirety of Western civilization. Because compliance has always been posited as voluntary, nobody has been alarmed enough to look any further at it. However, I will point out that almost ev- ery global imposition has been based on the *voluntary* aspect of

165   Ibid. p. 231.
166   Ibid. p. 232.

Reflexive Law. For instance, Agenda 21 depends upon voluntary compliance, which is often referred to as "soft law" among its critics who have not perceived the deeper meaning of Reflexive Law. Common Core education standards were introduced as a voluntary program. Sustainable Development in general is always proposed as a voluntary program. All of these are based on the theory of Reflexive Law. But, once it gets its tentacles into your personal property and local community, you will be involuntarily squeezed until you "voluntarily" comply. There is no legal process available to defend yourself, your property, or your rights. There is no appeal from the damage done to your rights or property.

Another example of Reflexive Law revealing itself is seen in an article in the *New York Times*, "Obama Pursuing Climate Accord in Lieu of Treaty". The article states that "the negotiators are meeting with diplomats from other countries to broker a deal to commit some of the world's largest economies to enact laws to reduce their carbon pollution."[167] The self-decided social norm is that carbon pollution is bad and that society must cut back or risk running out of resources altogether. The problem is the Constitution which bars the President from signing any legally binding treaty without a two-thirds vote from the Senate. The article then offers the Reflexive Law solution:

> To sidestep that requirement [two-third vote of the Senate], President Obama's climate negotiators are devising what they call a "politically binding" deal that would "name and shame" countries into cutting their emissions. The deal is likely to face strong objections from Republicans on Capitol Hill and from poor countries around the world, but negotiators say it may be the only realistic path.[168]

Name and shame? Politically binding but not legally binding? Knowing that the Senate would never vote on such shenanigans, the negotiators conclude that "it may be the only realistic path." Thus, President Obama is delivering us into an international Reflexive Law treaty that has no actual legal basis in fact, and that is why they think they are justified in ignoring the Senate. After

---

167   "Obama Pursuing Climate Accord in Lieu of Treaty", *New York Times*, August 26, 2014.
168   Ibid.

all, the Senate deals with "hard law" while the White House deals with "Reflexive Law". Furthermore, they will use the principal "name and shame" policy tool of Reflexive Law to smoke out the resistance for public shaming. Subsequently, from what is now known about how Reflexive Law is enforced in the end, those holdouts will be offered a "deal that they cannot refuse", namely, much worse regulatory outcomes, international lawsuits and entanglement, trade sanctions, etc.

The *NYT* elaborates further:

American negotiators are instead homing in on a hybrid agreement — a proposal to blend legally binding conditions from an existing 1992 treaty with new voluntary pledges. The mix would create a deal that would update the treaty, and thus, negotiators say, not require a new vote of ratification.

Countries would be legally required to enact domestic climate change policies — but would voluntarily pledge to specific levels of emissions cuts and to channel money to poor countries to help them adapt to climate change. Countries might then be legally obligated to report their progress toward meeting those pledges at meetings held to identify those nations that did not meet their cuts.[169]

There is not a single shred of doubt that anything other than Reflexive Law is pictured here. It spits in the face of traditional Rule of Law that our country was founded upon and operated under until 1983 when this treasonous legal system was conceived - by a German, no less. For all intents and purposes, Reflexive Law is causing the utter collapse of the Rule of Law as we know it.

Don't even begin to think this is anything less than blatant, for the article concludes with the frank braggadocio :

"There's some legal and political magic to this," said Jake Schmidt, an expert in global climate negotiations with the Natural Resources Defense Council, an advocacy group. "They're trying to move this as far as possible without having to reach the 67-vote threshold" in the Senate.[170]

Magic, indeed. *Merriam-Webster* defines magic as "the art of

169   Ibid.
170   Ibid.

producing illusions by sleight of hand." From a layman's point of view, that perfectly describes the heart and intent of Reflexive Law. One critical legal scholar sums it up this way:

> *Looking at many of the recent innovations in reflexive regulation suggests that the effects of "reflective" approach might lie in stimulating new ways of avoiding laws rather than in enhancing compliance with them.* [171]

---

[171]   Blankenburg, "The Poverty of Evolutionism: A Critique of Teubner's Case For 'Reflexive Law'", *Law & Society Review*, p. 288, 1984.

CHAPTER 8

TRANSFORMING ENERGY: GLOBAL SMART GRID

A key requirement in the implementation of Technocracy is control over energy, both distribution and consumption. However, you cannot control what you cannot monitor and measure, and this is where Smart Grid weighs in. Howard Scott and M. King Hubbert clearly delineated this in the first two requirements listed in *Technocracy Study Course*:

- *Register on a continuous 24 hour-per-day basis the total net conversion of energy*
- *By means of the registration of energy converted and consumed, make possible a balanced load[172]*

The technology required to achieve these goals did not exist in the 1930s, but it does exist today. It's called Smart Grid.

What is Smart Grid?

Smart Grid is a broad technical term that encompasses the generation, distribution and consumption of electrical power, with an inclusion for gas and water as well. Smart Grid is an initiative that seeks to completely redesign the power grid using advanced digital technology, including the installation of new, digital meters on every home and business.

Using wireless communication technology, these digital meters provide around-the-clock monitoring of a consumer's energy consumption using continuous two-way communication between the utility and the consumer's property. Furthermore, meters are able to communicate with electrical devices within the residence in order to gather consumption data and to control certain devices directly without consumer intervention.

According to a U.S. Department of Energy publication,

---

172   Hubbert & Scott, p. 232.

The Department of Energy has been charged with orchestrating the wholesale modernization of our nation's electrical grid.... Heading this effort is the Office of Electricity Delivery and Energy Reliability. In concert with its cutting edge research and energy policy programs, the office's newly formed, multi-agency Smart Grid Task Force is responsible for coordinating standards development, guiding research and development projects, and reconciling the agendas of a wide range of stakeholders.[173]

The Office of Electricity Delivery and Energy Reliability was created in 2003 under President George W. Bush and was elevated in stature in 2007 by creating the position of Assistant Secretary of Electricity Delivery and Energy Reliability to head it.

It is not stated who "charged" the Department of Energy to this task, but since the Secretary of Energy answers directly to the President as a cabinet position, it is self-evident that the directive came from the President, whether Bush or Obama. In any case, there was no Congressional legislation that required it, nor has there been any Congressional oversight controlling it.

Implementation

On October 27, 2009, the Obama administration unveiled its Smart Grid plan by awarding $3.4 billion to 100 Smart Grid projects.[174] According to the Department of Energy's first press release, these awards were to result in the installation of

- more than 850 sensors called "Phasor Measurement Units" to monitor the overall power grid nationwide
- 200,000 smart transformers
- 700 automated substations (about 5 percent of the nation's total)
- 1,000,000 in-home displays
- 345,000 load control devices in homes

This was the "kick-start" of Smart Grid in the U.S. On January

---

173   "The Smart Grid: An Introduction", *Department of Energy publication*, (2010), P. 1. (http://energy.gov/sites/prod/files/oeprod/DocumentsandMedia/DOE_SG_Book_Single_ Pages%281%29.pdf).

174   "Recovery Act Selections for Smart Grid Investment Grant Awards", *Department of Energy*, 2010.

8, 2010, President Obama unveiled an additional $2.3 billion Federal funding program for the "energy manufacturing sector" as part of the $787 billion American Reinvestment and Recovery Act. Funding had already been awarded in advance to projects in 43 states, pending Obama's announcement.

One such project in the northwest was headed by Battelle Memorial Institute, covering five states and targeting 60,000 customers. The project was actually developed by the Bonneville Power Administration (BPA), a federal agency under the Department of Energy. Since it is pointedly illegal for a federal agency to apply for federal funds, BPA passed the project off to Battelle, a non-profit and non-governmental organization (NGO), which was promptly awarded $178 million.

It is important to note that BPA takes credit for originating the Smart Grid concept in the early 1990s which it termed "Energy Web". This alone is evidence that the wheels of Technocracy were turning years before the turn of the century. It is also interesting to note that Washington state was a hotbed of Technocracy membership and supporters in the 1930s and is currently home to the headquarters of Technocracy, Inc.

According to Battelle's August 27, 2009 press release,

The project will involve more than 60,000 metered customers in Idaho, Montana, Oregon, Washington and Wyoming. Using smart grid technologies, the project will engage system assets exceeding 112 megawatts, the equivalent of power to serve 86,000 households.

"The proposed demonstration will study smart grid benefits at unprecedented geographic breadth across five states, spanning the electrical system from generation to end-use, and containing many key functions of the future smart grid," said Mike Davis, a Battelle vice president, *"The intended impact of this project will span well beyond traditional utility service territory boundaries, helping to enable a future grid that meets pressing local, regional and national needs."*[175]

Battelle and BPA worked closely together, and there was an

---

175   "Northwest team bids on $178 million regional smart grid demonstration project", Battelle News Release, August 27, 2009.

obvious blurring as to who was really in control of the project's management during the test period. In a "For Internal Use Only" document written in August 2009, BPA offered talking points to its partners: "Smart Grid technology includes everything from interactive appliances in homes to smart meters, substation automation and sensors on transmission lines."

Venture capitalists who saw the coming feeding frenzy invested close to $2 billion in 2010-2012, and the largest providers invested billions more in increased capacity. These included global players like IBM, Siemens, GE, Cisco, Panasonic, Kyocera, Toshiba, Mitsubishi and others.

The resulting bonanza of investment has pushed Smart Grid past the trial stage and well into the roll-out phase. Between 2012 and 2020, total aggregate spending on Smart Grid will likely exceed $500 billion.

The data-tracking element of Smart Grid is a second element of concern. Annual spending on software systems and data tracking were estimated to reach $1.1 billion in 2013 and as much as $3.8 billion by 2020. According to one analyst, "With the influx of big data, the potential of smart grid has shifted dramatically from the original aim of adding a myriad of new devices toward a complete re-invention of the way utilities do business."[176]

The dynamics of hardware/software interaction dramatically reinforces and accelerates the development cycle; the hardware (digital smart meters) representing the data collection system has hotly stimulated software development. In turn, the advanced software used to aggregate and analyze the data puts even more urgency into completing the physical infrastructure.

This acceleration dynamic between hardware and software is well known within the world of engineering and computer science. Engineers will push the envelope at every opportunity to improve both hardware and software as additional functionality is seen as beneficial. Thus, what Obama started as a seed project

---

176   Leopard, "Big data apps seen driving smart grid rollout", *EE Times*, December 12, 2012 (http://www.eetimes.com/design/power-management-design/4403367/-Big-data--).

in 2009 has now become a self-nourished behemoth with a life of its own.

Before we examine how the global Smart Grid is being built out, it will be helpful to understand a new technology called "Internet of Things" (IoT).

A Network of Things

Networks of various kinds are foundational to Technocracy, and this is especially true of the Internet of Things. As the World Wide Web is to people, the IoT is to appliances. This brand new technology creates a wireless (or in some cases, wired) network between a broad range of inanimate objects from shoes to refrigerators. This concept is "shovel ready" for Smart Grid implementation because appliances, meters and substations are all inanimate items that technocrats would have communicating with each other in autonomous fashion.

IoT is not only revolutionary in concept but also is exploding in every direction in society. It is made possible by an upgraded Internet addressing system called IPv6 which was initially formalized in 1998. Admittedly, it gets a little complicated to explain. All Internet traffic is routed from point to point based on a unique address assigned to each point. The original Internet communication was based on an older standard called IPv4, the capacity of which was limited to only 4.3 billion devices, e.g., computers, servers, routers and so forth. IPv4 is still used worldwide, but you can imagine the address availability crisis considering the many billions of computers, tablets and smart phones all vying for their own unique identity. The IPv6 standard expands the available address pool to 340 trillion trillion trillion, or more than we could ever conceivably use; or could we?

IPv6 is large enough to assign a unique address to every person, computer, and digital device known to exist, and barely break a sweat. Giving a unique address to your digital smart meter, plus every digital device in your home is miniscule. Every credit card, driver's license, RFID (Radio-Frequency IDentification) chip in the world could have its own address. When Wal-Mart sells tennis shoes, every pair could be "chipped" and uniquely addressed, and so on for all retail merchandise. Think about industrial machines and processes: factories, machines, software programs, algorithms, employees, ad infinitum, can be addressed.

Furthermore, every device in the world that can receive a unique address under IPv6 can be cataloged and described. You will wonder why this matters, but it does, and here's why. With IPv4 and Smart Grid, the appliances within your home or business can only be controlled by first accessing your external Smart Meter. Your internal appliances can then be reached by their assigned "pseudo-addresses" that are known only within your home. This is a semi-manual process and totally blocks the technocrat dream of controlling everything automatically via remote software.

However, if all of your appliances have unique and cataloged IPv6 addresses, then all washing machines, for instance, could be accessed as a class of devices with a universal command to turn them on or off... or limit their usage to certain times of the day. With IoT, accessing remote resources via class, type, group, etc., is a technocrat's nirvana. Usage and consumption policies can then be set at the top level and executed automatically across the entire population of a region, country or even the entire world!

Here is a hypothetical example. The Department of Energy (DOE) is trying to balance the load between supply and demand during the hot month of July. It also knows that air conditioners are the primary consumers of electricity during this period. For the last 5 years, the DOE has been pushing energy efficient air conditioners that use 10 percent less energy than other classes of units, and it promised to "reward" purchasers of these new units. DOE further knows who has all the other "dirty, power hog" units and in particular a few brands that it really dislikes. A summertime policy decision is then made to give everyone the same allocation of energy regardless of unit owned to keep the baseline thermostat reading at 75 degrees. The most efficient units undershoot that mark and can set their thermostats to 70 degrees while meeting their allocation. The least efficient units can only run at 80 degrees given the same amount of energy. As the command is issued to "make it so", the DOE's super computer instantly identifies every air conditioner in the country by its IPv6 address, owner, manufacturer, model and install date, and simultaneously issues a command to "speak" to each IPv6-addressed thermostat and adjust it accordingly. Ten seconds later, every thermostat in the nation has been "balanced".

Well, here is how it is intended to work in the real world. In 2008 the Pacific Northwest National Laboratory (PNNL) developed a small circuit board called a "Grid Friendly Appliance Controller". According to a Department of Energy brochure,

> *The GFA Controller developed by Pacific Northwest National Laboratory is a small circuit board built into household appliances that reduces stress on the power grid by continually monitoring fluctuations in available power. During times of high demand, appliances equipped with the controller automatically shut down for a short period of time, resulting in a cumulative reduction that can maintain stability on the grid.*[177]

Furthermore, according to PNNL's website,

> *The controller is essentially a simple computer chip that can be installed in regular household appliances like dishwashers, clothes washers, dryers, refrigerators, air conditioners, and water heaters. The chip senses when there is a disruption in the grid and turns the appliances off for a few seconds or minutes to allow the grid to stabilize. The controllers also can be programmed to delay the restart of the appliances. The delay allows the appliances to be turned on one at a time rather than all at once to ease power restoration following an outage.*[178]

You can see how automatic actions are intended to be triggered by direct interaction between objects, without human intervention. The rules will be written by programmers under the direction of technocrats who create the policies which are then downloaded to the controllers as necessary. Thus, changes to the rules can be made on the fly, at any time, and without the homeowner's knowledge or permission.

---

177 "Department of Energy Putting Power in the Hands of Consumers Through Technology", DOE, January 9, 2008.
178 Pacific Northwest National Laboratory website (http://www.pnl.gov/).

PNNL is not a private enterprise, however. It is "owned" by the U.S. Department of Energy and operated by Battelle Memorial Institute!

All of this technology will be enabled with Wi-Fi circuitry that is identical to the Wi-Fi-enabled network modems and routers commonly used in homes and businesses throughout the world. Wi-Fi is a trademark of the Wi-Fi Alliance that refers to wireless network systems used in devices from personal computers to mobile phones, connecting them together and/or to the Internet.

According to the Wi-Fi Alliance, "the need for Smart Grid solutions is being driven by the emergence of distributed power generation and management/monitoring of consumption." In their white paper, *Wi-Fi for the Smart Grid*, they list the specific requirements for interoperability posted by the Department of Energy:

- *Provide two-way communication among grid users, e.g. regional market operators, utilities, service providers and consumers*

- *Allow power system operators to monitor their own systems as well as neighboring systems that affect them so as to facilitate more reliable energy distribution and delivery*

- *Coordinate the integration into the power system of emerging technologies such as renewable resources, demand response resources, electricity storage facilities and electric transportation systems*

- *Ensure the cyber security of the grid.*[179]

Thus, the bi-directional and real time Smart Grid communications network will depend on Wi-Fi from end to end. While the consumer is pacified with the promise of lower utility costs, it is the utility company who will enforce the policies set by the regional, national and global regulators. Thus, if a neighboring system has a shortage of electricity, your thermostat might automatically be turned down to compensate; if you have exceeded your monthly daytime quota of electricity, energy-consuming

---

179   "WiFi for the Smart Grid", *WiFi Alliance*, September 2010, (http://www.wi-fi.org/sites/default/files/membersonly/wp_wifi_smart_grid_with_security_faq_20100912.pdf).

tasks like washing and drying clothes could be limited to over-night hours.

Here is another hypothetical example of how the IoT might work. Let's say that all IoT devices in your utility area are happily communicating with each other and the local controlling device. A sophisticated program policy is in effect to limit aggregate consumption in each home according to types of appliances, insulation efficiency and square footage of the home. Accordingly, the controller device contains a baseline consumption value for each home in the utility area. When a neighborhood home exceeds its baseline consumption, internal devices are "taken over" to reduce your load; this might mean changing the thermostat, limiting washers and dryers to off-peak hours, etc.

When Smart Grid promises of lower utility costs are examined in the real world, we find a completely different story, namely, record high electricity prices:

For the first time ever, the average price for a kilowatthour (KWH) of electricity in the United States has broken through the 14-cent mark, climbing to a record 14.3 cents in June.[180]

To add insult to injury, the International Monetary Fund (IMF) simultaneously called for higher energy prices in order to fight climate change.[181] The consumer is obviously not in view here; talk of lower utility costs refers to the utility companies.

Smart Grid Goes Global

A prominent business journal stated on November 16, 2009 that "After several false starts, 2010 finally could be the year when smart meters go global."[182] Indeed, it was:

- Italy had already implemented Smart Grid technology in 85 percent of its homes nationwide.
- Earth2Tech reported that Smart Grid will generate $200 billion of global investment in the next few years.
- The International Electrotechnical Commission (IEC) has laid out a global roadmap to insure interoperability of Smart Grid systems among nations.

---

180   "Average Price Of Electricity Climbs To All-Time Record", *CNS News*, July 29, 2014.
181   "IMF urges higher energy taxes to fight climate change", *Reuters*, July 31, 2014.
182   "How Italy Beat the World to a Smarter Grid", *Business Week*, November 16, 2009.

- China is spending $7.32 billion to build out Smart Grid in Asia.

Other countries with Smart Grid pilot projects that were already launched included Germany, France, England, Russia, Japan, India, Australia, South Africa and a host of others. Regional organizations such as *SMARTGRIDS Africa* were set up to promote Smart Grid in smaller countries. The global rush was truly underway. In every case, Smart Grid was being accelerated by government stimulus spending, and the global vendors were merely lining up their money buckets to be filled up with taxpayer funds.

As is the case in the U.S., there was little, if any, preexisting or latent demand for Smart Grid technology. Demand had been artificially created by the respective governments of each country. Could it have been random chance that so many nations chose to kick-start Smart Grid at the same time with the same kind of funding, that is, taxpayer funded stimulus money?

One organization dedicated to the creation of a global Smart Grid stated, "There is a new world wide web emerging right before our eyes. It is a global energy network and, like the internet, it will change our culture, society and how we do business. More importantly, it will alter how we use, transform and exchange energy."[183] Statements like this allude to the grandiose nature of a global Smart Grid: As big as the Internet and able to transcend borders, cultures and entire societies. With the stakes this high, the technocratic global elite went all in to build a global infrastructure and create standards to control the energy distribution and consumption across the entire planet.

Proponents of Smart Grid have claimed that it will empower the consumer to better manage his or her power consumption and hence, costs. The utility companies will therefore be more efficient in balancing power loads and requirements across diverse markets. However, like carnival barkers, these Smart Grid hucksters never revealed where or how SmartGrid came into being, nor what the ultimate endgame might be.

The reader should again note that the reasons for the existence of the Technocracy movement in the 1930s are the same reasons given today: energy efficiency, load balancing, fairness,

---

183   Terrawatts.com home page, 2009 (http://www.terrawatts.com).

alleviating poverty and hunger, etc. The feigned concern for those in poverty and hunger in the underdeveloped nations is hollow. Technocracy is pointedly amoral in its practice: the means (their Scientific Method/process) justifies the end, whatever the end might turn out to be.

In addition to European and Asian countries and the United States, Smart Grid is also being implemented in both Canada and Mexico, and planners have been working on standards that will integrate all of North America into a single, unified Smart Grid system. This "continental" grid is designed to integrate with other continental systems to create a unified global Smart Grid.

One leader in this planetary Smart Grid is the Global Energy Network Institute (GENI). It has created a Dymaxion (tm) Map of the world from the perspective of the North Pole that reveals the global grid currently under construction. The only part of planet earth left untouched is Antarctica. High-voltage electrical transmission links are displayed that are capable of transferring large amounts of energy from continent to continent to balance global supply and demand.

The GENI project has gathered momentum and is endorsed by global leaders such as the Dalai Lama, Archbishop Desmond Tutu, Sen. James Jeffords (I-VT) and Noel Brown (North American Director, United Nations Environmental Program), the United Nations and by the governments of Canada, New Zealand, Switzerland, and China, among others.

According to GENI, the conceptual design for the global Smart Grid is credited to a brilliant architect, system theorist, designer and futurist, R. Buckminster Fuller (1895-1983). Although Fuller was not a joiner, he was a dyed-in-the-wool technocrat:

Fuller encountered technocratic thinking through personal relationships with leading technocrats, including Scott, Chase, and the Committee on Technocracy member Frederick Ackerman, as well as with their less prominent associates such as the engineers Clarence Steinmetz and Irving Langmuir.... Fuller would later characterize himself as "a life-long friend of Howard Scott and Stuart Chase" and explain that although never a member of Technocracy, Inc., he was "thoroughly fa-

miliar with its history and highly sympathetic with many of the views of its founders."[184]

In his 1982 book, *Critical Path*, Fuller wrote,

This world electric grid, with its omni-integrated advantage, will deliver its electric energy anywhere, to anyone, at any one time, at one common rate. This will make a world-around uniform costing and pricing system for all goods and services based realistically on the time-energy metabolic accounting system of Universe.

In this cosmically uniform, common energy-value system for all humanity, costing will be expressed in kilowatt-hours, watt-hours and watt-seconds of work. Kilowatt-hours will become the prime criteria of costing the production of the complex of metabolic involvements per each function or item. These uniform energy valuations will replace all the world's wildly inter-varying, opinion-gambled-upon, top-power-system-manipulatable monetary systems. The time-energy world accounting system will do away with all the inequities now occurring in regard to the arbitrarily maneuverable international shipping of goods and top economic power structure's banker-invented, international balance-of-trade accountings. It will eliminate all the tricky banking and securities-markets exploitations of all the around-the-world-time-zone activities differences in operation today, all unbeknownst to the at-all-times two billion humans who are sleeping.[185]

If this sounds familiar, it should. It is an unvarnished re-hash of 1930s-style Technocracy, except on a global, versus continental, scale. Electricity is delivered equally to all, and the price-based economic system is replaced by a "time-energy world accounting system" based on kilowatt-hours, watt-hours and watt-seconds.

There is no evidence that such a system will actually work, but that hasn't stopped global groups from rushing headlong into this global initiative. Take, for instance, the World Economic Forum....

---

184   Chu, "New views on R. Buckminster Fuller", (Stanford University Press, 2009), p. 109.

185   Buckminster Fuller, *Critical Path*, (Saint Martin's Griffin 1982).

World Economic Forum and Climate Change

If a skeptic were to question the seriousness of organizations like Terrawatts and GENI, they should consider that the elitist World Economic Forum (WEF) has thrown its collective weight behind the initiative and has managed to link the advancement of Smart Grid to the reduction of carbon emissions, thus promising a tangible way to fight global warming.

Founded in 1971, the WEF meets annually in Davos, Switzerland and attendees are mostly the "who's who" of the global elite. In January 2011, the WEF presented a major progress report that stated,

> *Accelerating Successful Smart Grid Pilots, a World Economic Forum report developed with Accenture and industry experts, sets out the centrality of smart grids as key enablers for a low-carbon economy and in response to increasingly growing energy demands. Over 60 industry, policy and regulatory stakeholders were engaged in the Accelerating Successful Smart Grid Pilots report, to identify the factors that determine the success, or otherwise, of smart grid pilots.... There is an opportunity to launch the next wave of development towards a lower carbon energy system, and **successful smart grid pilots will be a key step in this process.**[186]* [Emphasis added]

Mark Spelman, Global Head of Strategy at Accenture, participated in the WEF's Smart Grid Workshop in 2010. When asked the question, "What value can Smart Grid add in the next 30 years?" Spelman replied, "Smart Grids are absolutely fundamental if we are going to achieve some of our climate change objectives. Smart Grids are the glue, they are the energy internet of the future and they are the central component which is going to bring demand and supply together."[187]

Spelman may not call himself a Technocrat, but he certainly knows his way around the language of Technocracy.

The IEEE Standards Association

The global energy network, or Smart Grid, will operate ac-

---

186   "Energy Industry Partnership Programme", *World Economic Forum*, January 2011.
187   Interview with Mark Spelman, WEF, Smart Grid Workshop, Davos, Switzerland, 2010

cording to universally accepted engineering standards that make data and energy flows compatible with each other. Who will supply such standards? The venerable Institute of Electrical and Electronics Engineers, or IEEE.

The IEEE claims that it is "the world's largest professional association dedicated to advancing technological innovation and excellence for the benefit of humanity." Founded in 1884, it has been involved with electricity standards and development since Thomas Edison invented the light bulb. Today, however, the IEEE is massively global with 395,000 members in 160 countries, and it supports approximately 900 active standards in various fields of engineering and electronics. As it states on its Smart Grid website, the IEEE has staked its claim, in clear language, on the global energy initiative:

> There's no global organization to oversee all nations' energy systems transformations, it is a vast movement and it's in its infancy. With our 38 societies and seven councils IEEE is positioned to lead the smart grid initiative. Through them and our 395,000 members, who work in the world's academic, government and private sectors, IEEE touches virtually every aspect of the smart grid.
>
> We leverage our strong foundation and inclusive collaboration to evolve standards, share best practices, publish developments and provide related educational offerings to further the smart grid. We are at the forefront of advancing technology and facilitating successful deployments throughout the world. Working hand in hand with other leading organizations to create one set of standards for the smart grid is the way we can ensure success.[188]

IEEE's bravado is not unwarranted. It truly is the *only* global organization capable of such a monumental task. When given the challenge to unify the global energy network, 395,000 engineers should be enough to complete the mission! The IEEE Student Branch at Northern Illinois University notes on their web site that the "IEEE has managed to bring technocrats from all over the world on a single platform." Indeed.

---

188   IIE Website, (http://smartgrid.ieee.org/standards).

The IEEE-SA (SA stands for Standards Association) is also dedicated to bringing IoT to life: "With WIFI and other well-known standards under their belt, the IEEE-SA is now putting their attention on the Internet of Things (IoT) to ensure that the dream of everything connected can come to fruition."[189]

It is not clear who will oversee any or all facets of the global Smart Grid. The implied suggestion is that it will be the same engineers and global corporations that are currently developing it. There is no suggestion anywhere in literature that there is a plan for a hand-off of the resulting system to a political structure that serves the people.

The negative aspects of Smart Grid are seldom mentioned. Take cyber-security, for instance. Picture a tech-savvy criminal who breaks into your energy profile data by hacking the computers at your local substation. Based on your power usage, he knows when you are home and when you are not home, when you are awake and when you are asleep, whether you have a security system turned on or off, etc. Armed with such information, your possessions and personal safety would be at his disposal.

In the United States, Smart Grid is escalating without any legislative oversight or involvement; in other words, it is being implemented exclusively by Executive Branch fiat. The same is true in other countries. There is obviously a small group of master planners or orchestrators, most likely to be found in the bowels of elite organizations like the World Economic Forum.

In summary, without a functioning global Smart Grid, Technocracy would have no chance of succeeding because there would be no means of controlling the distribution and consumption of energy. Conversely, the completion and activation of Smart Grid will all but guarantee the full and immediate implementation of Technocracy. If you have any doubt, just remember these two specific requirements from *Technocracy Study Course*:

- *Register on a continuous 24 hour-per-day basis the total net conversion of energy.*

---

189 "Standards: The Connective Tissue Behind the Internet of Things", *TechVibes*, March 22, 2013 (http://www.techvibes.com/blog/connective-tissue-internet-of-things-2013-03-22).

- *By means of the registration of energy converted and consumed, make possible a balanced load.*[190]

If you are wondering why you haven't heard more about Smart Grid in recent years, it is because the technocratic engineers and technicians are operating at a level far above the understanding or awareness of politicians, the media and the general public. Whenever concerns are raised as to motive and agenda, criticism is deflected with the "It's good for the consumer!" mantra. It is claimed that they are helping to lower energy costs, giving more options to consumers and more fairly distributing limited resources for economic progress. Perhaps technocrats believe this themselves, but I don't and neither should you.

Carbon Currency

Control over energy makes possible the original Technocracy goal of implementing a carbon-based energy certificate that would replace the existing price-based currencies of the world. Such a currency would also be the life blood of a "green economy" based on Sustainable Development.

It is plainly evident today that the world is laboring under a dysfunctional system of price-based economics as evidenced by the rapid decline of value in paper currencies. The era of fiat (irredeemable paper currency) was introduced in 1971 when President Richard Nixon decoupled the U.S. dollar from gold. Because the dollar-turned-fiat was the world's primary reserve asset, all other currencies eventually followed suit, leaving us today with a global sea of paper that is increasingly undesired, unstable and unusable. The deathly economic state of today's world is a direct reflection of the sum of its sick and dying currencies, but this could soon change.

Forces are already at work to position a new Carbon Currency as the ultimate solution to global calls for poverty reduction, population control, environmental control, global warming, energy allocation and blanket distribution of economic wealth. Unfortunately for individual people living in this new system, it will also require authoritarian and centralized control over all aspects of life, from cradle to grave.

---

190   Hubbert & Scott, p. 232.

What is Carbon Currency and how does it work? In a nutshell, Carbon Currency will be based on the regular allocation of available energy to the people of the world. If not used within a period of time, the Currency will expire (like monthly minutes on your cell phone plan) so that the same people can receive a new allocation based on new energy production quotas for the next period.

Because the energy supply chain is already dominated by the global elite, setting energy production quotas will limit the amount of Carbon Currency in circulation at any one time. It will also naturally limit manufacturing, food production and people movement.

Local currencies could remain in play for a time, but they would eventually wither and be fully replaced by the Carbon Currency, much the same way that the Euro displaced individual European currencies over a period of time. Technocracy's keen focus on the efficient use of energy is likely the first hint of a sustained ecological/environmental movement in the United States. *Technocracy Study Course* stated, for instance,

> *Although it (the earth) is not an isolated system the changes in the configuration of matter on the earth, such as the erosion of soil, the making of mountains, the burning of coal and oil, and the mining of metals are all typical and characteristic examples of irreversible processes, involving in each case an increase of entropy.*[191]

Modern emphasis on curtailing carbon fuel consumption that causes global warming and CO2 emissions is essentially a product of early technocratic thinking.

As scientists, Hubbert and Scott tried to explain (or justify) their arguments in terms of physics and the law of thermodynamics which is the study of energy conversion between heat and mechanical work.

Again, entropy is a concept within thermodynamics that represents the amount of energy in a system that is no longer available for doing mechanical work. Entropy thus increases as matter and energy in the system degrade toward the ultimate state of inert uniformity.

---

191   Ibid., p. 49.

In layman's terms, entropy means once you use it, you lose it for good. Furthermore, the end state of entropy is "inert uniformity" where nothing takes place. Thus, if man uses up all the available energy and/or destroys the ecology, it cannot be repeated or restored ever again.

The technocrat's avoidance of social entropy is to increase the efficiency of society by the careful allocation of available energy and measuring of subsequent output in order to find a state of "equilibrium", or balance. Hubbert's focus on entropy is evidenced by Technocracy, Inc.'s logo, the well-known Yin Yang symbol that depicts balance.

To facilitate this equilibrium between man and nature, Technocracy proposed that citizens would receive Energy Certificates in order to operate the economy:

> *Energy Certificates are issued individually to every adult of the entire population. The record of one's income and its rate of expenditure is kept by the Distribution Sequence, so that it is a simple matter at any time for the Distribution Sequence to ascertain the state of a given customer's balance.... When making purchases of either goods or services an individual surrenders the Energy Certificates properly identified and signed.*

> *The significance of this, from the point of view of knowledge of what is going on in the social system, and of social control, can best be appreciated when one surveys the whole system in perspective. First, one single organization is manning and operating the whole social mechanism. The same organization not only produces but also distributes all goods and services.*

> *With this information clearing continuously to a central headquarters we have a case exactly analogous to the control panel of a power plant, or the bridge of an ocean liner.*[192]

Two key differences between price-based money and Energy Certificates are that a) money is generic to the holder while Certificates are individually registered to each citizen and b) money persists while Certificates expire. The latter facet would

---

192   Ibid., p. 238-239.

greatly hinder, if not altogether prevent, the accumulation of wealth and property.

Transition

At the start of WWII, Technocracy's popularity dwindled as economic prosperity returned; however, both the organization and its philosophy survived.

Today, there are two principal websites representing Technocracy in North America: Technocracy, Inc., located in Ferndale, Washington, is represented at www.technocracy.org. A sister organization in Vancouver, British Columbia is Technocracy Vancouver and can be found at www.technocracyvan.ca.

While Technocracy's original focus was exclusively on the North American continent, it is now growing rapidly in Europe and other industrialized nations. For instance, the *Network of European Technocrats* (NET) was formed in 2005 as "an autonomous research and social movement that aims to explore and develop both the theory and design of technocracy."[193] The NET website claims to have members around the world.

Of course, a few minor league organizations and their websites cannot hope to create or implement a global energy policy, but it's not because the ideas aren't still alive and well. A more likely influence on modern thinking is due to Hubbert's Peak Oil Theory (e.g., the earth was running out of oil) introduced in 1954. It has figured prominently in the ecological/environmental movement. In fact, the entire global warming movement indirectly sits on top of the Hubbert Peak Theory. As the Canadian Association for the Club of Rome recently stated, "The issue of peak oil impinges directly on the climate change question."[194]

The Modern Proposal

Because of the connection between the environmental movement, global warming and the Technocratic concept of Energy Certificates, one would expect that a Carbon Currency would be suggested from that particular community, and in fact, this is

---

193   See http://www.eoslife.eu/. Name changed to Earth Organization for Sustainability.
194   John H. Walsh, "The Impending Twin Crisis: One Set of Solutions?", (Canadian Association for the Club of Rome), p.5.

the case. In 1995, Judith Hanna wrote in *New Scientist, Toward a Single Carbon Currency*, "My proposal is to set a global quota for fossil fuel combustion every year, and to share it equally between all the adults in the world."[195]

In 2004, the prestigious *Harvard International Review* (HIR) published *A New Currency* and stated,

> For those keen to slow global warming, **the most effective actions are in the creation of strong national carbon currencies**. For scholars and policymakers, the key task is to mine history for guides that are more useful. Global warming is considered an environmental issue, but its best solutions are not to be found in the canon of environmental law. Carbon's ubiquity in the world economy demands that cost be a consideration in any regime to limit emissions. Indeed, emissions trading has been anointed king because it is the most responsive to cost. And since trading emissions for carbon is more akin to trading currency than eliminating a pollutant, policymakers should be looking at trade and finance with an eye to how carbon markets should be governed. We must anticipate the policy challenges that will arise as this bottom-up system emerges, including the governance of seams between each of the nascent trading systems, liability rules for bogus permits, and judicial cooperation.[196] [Emphasis added]

HIR concludes that "after seven years of spinning wheels and wrong analogies, the international regime to control carbon is headed, albeit tentatively, down a productive path."[197]

In 2006, UK Environment Secretary David Miliband spoke to the Audit Commission Annual Lecture and flatly stated,

> Imagine a country where **carbon becomes a new currency**. We carry bankcards that store both pounds and carbon points. When we buy electricity, gas and fuel, **we use our carbon points**, as well as pounds. To help reduce carbon emissions, the Government would set limits on the amount of carbon that could be used.[198] [Emphasis added]

---

195   Judith Hanna, "Toward a single carbon currency", *New Scientist*, April 29, 1995.
196   "A New Currency", *Harvard International Review*, May 6, 2006.
197   Ibid.
198   "Pollute Less and You Could Cash In, Britons Told", *World Environment News*, July

In 2007, *New York Times* published "When Carbon Is Currency" by Hannah Fairfield. She pointedly stated "To build a carbon market, its originators must create a currency of carbon credits that participants can trade."[199]

PointCarbon, a leading global consultancy, is partnered with Bank of New York Mellon to assess rapidly growing carbon markets. In 2008 they published "Towards a Common Carbon Currency: Exploring the Prospects for Integrated Global Carbon Markets." This report discussed both environmental and economic efficiency in a similar context as originally seen with Hubbert in 1933.

Finally, on November 9, 2009, the *Telegraph (UK)* presented an article: "Everyone in Britain could be given a personal 'carbon allowance'" that suggested,

Implementing individual carbon allowances for every person will be the most effective way of meeting the targets for cutting greenhouse gas emissions. It would involve people being issued with a unique number which they would hand over when purchasing products that contribute to their carbon footprint, such as fuel, airline tickets and electricity. Like with a bank account, a statement would be sent out each month to help people keep track of what they are using. If their "carbon account" hits zero, they would have to pay to get more credits.[200]

As you can see, these references are hardly minor league in terms of either authorship or content. At the very least, the undercurrent of early Technocratic thought has finally reached the shore where the waves are lapping at the beach, with the potential to morph into a riptide under the right circumstances.

Technocracy's Energy Card Prototype

In July 1937, an article by Howard Scott in *Technocracy Magazine* described an Energy Distribution Card in great detail. It declared that using such an instrument as a "means of accounting is

20, 2006.

199   Hannah Fairfield, "When Carbon Is Currency", *The New York Times*, May 6, 2007.
200   "Everyone in Britain could be given a personal 'carbon allowance'", *The Telegraph (UK)*, November 9, 2009.

a part of Technocracy's proposed change in the course of how our socioeconomic system can be organized."[201]

Scott further wrote,

The certificate will be issued directly to the individual. It is nontransferable and nonnegotiable; therefore, it cannot be stolen, lost, loaned, borrowed, or given away. It is noncumulative; therefore, it cannot be saved, and it does not accrue or bear interest. It need not be spent but loses its validity after a designated time period.[202]

This may have seemed like science fiction in 1937, but today it is wholly achievable. In 2010 Technocracy, Inc. offered an updated idea of what such an Energy Distribution Card might look like. Their website states,

It is now possible to use a plastic card similar to today's credit card embedded with a microchip. This chip could contain all the information needed to create an energy distribution card as described in this booklet. Since the same information would be provided in whatever forms best suits the latest technology, however, the concept of an "Energy Distribution Card" is what is explained here.[203]

The card would also serve as a universal identity card and contain a microchip. This reflects Technocracy's philosophy that each person in society must be meticulously monitored and accounted for in order to track what they consume in terms of energy and also what they contribute to the manufacturing process.

Carbon Market Players

The modern system of carbon credits was an invention of the Kyoto Protocol and started to gain momentum in 2002 with the establishment of the first domestic economy-wide trading scheme in the U.K. After becoming international law in 2005, the trading market is now predicted to reach $3 trillion by 2020 or earlier.

Graciela Chichilnisky, director of the Columbia Consortium for Risk Management and a designer of the carbon credit text of

---

201   Howard Scott, "An Energy Distribution Card", *Technocracy Magazine*, 1937
202   Ibid.
203   "An Energy Distribution Card", *Technocracy, Inc.*, website, 2009.

the Kyoto Protocol, states that the carbon market "is therefore all about cash and trading" but it is also a way to a profitable and greener future.[204]

Who are the "traders" who provide the open door to all this profit? Currently leading the pack are JPMorgan Chase, Goldman Sachs and Morgan Stanley.

Bloomberg noted in "Carbon Capitalists" on December 4, 2009 that

The banks are preparing to do with carbon what they've done before: design and market derivatives contracts that will help client companies hedge their price risk over the long term. They're also ready to sell carbon-related financial products to outside investors.[205]

At JP Morgan, the woman who originally invented Credit Default Swaps, Blythe Masters, is now head of the department that will trade carbon credits for the bank. Considering the sheer force of global banking giants behind carbon trading, it's no wonder analysts are already predicting that the carbon market will soon dwarf all other commodities trading.

If M. King Hubbert and other early architects of Technocracy were alive today, they would be very pleased to see the seeds of their ideas on energy allocation grow to bear fruit on such a large scale. In 1933, the technology didn't exist to implement a system of Energy Certificates. However, with today's ever-advancing computer technology, the entire world could easily be managed on a single computer.

Of course, a currency is merely a means to an end. Whoever controls the currency would also control the economy and the governance system that goes with it. Technocracy and energy-based accounting are not idle or theoretical issues. If the global elite intends for Carbon Currency to supplant national currencies, then the world economic and political systems will also be fundamentally changed forever.

---

204 Graciela Chichilnisky, "Who Needs A Carbon Market?", *Environmental Leader*, January 10, 2010.
205 "Carbon Capitalists Warming to Climate Market Using Derivatives", *Bloomberg*, December 4, 2009.

CHAPTER 9

THE TOTAL SURVEILLANCE SOCIETY

Provide specific registration of the consumption of each individual, plus a record and description of the individual.[202] *- Technocracy Study Course*

Virtually everyone knows that some type of spy machine in Washington is collecting untold amounts of information on every citizen: Emails, phone calls, credit card transactions, health records, biometric information and so on. Most are in denial as to the nature and scope of it.

Among the National Security Agency (NSA), Federal Bureau of Investigation (FBI), the Central Intelligence Agency (CIA) and the Department of Homeland Security (DHS), no stone is left unturned to harvest all available electronic data. But, what is available? According to documents leaked by whistle-blower Edward Snowden, the NSA's top-secret Project Prism has relationships with nine principal Internet companies, including Microsoft, Google, Yahoo!, Facebook, PalTalk, YouTube, Skype, AOL and Apple, to collect all email, private messaging and other private communications.[203]

Such a realization flies in the face of official NSA propaganda. Even two years after the initial Snowden revelations, the NSA's official website still states the following in a Q&A section on oversight:

[Q] How can I find out if the government has records on me?

*[A] Both the Freedom of Information Act (FOIA) and the Privacy Act (PA) establish procedures for individuals to seek access to government records. The FOIA is a statute that gives anyone the right to seek access to government records. Since NSA is **authorized by law to collect only foreign intelligence information, we would not ordinarily expect to find***

---

202   Hubbert & Scott, 1934, p. 225.
203   "NSA slides explain PRISM", *The Washington Post*, June 6, 2013.

intelligence information about U.S. persons. Although you may submit a FOIA request for intelligence records, because our intelligence activities are classified, **we generally are unable to acknowledge whether or not we hold intelligence information on individuals.**[204] [Emphasis added]

Thus, even if the NSA is breaking the law (which it is) by collecting mountains of data on U.S. Citizens (which they are), don't expect to ever find out about *your* records because they are classified and therefore none of your business. On the surface of it, it may seem that the NSA has "gone rogue" and has taken on a life form of its own. We will soon discover that nothing could be further from the truth.

An earlier whistle-blower, retired AT&T technician Mark Klein, revealed that the NSA had installed a secret "listening room" at a major trunk facility owned by AT&T in San Francisco. Every phone call passing through the call center was secretly siphoned off by the NSA for storage and analysis.[205] The NSA was slapped hard by public outcries and even Congressional inquiry, but it did nothing to stop the phone call collection program; in fact, within two years, major AT&T trunk facilities in other cities had been set up and the collection expanded. By 2013, it was revealed that Verizon had also become part of the spy network. According to *The Guardian (UK)*,

The National Security Agency is currently collecting the telephone records of millions of US customers of Verizon, one of America's largest telecoms providers, under a top secret court order issued in April.... The order, a copy of which has been obtained by the Guardian, requires Verizon on an "ongoing, daily basis" to give the NSA information on all telephone calls in its systems, both within the US and between the US and other countries.[206]

There were lawsuits filed by citizen groups against the outrageous betrayal by commercial entities like AT&T, Verizon and Microsoft, but they were futile because in 2008, Congress ret-

---

204 (http://www.nsa.gov/about/faqs/oversight.shtml).
205 "The NSA Wiretapping Story That Nobody Wanted", *PC World*, July 17, 2009.
206 "NSA collecting phone records of millions of Verizon customers daily", *The Guardian (UK)*, June 5, 2003.

roactively amended the Foreign Intelligence Surveillance Act of 1978 to read,

> *Release from liability.—No cause of action shall lie in any court against any electronic communication service provider for providing any information, facilities, or assistance in accordance with [an order/request/directive issued by the Attorney General or the Director of National Intelligence.]*[207]

Case closed. The door was thrown wide-open for a complete co-opting of all communication and Internet companies by the Executive Branch of the U.S. Government. Do you have Verizon or AT&T? Every phone call is being recorded. Do you have a Gmail or AOL account? Every email is being recorded. Do you use Facebook, LinkedIn or Twitter? Every post is recorded. And, needless to say, it is all tied to your master file, providing for a convenient warrantless search at any time in the future.

All of this data is being siphoned off and stored in massive data centers, recently constructed, to prepare for the next phase of the operation which will focus on analysis. Fortunately for us, it is estimated that only one percent of all collected data is currently being analyzed, and the reason for this is that data storage technology has raced ahead of raw computer processing power and the algorithms necessary for analyses. This imbalance will not last for long since massive projects are already underway to create super-computers that will be able to process huge amounts of data within seconds. In addition, brand new computing technologies are being developed, such as quantum computing, that will increase existing computing power by a factor of several thousand times. To reiterate, the collection of data is already a fait accompli, but the analysis of the data is still ahead. To a technocrat, what the data says in a nominal way is a trivial issue. Rather, the elements of control come into focus only when he learns what the data means and what it can predict about the future. Such knowledge will be a product of analysis and not collection.

---

207 "FISA Amendments Act of 2008" – Section 702, subsection h, paragraph 3; Section 703, subsection e, (http://www.gpo.gov/fdsys/pkg/BILLS-110hr6304enr/pdf/BILLS-110hr6304enr.pdf).

Enter Big Data

When computer engineers talk about "big data", it engenders a mental disconnect with most people. What is big data? And what would anyone want to do with it?

The simplest concept of big data refers to any database that is too large for traditional data management tools to be used for storage, retrieval, correlation and analysis. The question is, what is too large to be "big".

When the original Apple Macintosh computer was unveiled in 1984, it contained a 3 1/2 inch floppy disk that could hold 400,000 bytes of information, or 400K. The "K" denotes Kilobytes, or thousands of bytes, and a single byte was enough to express one letter in the English alphabet. In 1986, the world eagerly received the next Macintosh version that expanded storage to 800K. At about the same time, the PC industry introduced the 1,440K floppy disk that then became the standard of portable disks for several years thereafter. The colloquial term used to describe this latter disk was 1.44MB, where the MB means Megabytes.

When IBM came out with the first 5MB hard drive, there was real excitement. Programmers were ecstatic because they now had room to work with some "real data".

Most of us can relate to these smaller numbers, and perhaps a little larger. After the 1,000MB threshold was broken, the industry started talking about Gigabytes. A hard drive with 5GB of storage simply meant 5,000MB. The starting size for new personal computers today is around the 500GB range, even for most laptop computers. So you may be thinking how could life get any better and what would you need any more storage for anyway?

We are getting closer to big data, but not close enough. Because of a need to store commercial video files, I recently purchased a whopping 4,000GB disk drive that was billed in terms of Terabytes as a 4TB monster. If it were not for storing large video and graphics files, I have no idea how I would use that much space! Whereas the original 400K floppy could store the equivalent of a 100 page book, just three of my 4TB drives could store the entire contents of the Library of Congress. Needless to say, Terabytes means serious business when it comes to massive data storage, but we have barely touched the realm of "big data".

To summarize and extend this progression of thinking,

Size	Term
1,000 Bytes	Kilobyte (KB)
1,000 Kilobytes	Megabyte (MB)
1,000 Megabytes	Gigabyte (GB)
1,000 Gigabytes	Terabyte (TB)
1,000 Terabytes	Petabyte (PB)
1,000 Petabytes	Exabyte (EB)
1,000 Exabytes	Zettabyte (ZB)
1,000 Zettabytes	Yottabyte (YB)

Consider what you can do at the Petabyte level:

- One Petabyte can store the DNA of every man, woman and child in the United States, three times over.
- The human brain can store about 2.5 Petabytes of data.
- One Petabyte of MP3-encoded music would take 2,000 years to play.
- A one Petabyte file could contain a 3 Megabyte profile of every person in America.

When we get to the Zettabyte level, it is almost inconceivable. A study was conducted in 2012 showing that the digital content of the entire world was 2.8 Zettabytes and that it would double that size about every 30 months. Now this is big data! One Zettabyte is represented by the number 10 with 21 zeros after it. It represents one billion Terabytes or one trillion Gigabytes. Let's not even think about Yottabytes.

As of 2011, no organization in the world was able to house even one Zettabyte of data. However, by fall of 2013, the National Security Agency (NSA) finished its new $1.5 billion spy center in Utah that alone has a reported capacity of 5 Zettabytes or almost twice the size of all digital data in the world. Now you can see why the NSA vacuums up all the data in sight: Because it can.

The NSA's Utah data center has had a lot of criticism, none of which has slowed its progress in the slightest. However, note that

Reuters reported in 2013 a vital connection to an even higher intelligence operation:

> **The NSA is the executive agent for the Office of the Director of National Intelligence**, *and will be the lead agency at the facility, but the center will also help other agencies, including the Department of Homeland Security, in protecting national security networks, according to a NSA news release.*[208] [Emphasis added]

Here we see two key points. First, the Utah facility doesn't belong to the NSA at all! Instead, it really belongs to the Office of the Director of National Intelligence (ODNI) with the NSA being only the "lead agency" at the facility. Second, we see that the NSA is only an agency of the ODNI and reports directly to it. In other words, the ODNI is where marching orders, funding and oversight come from. It is therefore worthwhile to examine the ODNI more closely.

Office of the Director of National Intelligence

The Intelligence Reform and Terrorism Prevention Act of 2004 (IRTPA) provided sweeping reform to the U.S. Intelligence community. With the experience of 9/11 still fresh in mind and a seemingly impotent intelligence apparatus, Congress passed the 235-page IRTPA with overwhelming support from both Democrats and Republicans. However, IRTPA opened the floodgate for the unbridled collection of data in order to build a national repository of information on virtually every person in the United States.

Title I, Subtitle A of IRTPA was labeled *Establishment of Director of National Intelligence* and was created for the "reorganization and improvement of management of the intelligence community." The Director of National Intelligence (DNI) was to be appointed by the President with advice and consent from the Senate. The appointee answered directly to the President but was not a member of the President's Cabinet. Authority was granted to serve as the undisputed head of the intelligence community with direct responsibility over all 16 intelligence agencies scattered throughout government; notably, this included the CIA, FBI and Homeland Security. The DNI's authority was sweeping:

---

*The Director of National Intelligence shall have access to **all national intelligence** and intelligence related to the national security which is **collected by any Federal department, agency, or other entity,** except as otherwise provided by law or, as appropriate, under guidelines agreed upon by the Attorney General and the Director of National Intelligence.*[209] [Emphasis added]

Further, the intelligence gathered and made possible by the DNI was to be first provided to the President, then to heads of departments and agencies of the executive branch, then to the Chairman of the Joint Chiefs of Staff and senior military commanders, and finally to the Senate and House of Representatives.

The czar-like status of the DNI is underscored by the fact that he is responsible for not only overall intelligence strategy but also operational management, funding and allocation of programs in all sub-agencies. The IRTPA further stated that *"The Director of National Intelligence shall -*

(A) establish uniform security standards and procedures;

*(B) **establish common information technology standards, protocols, and interfaces;***

*(C) ensure **development of information technology systems** that include multi-level security and intelligence integration capabilities;*

*(D) establish policies and procedures to resolve conflicts between the need to share intelligence information and the need to **protect intelligence sources and methods;***

*(E) **develop an enterprise architecture for the intelligence community and ensure that elements of the intelligence community comply with such architecture;** and*

*(F) have **procurement approval authority** over all enterprise architecture-related information technology items funded in the National Intelligence Program.*[210] [Emphasis added]

The earlier statement that the "NSA is the executive agent for

---

209   IRTPA, Sec. 102A, p. 7.
210   Ibid., p.13.

the Office of the Director of National Intelligence" now makes perfect sense. In short, the head of the NSA answers directly to the Director of National Intelligence and receives from him direction and strategy, funding and oversight. Who ordered and approved the $1.5 billion budget for the NSA's massive five Zettabyte data center in Utah? The Director. Who ordered and approved the data center's operational objectives and policies? The Director. Who ordered and approved massive spying operations involving AT&T, Verizon, Microsoft, Facebook, Apple, Skype, etc.? The Director. Who ordered and created the overall strategy of building a national database with all this data in the first place? The Director.

So, who *was* the first Director that initially created, staffed, funded and organized the original Office of the Director of National Intelligence in 2005? It was none other than Trilateral Commission member **John Negroponte**, appointed by then-President George W. Bush. Bush was never a member of the Trilateral Commission, but his father, **George H.W. Bush** was. Most notably, Bush's Vice-President, **Dick Cheney,** was also a member.

Negroponte held his DNI position from April 21, 2005 through February 13, 2007, or almost two years. Bush then appointed Vice Admiral John McConnell who held on until January 27, 2009, or eight days into the first Obama administration when he was sacked. Obama obviously wanted to have his "own guy" as DNI but who did he appoint? You might already have guessed it was yet another member of the Trilateral Commission, **Admiral Dennis C. Blair**!

It would be stating the obvious that Technocracy and the Trilateral Commission are always seen above the two-party continuum, neither Republican or Democrat. With equal aplomb, their members surrounded Obama just as easily as they did Bush. As far as the technocratic intelligence community was concerned, a change in political leadership meant nothing in terms of pushing forward with their pre-conceived Total Surveillance Society; one might rightly wonder who is in control of whom. In fact, measuring and monitoring is the life-blood of Technocracy, remembering that the fifth requirement as noted earlier is to "Provide specific registration of the consumption of each individual, plus a record and description of the individual." The current total surveillance mentality is a hand-in-glove fit!

Americans were warned of the dangers of such technology being used against the American people. In 1975, Sen. Frank Church (D-Idaho) clearly and pointedly stated,

> The chairman of the Senate panel probing U.S. Intelligence agencies says **the government has the technological capacity to impose "total tyranny" if a dictator ever came to power.** "There would be no place to hide," Sen. Frank Church (D-Idaho), chairman of the committee, said Sunday on NBC's Meet the Press. Church said the eavesdropping technology given the government by intelligence agencies would enable the government to impose total tyranny "and **there would be no way to fight back because the most careful effort to combine together in resistance to the government, no matter how privately it was done, is within the reach of the government to know,** such is the capability of this technology."[211] [Emphasis added]

In 1961, outgoing President Dwight D. Eisenhower warned in his farewell speech,

> ...in holding scientific research and discovery in respect, as we should, we must also be alert to the equal and opposite danger that public policy could itself become the captive of a scientific-technological elite.[212]

In 1975 and 1961, nobody had any idea of what Church or Eisenhower were talking about. In 2014, however, the fruit of a "scientific-technological elite" is all too evident and all too encompassing. If Hitler could have somehow grabbed hold of today's surveillance technology back in 1935, the whole world would be speaking German today, and all of his perceived enemies would have been summarily destroyed.

Data Fusion and Fusion Centers

Most of the data collection network established by the DNI operates on a national and international scale. For instance, col-

---

211   "Dictator Could Impose Total Tyranny in U.S., Church Says", *The Times-News*, August 16, 1975.
212   Eisenhower's Farewell Address to the Nation, January 17, 1961.

lecting phone calls, email and messaging records only requires a small number of entry points, such as phone companies and email services. Since email records are virtually identical across all email providers, there is no data inconsistency in vacuuming everything up and putting it into a common database. The same applies for phone calls, banking records and consumer transactional data.

At the state level where volumes of critical data are found, such standardization is seldom seen. Most state data systems were "home grown" and hence, different from state to state. To further exacerbate the problem, communities within each state built their own local systems that had little in common with a neighboring city or county. Over the years, a myriad of software companies offered different flavors of database software, some radically different than others. Programmers have used different techniques to define and describe the same data from project to project. In short, you cannot just throw all of this data into a melting pot and expect anything other than meaningless garbage to come out the other end.

This is where the concept of "data fusion" is applied, where different databases are compared so that a) connectors can be built to bridge the differences and b) missing pieces of data in one database can be fabricated in another. In fact, creating missing data elements out of thin air, based on implications from other pieces of data, is a key concept in the "fusion" process.

The Federal intelligence juggernaut saw fit to go after all of this state-level data and thus created the concept of Fusion Centers that would survey, map, collect and coordinate the transmission of local information to the national level. Each state in America has at least one local Fusion Center. In fact, according to the Department of Homeland Security (DHS) website, there were 78 Fusion Centers operating in the United States as of January 2014.

Former DHS head Janet Napolitano described Fusion Centers in testimony before the House of Representatives Subcommittee on Homeland Security in 2012:

These centers analyze information and identify trends to share timely intelligence with federal, state, and local law enforcement including DHS, which then further shares this information with other members of the Intelligence Community. In turn, DHS provides relevant and appropriate threat information from the Intelligence Community back to the fusion centers. Today, there are 72 state- and locally-run fusion centers in operation across the nation, up from a handful in 2006. Our goal is to make every one of these fusion centers a center of analytic excellence that provides useful, actionable information about threats to law enforcement and first responders.[213]

However, Napolitano's rhetoric did not hold up to scrutiny for long. On October 3, 2012, the Senate's Permanent Subcommittee on Investigations released its scathing report, *Federal Support For And Involvement In State And Local Fusion Centers.* Judicial Watch summarized this 141-page report as follows:

Nine years and more than $300 million later, the national [fusion] centers have failed to provide any valuable information, according to investigators. Instead they have forwarded "intelligence of uneven quality – oftentimes shoddy, rarely timely, sometimes endangering citizens' civil liberties and Privacy Act protections, occasionally taken from already-published public sources, and more often than not unrelated to terrorism." A review of more than a year of fusion center reports nationwide determined that they were irrelevant, useless or inappropriate. None uncovered any terrorist threats nor did they contribute to the disruption of an active terrorist plot, the report says. In fact, DHS officials acknowledged that the information produced by the fusion centers was "predominantly useless". One branch chief actually said, "a bunch of crap is coming through."[214]

This writer suggests that the criteria for judging the DHS's Fusion Centers may have been wrong. Instead of using Napolitano's baseline, perhaps they should have paid closer attention to this 2006 Department of Justice document:

---

213   Testimony of DHS Secretary Janet Napolitano Before the United States House of Representatives Committee on Homeland Security, "Understanding the Homeland Threat Landscape - Considerations for the 112th Congress".

214   "DHS Covers Up Failures of U.S. Counterterrorism Centers", *Judicial Watch*, Oct. 3, 2012.

Fusion centers will allow information from all sources to be readily gathered, analyzed, and exchanged, based upon the predicate, by **providing access to a variety of disparate databases that are maintained and controlled by appropriate local, state, tribal,** *and federal representatives at the fusion center.*[215] [Emphasis added]

Thus, the true role of Fusion Centers is to simply "fuse" data from disparate databases at the local and state level and feed the result to the national level. No publicly available studies using this criteria have been found that measure the value of the Fusion Center network to Federal agencies like the NSA. Perhaps actions speak louder than words: The Fusion Center program is still fully funded and six more Fusion Centers have been added since Napolitano's testimony!

Conclusion

Any engineer knows that you cannot control what you cannot monitor. Thus, Technocracy requires an all-encompassing data collection and intelligence function in order to monitor and control all elements of society and economic activity. To a technocrat, there is no such thing as "too much data". When collecting becomes an end in itself, participants quickly display symptoms of classical hoarding disorder as described by Mayo Clinic:

A persistent difficulty discarding or parting with possessions because of a perceived need to save them. A person with hoarding disorder experiences distress at the thought of getting rid of the items. Excessive accumulation of items, regardless of actual value, occurs.

Such is the state of today's Total Surveillance Society, created to serve Technocracy only, while excluding any benefit for individuals, groups or even society at large. While this may seem completely irrational to you, it is perfectly rational to a technocrat.

It is also noteworthy that the guardians of the technocrat chickens are technocrat foxes themselves, and together they have successfully removed themselves from any effective oversight or

---

215 "Fusion Center Guidelines", Department of Justice and Department of Homeland Security, August 2006.

control by Congress, state or local officials, all of which have been completely ineffective at reigning in their data vacuum juggernaut.

CHAPTER 10

TRANSFORMING HUMANITY

The master strategy of Technocracy and its goal of global transformation has already been detailed in the chapters Transforming Economics, Transforming Government and Transforming Religion. But, there is one last consideration: What about the people of the world themselves? Are they suited to live in a Technocracy without further changing the very fabric of life itself? Or, perhaps is it just the elite technocrats who need to be changed? This brings us to an important discussion on Transhumans, Posthumans and Transhumanism, without which this book would simply be inadequate. One prominent leader in the movement defines transhumanism as

> ...a commitment to overcoming human limits in all their forms including extending lifespan, augmenting intelligence, perpetually increasing knowledge, achieving complete control over our personalities and identities and gaining the ability to leave the planet. Transhumanists seek to achieve these goals through reason, science and technology.[215]

Another puts it this way:

> Philosophies of life that seek the continuation and acceleration of the evolution of intelligent life beyond its currently human form and human limitations by means of science and technology, guided by life-promoting principles and values.[216]

A Transhuman is a person who believes in transhumanism, and views himself as "in transition" toward becoming posthuman, a state which no one has actually achieved as yet; according to the following definition, you can see why:

> "Posthuman" is a term used by transhumanists to refer to what humans could become if we succeed in using technology to remove the limitations of the human condition. No one

---

215 Attributed to Natasha Vita-More,
216 Attributed to Max More

can be certain exactly what posthumans would be like but
we can understand the term by contrasting it with "human":
Posthumans would be those who have overcome the biologi-
cal, neurological, and psychological constraints built into hu-
mans by the evolutionary process. Posthumans would have
a far greater ability to reconfigure and sculpt their physical
form and function; they would have an expanded range of
refined emotional responses, and would possess intellectual
and perceptual abilities enhanced beyond the purely human
range. Posthumans would not be subject to biological aging
or degeneration.[217]

You might be thinking that somebody has been watching too many science fiction movies lately, but you would be wrong. Transhumans are deadly serious about becoming posthuman by using advanced technology (e.g., NBIC) that is now well under development at major universities and research centers throughout the world, and there is just enough substance to court a loyal and growing following of would-be posthumans. Since all of this is squarely based on Scientism (discussed in Chapter 1), it is thus directly related to Technocracy and must be explored in some detail. Again, the question is, do technocratic strategists intend for their newly-transformed world to be populated with humans or posthumans?

Julian Huxley (1887-1975), brother of the utopian science fiction writer Aldous Huxley (*Brave New World*, 1932), was the first person to use the word Transhumanism in his 1957 book *New Bottles For New Wine*:

It is as if man had been suddenly appointed managing direc-
tor of the biggest business of all, the business of evolution —
appointed without being asked if he wanted it, and without
proper warning and preparation. What is more, he can't re-
fuse the job. Whether he wants to or not, whether he is con-
*scious of what he is doing or not, **he is in point of fact de-***
termining the future direction of evolution on this earth.
That is his inescapable destiny, and the sooner he realizes it
and starts believing in it, the better for all concerned.

---

217 Transhumanist FAQ, (http://www.extropy.org).

*The human species can, if it wishes, transcend itself —not just sporadically, an individual here in one way, an individual there in another way, but in its entirety, as humanity. We need a name for this new belief. Perhaps **transhumanism** will serve: **man remaining man, but transcending himself,** by realizing new possibilities of and for his human nature.*

"I believe in transhumanism": once there are enough people who can truly say that, the human species will be on the threshold of a new kind of existence, as different from ours as ours is from that of Peking man. It will at last be consciously fulfilling its real destiny. [218] [Emphasis added]

Huxley was a professing humanist, having signed the original Humanist Manifesto in 1933 and served as the first president of the British Humanist Association upon its founding in 1963. In 1962, Huxley received the "Humanist of the Year" award from the American Humanist Association. He was deeply committed to Darwin's theories of evolution and eugenics as an evolutionary biologist by education and profession. He became the first Director-General of the United Nations Educational, Scientific and Cultural Organization (UNESCO) in 1946 and was president of the British Eugenics Society from 1959-1962. He was also a founding member of the World Wildlife Fund in 1961. In short, Huxley lived a life totally immersed in Sustainable Development before the term even existed. However, as a visionary he saw beyond the valley of transformation to the mountain peaks afar off, where the ultimate goal of man might be realized: Taking direct control of evolution in order to launch mankind to a "new kind of existence", one achieved by "transcending himself", and thus finally fulfilling his "real destiny". Could it be that Huxley had a glimpse of the Human Genome Project to map the human genome in the 1990s? Or thoughts about Ray Kurzweil's prediction of Singularity in the 21st century? Whether he did or did not, Huxley is considered to be an important "founding father" of modern transhumanism by Transhumanists themselves.

Although there are many Transhumanist organizations around the world all espousing very consistent philosophical and religious views, there is none more representative and authoritative

---

218 Julian Huxley, *New Bottles for New Wine*, (Peters Fraser & Dunlop, 1957), p.17.

than Humanity Plus, or H+, led by Max More and his wife, Natasha Vita-More, who authored the *Transhuman Manifesto* in 1983. Max co-founded the original Transhumanist magazine *Extropy* in 1988 and the Extropy Institute in the early 1990s. The first point of their Transhumanist Declaration states,

*Humanity stands to be profoundly affected by science and technology in the future. We envision the possibility of broadening human potential by **overcoming aging, cognitive shortcomings**, involuntary suffering, and our confinement to planet Earth.*[219] [Emphasis added]

Essentially, the Transhuman envisions that ultimately he will be able to recreate himself as a "superman" with unlimited intelligence and information at his disposal (on-demand omniscience), to escape his human form to travel the universe in electronic form (multi-presence if not omnipresence), to modify physical creation to suit his personal taste (omnipotence) and to escape physical death (immortality).

The fact that these are God-like qualities is not lost on would-be posthumans. On October 1, 2010, a conference titled *Transhumanism and Spirituality* was hosted by the University of Utah in Salt Lake City where Transhuman movement leaders from around the world convened to discuss the "evolutionary transition to divinity through technology...", that is, man becoming God. Attendees represented a mix of Mormonism, Buddhism, Atheism and Christianity. Although Hinduism wasn't officially represented, the concept was evident.[220] Transhumanism has a wide appeal to many different religions around the world, especially those that espouse a road to becoming gods; transhumanism simply offers a way to achieve it - through technology developed by leading scientists and engineers in the world's top universities. Indeed, the language of divinity, or men becoming gods, is seen throughout the scientific community as well. If there is any reason why you have never heard about this, it is because scientists and engineers avoid publicity, and the media does not perceive a story anyway.

To restate: Whereas Humanism relied on a metaphysical fan-

---

219 Transhumanist Declaration, (http://humanityplus.org/philosophy/transhumanist-declaration/).

220 Eyewitness testimony from Christian researcher and apologist, Carl Teichrib who was allowed to attend the conference as an observer. (see www.ForcingChange.com)

tasy to achieve its goals, Transhumanism fortifies its metaphysical wish-list with supposedly objective science. Never mind that much, if not most, of that objective science hasn't been invented yet. To the Transhuman psyche, just the mere promise of future science is enough for them to count it as a fait accompli.

Converging Technologies

In June 2002, the National Science Foundation published a major 482-page report called, *Converging Technologies for Improving Human Performance*. It called for the integration of four branches of physical science for the sole purpose of enhancing the human condition. Specifically, the converging disciplines are Nanotechnology, Biotechnology, Information Technology and Cognitive Science, and they have given rise to the acronym NBIC. In common use among its advocates, the word "Convergence" is often used as a noun.

Why these four particular areas of study? Let's briefly explore each one.

First, *Nanotechnology* has recently discovered how to manipulate the building blocks of matter at the atomic and molecular level. A nanometer is one billionth of a meter and is comparable to the size of a marble verses the size of Earth. Nanotechnology is already producing a number of sub-disciplines in the fields of medicine (drugs, diagnostics) and engineering (alloys, chemicals), for instance. The key to Nanotechnology in the Convergence, however, is in the ongoing and on-demand manipulation of matter through external means, such as through the use of computer technology.

Second, *Biotechnology* is concerned with the study of life and living organisms. Cells are the building blocks of all life, but scientists believe they have cracked the code to life by successfully mapping the human genome, or DNA, starting in 1990, and mostly completed in 2003. DNA is the essential building block of all life forms. Scientists subsequently noted how similar the DNA structure is to the principles and logic found in computer information technology.

Third, *Computer Information Technology* (CIT) is the most well known of these four technologies. Personal computers, smart phones, smart appliances and even automobiles have embedded micro-chips that control processes, collect and process data, enable communications, and so on. Applied computer science is absolutely necessary to design, build and control DNA sequences and nano-sized atomic and molecular material. Increasingly fast computer chips are now able to make split-second calculations that would have been completely impossible even 50 years ago. Thus, this CIT is enabling lightening-speed development and application of the other technologies.

Finally, *Cognitive Science* deals with the human mind, including psychology, artificial intelligence, philosophy, neuroscience, learning sciences, linguistics, anthropology, sociology and education.[221] The reader should note that this intersection of hard science with sociology (the study of human society) is reminiscent of the same phenomenon in the 1930s when sociology was crossed with science to produce Technocracy. At his 2013 State of the Union Address, President Obama alluded to Convergence when he stated,

Every dollar we invested to map the human genome returned $140 to our economy.... Today, our scientists are mapping the human brain.... Now is the time to reach a level of research and development not seen since the height of the Space Race.[222]

Thereafter, the White House quickly published the Fact Sheet: BRAIN Initiative, which elaborated,

*The BRAIN Initiative will accelerate the development and application of new technologies that will enable researchers to produce dynamic pictures of the brain that show how individual brain cells and complex neural circuits interact at the speed of thought. These technologies will open new doors to explore how the brain records, processes, uses, stores, and retrieves vast quantities of information, and **shed light on the complex links between brain function and behavior.***[223] [Emphasis added]

---

221 Paul Thagard, Edward N. Zalta (ed.), "Cognitive Science", *The Stanford Encyclopedia of Philosophy* (Fall 2008 Edition).

222 Barack Obama, "State of the Union Address", (2013) (http://www.whitehouse.gov/state-of-the-union-2013).

223 Fact Sheet: BRAIN Initiative, April 2, 2013, (http://www.whitehouse.gov/the-press-office/2013/04/02/fact-sheet-brain-initiative).

The BRAIN Initiative was immediately kick started with a one hundred million dollar Federal grant with the promise of billions more in future years as the project unfolds. The National Institutes of Health is leading the project, and the high-level working group in charge will be co-chaired by Dr. Cornelia Bargmann, a professor of neuroscience at Rockefeller University in New York City which was originally founded by John D. Rockefeller, Sr. in 1901 as the Rockefeller Institute for Medical Research.

Since there was no public demand for a project to map the human brain, nor would any career politician have a clue about the complexities or outcomes of such a project, one must conclude that some outside group put Obama up to it. Such a group could rightly claim incredible influence to be able to get a sitting president to announce and fund a scientific project such as this which only underscores my earlier claim that the scientists and engineers who aspire to a posthuman future for themselves are an incredibly powerful group and that they are dead serious about achieving their goals, especially if it is at taxpayer expense.

With the building blocks of matter and life at their disposal, coupled with advanced computer technology to help arrange them, technologists believe that they are on the fast-track to creating the final "quantum leap" where man takes direct control over evolution and launches mankind into a posthuman world. It is important to note that without the university framework, most of which is publicly funded, Convergence would generally be a moot issue and would remain in the fantasy world of science fiction writers. If government programs did not exist and private industry were left to develop technology for products designed to improve the human condition, it undoubtedly would do so, but it would be based on public demand and benefit rather than on spiritual, metaphysical and cult-like philosophies of scientists and engineers found within universities.

Singularity

The other key element of Transhuman hope is the futurist notion of scientific Singularity. Largely theorized and popularized by inventor and futurist Ray Kurzweil, the Singularity predicts a point in time (circa 2042) when computer intelligence will finally exceed that of humans, resulting in an unpredictable world where machines become autonomous, maintaining themselves and creating new technologies and new machine designs without human intervention. Discovery of new knowledge turns vertical on the chart, far outstripping human ability to keep up with it, much less direct it.

Singularity is often explained in relation to Moore's Law, named after Intel co-founder Gordon E. Moore, who described the advancing trend in technology in his 1965 paper, *Cramming more components onto integrated circuits.*[224] Moore's Law states that the number of transistors on an integrated circuit doubles approximately every two years. This has generally held true over the intervening years, and other elements of computer science have generally kept pace with Moore's Law as well, such as complexity in software engineering, speed in computer communications, etc. Using this logic to extrapolate technological advances in artificial intelligence has led Kurzweil and others to make such bold predictions.

In his 2005 book, *The Singularity is Near*, Kurzweil also reveals how biological evolution has extended through technological evolution and attaches a distinct spiritual connotation to the mix by stating,

> *The Singularity denotes an event that will take place in the material world, the inevitable next step in the evolutionary process that started with biological evolution and has extended through human-directed technological evolution. However, it is precisely in the world of matter and energy that* **we encounter transcendence, a principal connotation of what people refer to as spirituality.**[225] [Emphasis added]

It is important to point out that Kurzweil's vision of the future is an unproven theory, however plausible he can make it sound, and there is no hard evidence that he could be right. However, his strong and unwavering belief in his own theory has led him to seek to resurrect his beloved father back to life through a com-

---

224 Gordon E. More, "Cramming more components onto integrated circuits", *Electronics Magazine*, (1965), pp. 4.
225 Ray Kurzweil, *The Singularity is Near: When Humans Transcend Biology*, (Viking Press, 2005), p. 387.

puter avatar. As to the rest of the currently living, he forecasts,

> *The Singularity will allow us to transcend these limitations of our biological bodies and brains.* **We will gain power over our fates.** *Our mortality will be in our own hands. We will be able to live as long as we want. We will fully understand human thinking and will vastly extend and expand its reach. By the end of this century, the nonbiological portion of our intelligence will be trillions of trillions of times more powerful than unaided human intelligence.*[226] [Emphasis added]

When you take a little hard science produced by the Convergence and add to it a plausible but unproven theory of the Singularity, you have the modern equivalent of Darwin's primordial soup that produced the first edition of humanity. Whereas Darwin's theory of evolution was based on random chance, technological evolution will explicitly take control of the development of posthuman man, leading him to eventually become "gods of the universe" with incredible god-like powers.

That is a strong statement, but it is backed up by direct testimony. For instance, Dr. Richard Seed, a leading Transhuman, cloning researcher and nuclear physicist, was interviewed for a documentary on Transhumanism and rather angrily stated,

> *We are going to become Gods. Period. If you don't like it, get off. You don't have to contribute, you don't have to participate. But if you're going to interfere with ME becoming God, then we'll have big trouble; we'll have warfare. The only way to prevent me is to kill me. And you kill me, I'll kill you.*[227]

Since this book is about Technocracy and not Transhumanism, this brief discussion will have to suffice. The reader can ponder the question of how Posthumans and Technocracy will get along. But, since we see the multiple threads of Evolution, Humanism and Scientism through both, it is not unreasonable to suggest that one was made for the other and vice versa. Another reason to suggest this as a necessity is that today's humans may endorse Technocracy for a time, but in the end, as they see the nature of scientific dictatorship, they will reject it and attempt to throw it off society's back. In other words, the utopian promises of mod-

226 Ibid., p. 9.
227 Dr. Richard Seed, Technocalyps Part II - Preparing for the Singularity, 2006.

ern Technocracy may be appealing to the masses, but not *that* appealing. Adding the Transhuman carrot of becoming gods in the process will simply seal the deal by thoroughly deceiving man into thinking that the promises of Utopia actually exist and that they must patiently endure the inconveniences of Technocracy in order to realize them.

Chapter 11

Taking Action

When I use military terms such as enemies, defeat, battles and war, please understand that these are only analogies used to describe and explain our current condition. This chapter in no way proposes any kind of violence or illegal behavior toward any person, especially toward fellow American citizens. For those critics who will undoubtedly think it legitimate to lift a quote out of context, I warn you in advance that this paragraph states my clear intention: No guns. No knives. No blunt instruments. No bodily harm of any kind.

This may seem harsh to some, but Americans need to face the hard facts of reality. We find ourselves in our current situation because our enemies have had a clearly superior strategy from the start while we - the people - have had no coherent strategy at all. We have lost battle after battle and are almost to the point of losing the war altogether. We can work this dilemma backward by calling on General Sun Tzu (circa 500BC), the noted Chinese military strategist and philosopher. Tzu wrote *The Art of War*, a simple book that has been used by military strategists ever since, including those from the United States. Chapter Three states, in part,

> *If you know the enemy and know yourself, you need not fear the result of a hundred battles. If you know yourself but not the enemy, for every victory gained you will also suffer a defeat. If you know neither the enemy nor yourself, you will succumb in every battle.*[228]

By this analysis, the fact that we have "succumbed in every battle" (and yes, there are a few exceptions) is because we don't know the enemy and we don't know ourselves. So, who is the enemy? According to Tzu's philosophy, our enemies have succeeded in keeping all eyes off of them by encouraging useless infighting among our own citizens. Conservatives see liberals as the ene-

<hr>

228   Sun Tzu, *The Art of War*, circa 500BC.

my. Liberals see conservatives as the enemy. Libertarians see big government as the enemy. However, if you have picked up even one thing from reading this book, it should be that Technocracy has completely transcended political parties or philosophies. Trilateral Commission members have used and manipulated both sides of the political spectrum to get what they want while avoiding detection and hence, any effective resistance. Upon the election of Jimmy Carter in 1976, it can be accurately said that Trilateral Commission Technocrats literally hijacked the Executive Branch of the U.S. Government, and they have dominated every administration since then, up to and including that of Barack Hussein Obama. As we have progressed down this path, America has become more and more divided, contentious and many would even say, dysfunctional. And why not? When you know you are being attacked and things are falling apart, but you do not know who the enemy is, you strike out at any convenient target. This is the exact opposite of how Americans acted when Pearl Harbor was attacked at the start of our involvement in World War II because everybody knew who our enemies were and thus focused all of their attention on destroying them. Think what would happen today if Americans suddenly recognized who their true enemies were?

The next question is, "Who are we?" First off, most citizens of our nation are thoroughly deceived about the nature of our problems and how they have been perpetrated. Just the suggestion of this will undoubtedly trigger narrow-minded responses like "If only people knew about FEMA camps" or "We can't change our country unless we get rid of the Federal Reserve" or "The president must be impeached." Over the years, I have heard more arguments than can possibly be remembered, and they have all missed the mark. For all the effort put into these misguided pursuits, how much better off are we for it today? Our present condition speaks for itself: The nation is circling the drain because *we* have missed the mark. It is *we* who have been deceived by a crafty enemy who knew exactly what they were doing. This must stop.

Once we accept the fact that the problems we face are due to specific people pushing Technocracy on us, we will start to destroy this delusion. Who are these people? Again, the global leaders are members of the Trilateral Commission and their elitist cronies; the foot soldiers are the myriads of unelected and unaccountable technocrats at all levels of government and the corporate world who are specifically uninterested in politics unless it furthers their cause.

The second complaint about who we are is a failure to recognize that Congress has been neutered as far as controlling Technocracy and Trilateral hegemony is concerned. When I say "neutered", I mean impotent and ineffective. We have spent the last 40 years fighting to send good Representatives and Senators to Washington to steer our nation out of harm's way. Have they succeeded? No. However, like addicted gamblers who do not know when to stop putting coins in the machine, they double-down hoping to get their lost money back. Americans need to face the fact that the national political scene is largely a waste of valuable time and money and get beyond it.

Dismal as the above may seem, Americans need to just calm down, embrace tested and tried strategies to set things right, and then execute those strategies that will win battle after battle. They don't have to be "big" battles, either. If there were a thousand wins on even a small scale, it would have a huge impact on our nation as a whole.

What do I mean by a small scale? Let's say that your town is voting on a General Plan that is inspired, if not written, by the Agenda 21/Sustainable Development crowd. You take on the formidable task of rallying the citizens of the community to vote the General Plan down and at the same time, call out the city council members who supported it, the city manager who signed the consulting contracts, and all the planners who "wrote it up". Running your General Plan out of town will not make national news, but if enough towns did the same thing across the country, they would collectively send a huge message up the chain of technocrat command that they are being exposed and are at risk of being thrown out of their positions as well.

The citizens of our country are in no position to stop the National Security Agency from spying on them, as unconstitutional or illegal as that may be. We are in no position to rout the corruption out of the Internal Revenue Service and to stop it from being used as a political weapon against citizens. We are in no position to stop the Executive Branch from obstinately refusing to enforce existing immigration laws and close the border to illegal immigrants. While these truly are all critical issues, the real problem is that we simply have no power to overcome them at this time.

We need to listen a little harder to Sun Tzu to get some "street smarts" about developing strategies that lead to wins:

> *To fight and conquer in all your battles is not supreme excellence;* **supreme excellence consists in breaking the enemy's resistance without fighting.**
> - *Thus the highest form of generalship is to* **balk the enemy's plans;**
> - *the next best is to* **prevent the junction of the enemy's forces;**
> - *the next in order is to* **attack the enemy's army in the field;**
> - *and the* **worst policy of all is to besiege walled cities.**
> - *The rule is,* **not to besiege walled cities if it can possibly be avoided.**[229] [Emphasis added]

This is such a package of strategic wisdom. First, we are not in a street brawl where we just run into any fight and start throwing punches. The best thing is to break the enemy's will and resistance without a fight at all! Yes, that *is* possible. In order of importance, the best outcome is to scuttle the enemy's plans outright before a battle is even engaged; the worst scenario is laying siege to a walled city, that is, to an enemy who is already heavily entrenched and fortified by various layers of insulation and bureaucracy. The second-best outcome is to block the meet-up of various enemy forces coming to a battle from different directions, as is the case when environmental groups conspire with NGOs and local planning committees to force some policy down our throats.

On a national level, most top technocrats are definitely hardened by political battles where they have learned to repel or dodge resistance. On a local level, most Technocrats have never experienced any resistance from anyone, and hence, they are

---

229 Tzu, S., The Art of War, Dover Publications, 2002.

weak. Experience shows that they are utterly dismayed when someone suggests their ideas are stupid, shortsighted, unconstitutional, illegal or whatever. After all, they have been educated by a government school system that brainwashed them into thinking that *their beliefs* are shared by everyone in society. When confronted, especially in a public forum, they are often caught like the proverbial deer in the headlights, wide-eyed and clueless.

This is not to say that local technocrats are necessarily easy to dislodge from your community. After all, they are already there, and they are deeply invested in the work that they are doing. They will not just walk away from it all because you say so. On the other hand, they are virtually defenseless when their arguments and philosophies are confronted with hard facts and/or legal action.

The next most important element is to engage the enemy where *you* find him and do not engage those whom you do not know or cannot find. This might seem obvious, but it is often missed by most well-intentioned activists. The most overused and meaningless words in society are "them" and "they". When the enemy isn't identified, people simply use the impersonal substitution: "We must fight *them*." "*They* cannot get away with this." This has to stop: You simply cannot fight an unknown or unidentified enemy. To gain intelligence on the enemy, you must expend effort doing legwork and research. Attend public meetings, talk to local officials, research voting records, read planning documents, request access to city and county contracts, etc. In most communities, it will not take long to determine the who, what, when, where, why and how of your local situation. The point is, if you haven't done your homework to get this kind of information, you will be wasting your time shadow boxing with the hypothetical "them", always swinging and never landing a punch.

How can you identify a locally oriented Technocrat? If you can match up two or three characteristics from this list, you may have discovered a technocrat:

- Promotes pseudo-scientific ideas such as global warming/climate change or Sustainable Development
- Creates or enforces regulations or policies that are not subject to legislative, judicial or public approval

- Promotes or works with NGOs, environmental groups or any agency of the United Nations
- Promotes economic development or policies based on Smart Growth, urban renewal or Public-Private Partnerships
- Any elected or appointed official who is active in a Regional Governance program such as a Councils of Governments organization
- Unwilling to listen or shuts down any opposing positions or discussion

This is not meant to be exhaustive nor to send you on a witch hunt. If you have read and understood the rest of this book, you should be able to understand the technocrat mindset. You can be sure that most technocrats will not recognize themselves as such, and many may not even know what the word means. On the other hand, don't let innocence deceive you. Nice people can be misguided just as easily as anyone else. Accordingly, some people will easily recant their positions when exposed to the truth via gentle explanation or exhortation. Always look for people who are willing to seriously listen to you and who are willing to change if the motivation to do so is correct.

Technocrats will resist your efforts in one of two ways: overtly or passively. By overt resistance, I mean they will actively give you an argument as to why you are wrong and they are right. They might appear as ideologues instead of public servants, and they are always easy to identify. By passive resistance, I mean that they will appear to agree with you just to get you out of their face and will then proceed to do what they had already decided to do in the first place. The latter is more difficult to deal with than the former because precious time is wasted while you watch what they do in spite of what they have said. Furthermore, the passive resister is more difficult to pin down because he will pull the same trick on you (and others) over and over again, agreeing with you in word but doing just the opposite in action.

Since elected and unelected officials come from your own community, it is important to educate everyone about Technocracy and everything that it implies. It is obviously easier to groom a public servant before he or she is elevated to a position where policies are created and enforced. The most important reason for you to work on all local elections - city council, planning committees, school boards, fire district boards, etc. - is to get people into the system who can then rise to higher levels as time goes on. In the meantime, insiders are in a better position to influence their peers than you are, and if not, they can at least tell you where the logjams exist so that you can assist them in putting pressure in the right places.

How to Get a Technocrat Fired

First and foremost, let me point out that every local activist group *must have* good legal council. This is not optional. If you don't have access to a like-minded lawyer, recruit one to your cause. The law is not always clear and logical like you might think it should be. Further, people knowingly or unknowingly act outside of the law and need to be corrected with what the law actually says.

An elected official who acts in a way contrary to the best interests of those who are represented can certainly be threatened by political backlash and by being voted out of office. If the next election is far off, you must take other actions if you want to stop his or her behavior from doing more damage to your community. Isolation is one strategy: Persuade those immediately around the official to change their opinions and actions, requiring the official to work against his or her own peers. Enlisting official legal council is another strategy: Make your own case with your legal representative and then take it to the city or county attorney for action. In all cases, always seek to work with your local newspapers, radio and TV stations to publicize your case. The odds may be that they will not give you the time of day, but you set up a critical accountability to be used later by giving them the facts to report today.

Let's assume for a minute that you have worked the above strategy, hoping to get some particular result. Even though you are convinced, after talking with your own legal council, that laws are being or have been violated, you have hit the proverbial brick wall. The very next concept you need to become familiar with is *misprision.*

Misprision is a legal term that generally means failure of a public official to notify certain other officials when a criminal law has been broken. The official who should do this reporting is not a party to the crime but had clear knowledge that it was being or had been committed and took steps to conceal the crime. Both knowledge and concealment are necessary to prove misprision. When you have delivered clear proof of a felony crime to an duly elected or appointed official, and they make an conscious decision to ignore it, then they are taking action to conceal it. There are two types of misprisions that are relevant here: Misprision of Treason and Misprision of Felony. According to one law dictionary, Misprision of Felony occurs when

> *Whoever, having knowledge of the actual commission of a felony cognizable by a court of the U.S., conceals and does not as soon as possible make known the same to some judge or other person in civil or military authority under the U.S. 18 USC Misprision of felony, is the like concealment of felony, without giving any degree of maintenance to the felon for if any aid be given him, the party becomes an accessory after the fact.*[230]

Misprision of Treason is defined as

> *the concealment of treason, by being merely passive for if any assistance be given, to the traitor, it makes the party a principal, as there are no accessories in treason.*[231]

Understanding misprision requires very specific charges as to the felony or treason being committed. Has the Constitution, federal, state or local law been violated? Have you properly informed your local officials of these specific violations? Have they refused to act by reporting to appropriate authorities? If the answer is "Yes", then you can deliver an appropriate Misprision of Felony or Misprision of Treason to each official, putting them on official notice for future action against them. In the case of Misprision of Treason, the potential penalty would get anyone's attention:

---

230 Misprision, The 'Lectric Law Library Lexicon.
231 Ibid.

"Such person or persons, on conviction, shall be adjudged guilty of misprision of treason, and shall be imprisoned not exceeding seven years, and fined not exceeding one thousand dollars."[232]

To be clear, there have been no recent convictions anywhere in the U.S. on Misprision of Treason or Misprision of Felony, but the laws are nonetheless still valid and theoretically enforceable. Furthermore, there is no statute of limitation for misprision charges, so a notice delivered today may have legal consequences for the recipient years down the road.

Someone might be thinking, "I tried to explain the facts to my official, but they would not listen." In this case, deliver the facts to the public record in your community. This could mean delivering a clearly written explanation to the city or county recorder's office, or put into the official logs of your local city council's meeting. In addition, you could publish your explanation in a local newspaper, much like public notices of bankruptcies, deaths, legal actions, etc.

Let's not forget the unelected officials who are probably more directly responsible for crafting unconstitutional or illegal policies and regulations. Find out who they are, educate them as best as you can, and then serve them with the same notice of misprision. While they may wholeheartedly disagree with your positions, the mere fact that you have "called them out" will give them pause for their future behavior. As more successes are recorded throughout the nation, those who have been served with Misprision notices will indeed begin to sweat, even to the point of changing their mind, actions and allegiances.

Success Stories Are Building

Common Core State Standards were developed with private money (foundations like the Bill and Melinda Gates Foundation) and owned by a private organization (The National Governor's Association). Common Core prepares students for an Agenda 21- and Sustainable Development-dominated future. The standards have been widely adopted in most states, thanks to efforts by the National Governor's Association and certain NGOs. However, the

---

232 The Crimes Act of 1790 (or the Federal Criminal Code of 1790), formally titled *An Act for the Punishment of Certain Crimes Against the United States.*

resistance has been growing. Much to their own credit though, Indiana, Missouri, North Carolina, South Carolina and Oklahoma have already passed legislation to ban Common Core curriculum from their state. Ohio may soon become the fifth, and its legislation also intends to block any school from adopting other education standards that have been created by any entity outside of the state. In Louisiana, the governor executed an executive order requiring the state to develop its own education standards. There are anti-Common Core activists in all 50 states who are intent on reversing the tide in their local school systems. It is no small feat to get an entire state house and senate to craft such legislation, and it is certainly a clear warning to those who think only a few "narrow-minded" and otherwise ignorant citizens oppose Common Core.

The international sponsor of Agenda 21, Local Governments for Sustainability or ICLEI, formerly had over 600 cities as dues-paying members that agreed to adopt its policies. Resistance against ICLEI became so fierce that it removed its membership list from its website. From January 1, 2011 through June 30, 2012 - just 18 short months - 138 cities were forced by their own citizens to sever relations with ICLEI altogether. Many more have followed since then.

Lawsuits against Agenda 21 are springing up. In the San Francisco area two prominent local organizations, Freedom Advocates and the Post Sustainability Institute, launched a lawsuit against an Agenda 21-inspired *Plan Bay Area* created and imposed by the Association of Bay Area Governments (ABAG). ABAG is a member of the California Association of Councils of Government (CALCOG) and part of the larger unconstitutional network of regional government organizations. The Amended Complaint Brief of the lawsuit states, in part,

> *The [Post Sustainability] Institute has a beneficial interest in ensuring that public funds are not unlawfully wasted on statutes, plans, agreements, or programs that are in violation of rights held under the United States or California Constitutions. The Institute has also brought this action on behalf of the public interest; to vindicate the public's interest*

in land-use planning that is coherent and consistent with the California and United States Constitutions.[233]

Examples such as these should be an encouragement that some battles are being fought and won. In all cases of wins throughout the nation, you will see very professional and thorough activism that produced results. Someone might argue that these wins were only incidental and that they didn't see the whole picture correctly. Perhaps so. But, if incidental battles can be won by partially knowing themselves and/or the enemy, think what is possible from a cadre of Americans who know both in depth!

Indeed, all hope is not lost, but it is quickly fading. Americans have had ample opportunity over the last 40 years to stop the global transformation of America and have failed to do so. The two compelling reasons for this are that 1) they didn't know or understand their enemies and 2) they didn't know themselves. Hopefully, this chapter will completely remove both misconceptions.

---

233   Amended Complaint Brief, Superior Court of the State of California, Alameda County, Case # RG13699215, March 6, 2014.

CHAPTER 12

CONCLUSION

My hope is that this book has helped you to connect the dots in a world that is accelerating out of control. In fact, the problems we face as a society are not at all unrelated but rather are orchestrated by a very small global elite who wants to transform our society and the world into a utopian system called Technocracy. Further, every pillar of society is being radically transformed at the same time, each in synchrony with the other. The religious notions of Humanism and Scientism run throughout, pushing the world to become the first truly global and godless religion in history.

The first nation in history that attempted a full implementation of Technocracy was Nazi Germany during the reign of Adolf Hitler, and that ended very poorly with the mass genocide of millions of people. The technocrats who ran Hitler's war machine were glad to have a "host" where they could apply their amazing technology and know-how, but who Hitler was or what he did was of no concern to them. We learned from this that technocrats can thrive under any political system but that their presence will transform that system if they are left unchecked.

The second implementation of Technocracy was in China which was indeed a Communist nation until members of the Trilateral Commission got ahold of it. Remember that it was **Henry Kissinger** under Richard Nixon and **Zbigniew Brzezinski** under **Jimmy Carter** who normalized relations with Communist China and threw open the doors for Western multinational corporations to pursue massive economic development opportunities.[233] And so they did. Whether the Chinese knew it or not at the time, they were completely absorbed into the Trilateral vision of a "New International Economic Order", or Technocracy. Of the corporations who originally set up business there in the early days,

---

233   Patrick M. Wood, "Technocracy and the Making of China", *August Forecast & Review*, May 22, 2013.

almost all had at least one member of the Trilateral Commission on their board of directors, and some had several.

By 2001, just twenty years later, *Time Magazine* (itself tightly connected to the Trilateral Commission) documented the transformation in a byline titled "Made in China: The Revenge of the Nerds". It was a misleading title, but the story itself was spot on:

> *The nerds are running the show in today's China. In the twenty years since Deng Xiaoping's [1978-79] reforms kicked in, the composition of the **Chinese leadership has shifted markedly in favor of technocrats.** ...It's no exaggeration to describe **the current regime as a technocracy.***

> *After the Maoist madness abated and Deng Xiaoping inaugurated the opening **and reforms that began in late 1978, scientific and technical intellectuals were among the first to be rehabilitated.** Realizing that they were the key to the Four Modernizations embraced by the reformers, concerted efforts were made to bring the "experts" back into the fold.*

> *During the 1980s, technocracy as a concept was much talked about, especially in the context of so-called **"Neo-Authoritarianism" -- the principle at the heart of the "Asian Developmental Model" that South Korea, Singapore, and Taiwan had pursued with apparent success. The basic beliefs and assumptions of the technocrats were laid out quite plainly: Social and economic problems were akin to engineering problems and could be understood, addressed, and eventually solved as such.***

> *The open hostility to religion that Beijing exhibits at times -- most notably in its obsessive drive to stamp out the "evil cult" of Falun Gong -- has pre-Marxist roots. **Scientism underlies the post-Mao technocracy,** and it is the orthodoxy against which heresies are measured.*[234] [Emphasis added]

If you have absorbed what you have already read in this book, you will never see China in the same light again. Most observers, however, still look at China as a Communist Dictatorship, but only because it continues to be authoritarian and repressive. *Time*

---

234   Made In China: Revenge Of The Nerds, *Time Magazine*, June, 2001

Magazine simply tells us that this is just *Neo-Authoritarianism*, Technocracy-style. It looks the same on the surface as citizens continue to be oppressed, but the nature of the manipulation goes much deeper than it ever did before.

Then there is the Technocracy operating in the European Union. The co-founder of the Trilateral Commission, **David Rockefeller**, proudly stated in 1998,

> *Back in the early Seventies, the hope for a more united EUROPE was already full-blown - thanks in many ways to the individual energies previously spent by so many of the Trilateral Commission's earliest members.*[235]

This early influence apparently never abated because it was Trilateral Commissioner **Vallery d'Estaing** who authored the EU's Constitution in 2002-2003 when he was President of the Convention on the Future of Europe. Then in 2011, when Europe was hit by economic chaos and Greece and Italy were on the verge of total collapse, the European Commission summarily fired the elected prime minsters of both nations and appointed their replacements: **Mario Monti** was installed as prime minister in Italy and **Lukas Papademos** assumed the same title in Greece. To reiterate - they were *appointed* by the unelected and unaccountable European Union. Both were members of the Trilateral Commission and in the European press, most importantly, they were both widely hailed as "Technocrats". *Slate Magazine* immediately published a headline story titled "What's a Technocrat?" and proceeded to answer its own question:

> *Both men have been described as "technocrats" in major newspapers. What, exactly, is a technocrat?...An expert, not a politician. Technocrats make decisions based on specialized information rather than public opinion... The word technocrat can also refer to an advocate of a form of government in which experts preside.... in the United States, technocracy was most popular in the early years of the Great Depression. Inspired in part by the ideas of economist Thorstein Veblen, the movement was led by engineer Howard Scott, who proposed radical utopian ideas and solutions to the economic di-*

---

235   David Rockefeller, "In the Beginning; The Trilateral Commission at 25", *Trilateral Commission*, 1998, p.11.

saster in scientific language. His movement, founded in 1932, drew national interest.[236]

Slate nailed it and put in the proper context of historic Technocracy. So, we need to just get past the fluff and call the European Union what it is: *A Technocracy!* In this case, they installed two technocrat dictators over formerly proud democratic states. It is ironic that Western civilization was founded upon principles developed in these two countries, and yet they were the first two to succumb to outright dictatorship at the hands of neo-authoritarian technocrats.

How close is America to capitulating to Technocracy? Calls for it are already appearing if you know what to look for. For instance, *U.S. News & World Report* magazine waited until March 2012 to declare that "America Needs Leaders Like Greece's Papademos or Italy's Monti." The author elaborated,

> *What Papademos offered Greece and what Monti offered Italy was a chance for all parties, left, right, and center, to come together under technocratic and nonpolitical leadership to solve economic problems that threatened to spin out of control and damage democracy itself.*[237]

What the author fails to understand is that a dictatorship is mutually exclusive to a democracy. As to "nonpolitical leadership", we already see Technocracy operating within virtually every Federal agency and within every local community that is implementing Sustainable Development and Agenda 21 policies. It's just that nobody recognizes it for what it is, even though it is all around us. Worse, the noose is tightening rapidly.

Given the state of affairs in China and the European Union, should anyone be surprised that America would *not* be next on the list? Converting those nations to Technocracy took quite a bit of time, a lot of deception and persuasion to go along. It would require a different strategy and a different tactical plan. **Richard Gardner**, a professor at Columbia University and an original member of the Trilateral Commission, spelled this out in a 1974

---

236   "What's a Technocrat", *Slate*, November 11, 2011.
237   "America Needs Leaders Like Greece's Papademos or Italy's Monti", *U.S. News & World Report*, March 2, 2012.

paper published in the Council on Foreign Relations publication *Foreign Affairs*:

> In short, the "house of world order" would have to be built from the bottom up rather than from the top down. It will look like a great 'booming, buzzing confusion,' to use William James' famous description of reality, but an end run around national sovereignty, eroding it piece by piece, will accomplish much more than the old-fashioned frontal assault.[238]

Does today's world seem like a "booming, buzzing confusion" to you? Has our nation been picked apart piece by piece, effectively destroying national sovereignty in the process? Of course, the answer is emphatically Yes! The only reason it has taken longer to bring the U.S. to its knees is because the technocrats first needed to get through the sticky problems of "Rule of Law" and our concept of "unalienable rights" that so strongly define our Republic. There is no other nation in the world based squarely on these two principles. Furthermore, the technocrats needed to overturn America's Judeo-Christian ethical and moral base that said No! to relative truth, Evolution, Humanism and Scientism. Technocrats faced no such difficulties on other continents. China was already a godless dictatorship, and so only a single person needed to be convinced to go along. In Europe, the Judeo-Christian ethic and system of moral absolutes had already died several decades ago making the technocrat conquest an easy sport. Other countries with neither have fallen prey with zero resistance, like sheep being led to the slaughter. Indeed, America has posed a special obstacle for Technocracy in the past. The American people rejected it in the 1930s even as Nazi Germany eagerly embraced it at the same time. The "frontal attack" that did not work was replaced with an "end run around national sovereignty" that has been very effective without causing any alarm along the way - until perhaps now.

Critics are certain to argue the point that these nations are not transforming into Technocracies. I can only ask, "To what degree of transformation would it take for you to change your mind?" Today's issue is not necessarily that we have "arrived" but rather

---

238   Richard Gardner, "The Hard Road to World Order", *Foreign Affairs*, 1974, p. 558.

that we are "on the way" and may arrive sooner than anyone can imagine. Let me explain.

When studying the progression of Nazi Germany leading up to Hitler's assumption of complete power, I have often theorized that there was very likely a specific point in time when he realized that he had all the political, military, organizational and economic power necessary to declare himself dictator. Hitler had declared his intentions in his 1925 book, *Mein Kampf*, which was mostly ignored at the time because Hitler was viewed as a trouble-making rabble-rouser who was serving time in jail for what he claimed were political crimes. But, Hitler had a dream and a strategy to get there, and then he embarked on implementing that strategy. In 1933, after he clawed and connived his way into power, he pulled the plug and declared himself dictator; there was nothing anyone could do about it. To oppose him meant certain death or imprisonment. His work and strategy, like moving the pieces on a chessboard, had resulted in a doomsday checkmate. My point is that it didn't happen by accident or a even by a series of random events where one day he just woke up and thought, "I think I will announce my dictatorship after lunch today." Rather, Hitler was certainly gathering pieces of his empire all along, analyzing and plotting his victory with excruciating detail. As the necessary assets were lined up in a row under his control, Hitler knew exactly what it would take to get to the top, and he knew that he would know when he had arrived. Well, that day arrived, and history was changed forever.

Based on this thinking, if today's technocrats are meticulously working toward a scientific dictatorship and applying a specific strategy to get there, wouldn't you think that they have a specific list of criteria that must be met before "game over" can be called? Wouldn't you think that they are comparing such a list to the actual progress they are making in the world? Wouldn't you think that they are monitoring their progress and will recognize *when* the list has been fulfilled? If you can see my point here, then there are only two questions left: When that day comes, will the Technocrats have the guts to shut the old world order down and simply declare the "system" as dictator? If so, how long will it take them to act?

There have been science-fiction books written about Technocracy, the most famous of which is *Brave New World* (1932) by Aldous Huxley. Huxley pointedly concluded that Technocracy produces scientific dictatorship, not controlled by a single person, but by a system based on Scientific Method and designed to manipulate and micro-manage every human being in every detail of his life. The system itself became a god that was worshipped, and questioning any decision or outcome was tantamount to blasphemy. George Orwell finished *Nineteen Eighty Four* in 1949 and popularized the word *Orwellian* in the process. Both books were looking into the face of Technocracy. Orwell's theme, technocratic control, is not unlike what we face today:

> *In a way, the world-view of the Party imposed itself most successfully on people incapable of understanding it. They could be made to accept the most flagrant violations of reality, because they never fully grasped the enormity of what was demanded of them, and were not sufficiently interested in public events to notice what was happening. By lack of understanding they remained sane. They simply swallowed everything, and what they swallowed did them no harm, because it left no residue behind, just as a grain of corn will pass undigested through the body of a bird.*[239]

Some don't have the ability or capacity to understand, and we bear them no harm. Some refuse to understand. Some think they understand and don't care if they are ignorant. Only a few will admit that they don't understand and seek to do something about it. This book was written for you, and I encourage you to climb up to a higher peak to see the big picture instead of the various small fragments. The future belongs to us, and we alone must take responsibility for what we pass on to our children and grandchildren. If we choose to ignore and do nothing about Technocracy and its perpetrators, it is most certain that it will sweep over the entire world like a giant tsunami, pressing all of mankind into a scientific dictatorship that is devoid of any human capacity for things like compassion, mercy, justice, freedom and liberty.

Americans rejected Technocracy in the 1930s, and if we choose to, we can reject it today as well. Philosopher and states-

---

239   George Orwell, *Nineteen Eighty-Four*, (Signet Classic, 1950), Ch. 5.

man Edmund Burke (1729-1797) warned and reproved us from the past that "The people never give up their liberties but under some delusion."[240] This book has stripped away some of the delusion that has allowed the destruction of so many things that we hold most dear, so perhaps we will find ways to stop the destruction of liberty, and soon. If not us, then who? If not now, then when?

---

240   "Edmund Burke." BrainyQuote.com. Xplore Inc., 2014. 8 September 2014. http://www.brainyquote.com/quotes/quotes/e/edmundburk108344.html

APPENDIX I

TRANSFORMING CHRISTIANITY

The implications of Scientism, Technocracy and Transhumanism for the Christian church are, in this writer's opinion, quite profound. Two areas in particular are worth discussing. The first is the subject of Bible prophecy which has generally fallen out of favor with many Christian churches. The second is the repurposing of the Church to serve earthly and globalist ends rather than the God who saves in the first place. The worldly philosophy of Communitarianism, closely coupled to the philosophy of Technocracy, is the primary instrument that is bringing about this transformation.

The Rise and Fall of Bible Prophecy

When Hal Lindsey and Carole Carlson first published *The Late, Great Planet Earth* in 1970, interest in Bible prophecy skyrocketed. Over the next 20 years, their book sold no fewer than 28 million copies to make it the best-selling book in history, second only to the Bible itself.

The *Late, Great Planet Earth* was the first modern book that related specific Bible prophecies to current events. The Bible's books of Daniel, Isaiah, Ezekiel and Revelation played prominently, and events like the re-founding of Israel in 1948, the congealing of the European Economic Community, famines and earthquakes all appeared to be easily identified building blocks of the foretold "end times" and the visible return of Christ to the earth. In fact, Lindsey's and Carlson's arguments were so compelling that it led them to the conclusion that "the decade of the 1980s could very well be the last decade of history as we know it", and it ignited the spiritual inquiry of an entire generation of Christians around the world. The thought that Christ could come for His Church at any time was exhilarating.

Looking back over the last 45 years since the book first appeared, there are two key observations. First, Christ did not come during the 1980s, and many Christians were ultimately left in a dismayed condition thinking perhaps that somehow God had failed or let them down. Second, Christians were left with a fixation on current events as the "proof" that the end was near, and thus they continue to view today's events based on Lindsey's model of political structures and societal phenomenon. This has proved frustrating for many students of Bible prophecy even if it has not caused them to abandon their faith.

Taking a fresh look at the prophetical landscape and with this spotty past as a backdrop, one might conclude that people are simply looking in the wrong places today. The resulting frustration and waning interest in Prophecy has created a vacuum in the church that has been filled by globalization dogma along the lines already discussed in this book.

Where are some "better" places to look for prophetical relevance? Take, for instance, the topic of technology and a common language. The "Days of Noah" as mentioned in the New Testament are most often associated with the *pre-flood* condition of the world and rightly so because it was a period of great wickedness on the earth. However, Noah also lived for 350 years *after* the flood which should rightfully be included in the phrase "Days of Noah". Noah brought his three sons through the flood, with their wives, and they began to repopulate the earth. One of his sons, Ham, fathered a son named Cush who in turn sired a son named Nimrod:

> *He began to be a mighty one in the earth. He was a mighty hunter before the Lord wherefore it is said, Even as Nimrod the mighty hunter before the Lord. And the beginning of his kingdom was Babel, and Erech, and Accad, and Calneh, in the land of Shinar. (Genesis 10:8-10)*

The Bible doesn't record much about Nimrod, but it does note that the beginning of his kingdom was Babel, where the infamous Tower of Babel was constructed in rebellion against God.

The Old Testament account of the Tower of Babel in Genesis 11 first states, "And the whole earth was of one language, and of one speech." As they strategized on how to build a tower all the way to Heaven, they discovered a new technique for building

tall structures. Whereas rocks and mud had been used previously, now uniformly fired bricks and tar would prove far superior.
Simplistic as this sounds, it was a new technology to them, and
one so exciting that they were deceived into thinking they could
actually build that tower right into Heaven. But, why build it to
Heaven itself? The implications are that they intended to invade
Heaven and bring God down to earth, which of course, was abject
rebellion against God.

Before the tower was completed, however, God intervened
to break up the rebellion by "confusing" their language, causing
them to scatter to the four corners of the then-known world. My
only point here is to point out the connection between technology
and a common language that apparently enabled their rebellion.

Today we have a direct parallel that is almost universally *unrecognized* because it is not necessarily an event but rather the development of a process. Another reason is that there is very little
public awareness of science in general. Today's new NBIC technology largely being directed by advocates of Transhumanism is represented by the convergence of Nanotechnology, Bio-technology,
Information Technology and Cognitive Science. The Transhuman
dream is no less than to escape the laws of sin and death and to
assume qualities reserved for God, such as omniscience, omnipotence, omnipresence, eternality, etc. Thus, the NBIC technology
promises to deliver their dream of ultimate rebellion against God.
And the language used to construct this modern-day Tower of
Babel? It's not English, German, Latin or Esperanto. Rather, it is
digital. The human genome is compared to a master computer
with four building blocks that are digital in nature. The manipulation of matter at the atomic and molecular level is controlled by
digital computers. The mind is likened to a computer with billions of transistors that emulate a digital computer. If you were to
assemble a group of scientists from around the world to discuss
NBIC, you would find uneven ground with spoken languages, but
you would find perfect fluency with this new digital language.

Thus, this is the new common language spoken by those who
would build a modern Tower of Babel (i.e., Transhumanism) to
displace God in the same manner as the account in Genesis 11.
The clear implication of Prophecy for today is that God will not

deal with this current rebellion until the world enters the future 7-year period known as the Tribulation as described in the book of Revelation. The first rebellion ended in humanity being scattered throughout the world which was certainly inconvenient but not necessarily deadly. The second rebellion will end with all-consuming judgment.

Another unrecognized aspect of global Technocracy is that this is the first comprehensive system for global control that the world has ever seen. While Prophecy students have mostly examined political structures for clues to the future reign of antichrist, it is no wonder that they have been frustrated. There is a never-ending parade of changes in political alliances and structures. To think that the disparate political structures in the world will be merged into a single, functioning political system by themselves is simply futile. On the other hand, Technocracy promises to replace the nation-states of the world in one clean sweep. Indeed, if there is any kingdom being prepared by antichrist for the fulfillment of end-times events, it is one based on Scientism, Technocracy and Transhumanism - providing systematic and comprehensive control over every human being on earth without regard to geographic boundaries.

In this writer's opinion, topics like these should give rise to renewed interest in Bible prophecy, but unfortunately, the opposite has occurred. Instead, many prominent pastors and Christian leaders have abandoned the study of Prophecy altogether. Brian McLaren, a prominent leader in the emerging church movement concludes:

> *The book of Revelation is an example of popular literary genre of ancient Judaism, known today as Jewish apocalyptic. Trying to read it without understanding its genre would be like watching Star Trek or some other science fiction show thinking it was an historical documentary, or watching a sit-com as if it were a religious parable, or reading a satire as if it were a biography.*[241]

---

241   Brian D. Mclaren, *The Secret Message of Jesus: Uncovering the Truth That Could Change Everything,* (Thomas-Nelson, 2007), p. 175-176.

Rick Warren, megachurch pastor and global spokesman for "purpose-driven" church activism, is more pointed:

If you want Jesus to come back sooner, focus on fulfilling your mission, not figuring out prophecy.[242]

The former lead pastor of Mars Hill church, Mark Driscoll, elaborated:

We are not eschatological Theonomists or Classic Dispensationalists (e.g. Scofield) and believe that divisive and dogmatic certainty surrounding particular details of Jesus' Second Coming are unprofitable speculation, because the timing and exact details of His return are unclear to us.[243]

Perhaps these pastors arrived at their dim view of Bible prophecy for different reasons, but they arrived nonetheless, and their teachings and attitudes have swept Christendom like a wildfire that refuses to be contained. However, statements like these should bring to mind Biblical warnings such as,

Knowing this first, that there shall come in the last days scoffers, walking after their own lusts, and saying, Where is the promise of his coming? for since the fathers fell asleep, all things continue as they were from the beginning of the creation. (2 Peter 3:3-4)

Transforming the Church

As the careful study of Bible prophecy has largely been left in the dust, it has also led to the decline of the doctrine of Heaven that the church has held as a bedrock belief since its founding some 2000 years ago. With this decline has come a reorientation of worldview from heavenly to earthly things. One could argue (I would not do so, however) that there was no particular plot to discredit Bible prophecy and the doctrine of Heaven per se, but there is no argument against the fact that devilish forces immediately raced in to fill the vacuum. In order to understand these forces and the "replacement", it is necessary to review the philosophical background of Communitarianism and its major backers and proponents within the church.

---

242   Rick Warren, *The Purpose Driven Life*, (Zondervan, 2002), pp. 285-286.
243   Mark Driscoll, co-founder of Acts 29 Network, (http://www.acts29network.org/).

The *Merriam-Webster Dictionary* defines *Communitarian* as *"of or relating to social organization in small cooperative partially collectivist communities."* Some critics claim that Communitarianism is nothing more than Communism, but this is not likely the case, and Communitarians themselves reject this idea. Rather, it more likely reflects **Zbigniew Brzezinski's** Technetronic Era, his fourth and final stage of historical evolution, namely, "the ideal of rational humanism on a global scale - the result of American-Communist evolutionary transformations".[244] There is an apocalyptic flavor to Communitarianism due to the fact that when Capitalism (represented by America) and Communism collide head-on (i.e., toward Technocracy) the resulting chaos will cause all sides to surrender to a single ideology. Whether described from the perspective of Technocracy, Smut's Holism, Brzezinski's Technetronic Era, Brundtland's Sustainable Development or Communitarianism, the result is exactly the same: The individual ceases to have any intrinsic value and instead receives worth only in direct proportion to his or her position in, and contribution to, the community. All activity is directed toward the "common good".

One of the leading evangelists for Communitarianism in the last century was the famous management consultant and prolific author, Peter Drucker (1909-2005). In a 1999 letter to Drucker, **David Rockefeller** heaped praise on him by writing,

> *One of the pieces [articles] spoke of you appropriately as "the father of modern management". From my perspective, that was a fully justified accolade. Your approach to management always appealed to me as being more philosophical than dogmatic.... I learned more about how to be a manager from you than from anyone else I can think of.*[245]

Indeed, virtually every Fortune 500 company in the world has been thoroughly baptized in management theory created by Drucker, and countless millions of other managers have read his books, adapting themselves accordingly. Of course, anyone who has worked for such a corporation knows from direct experience that your value is determined solely by your contribution to the "common good". The day that you cease to contribute to the com-

---

244 Zbigniew Brzezinski, p. 246.
245 Correspondence from David Rockefeller to Peter Drucker, November 30, 1999, Claremont Colleges Digital Library.

mon good of that company will be the same day that you get fired. The corporate world is harsh in this respect. Corporations build on the same team mentality found in professional sports, and if you are "on the team" then you are expected to always contribute to the team and to *never* contribute to the success of any other team.

Drucker was steeped in Communitarianism and the application of General System Theory to all business problems. During the 1990s, he fine-tuned his "three-legged stool" doctrine that underscored the need for compatibility among political, economic and social sectors of society. During that time, he shifted his focus more toward the social sector as a way to shore up deficiencies he saw in the political and economic arenas. Accordingly, he wrote,

*Only the social sector, that is, the nongovernmental, nonprofit organization, can create what we now need, **communities for citizens** – and especially for the highly educated knowledge workers who increasingly dominate developed societies. One reason for this is that **only non-profit organizations can provide the enormous diversity of communities we need** – from **churches** to professional associations, from organizations taking care of the homeless to health clubs – if there are to be freely chosen communities for everyone. The nonprofit organizations also are **the only ones that can satisfy the second need of the city, the need for effective citizenship for its people.** Only social-sector institutions can provide opportunities to be a volunteer, and thus enable individuals to have both a sphere in which they are in control and a sphere in which they make a difference.*[246] [Emphasis added]

In particular, Drucker decided to focus on the church, and specifically, the megachurch. According to one writer,

*Peter Drucker calls the emergence of the large pastoral church – the "megachurch" in mediaese – "the most significant social event in America today." **He is its intellectual grandfather; he's been tutoring it for years through the agency of Bob Buford, a highly successful Dallas-based television ex-***

---

246   Peter F. Drucker, "Civilizing the City", *Leader to Leader*, 7 (Winter 1998): 8-10.

ecutive who in 1985 founded the Leadership Network.
"His Leadership Network," Drucker writes in his preface to
Buford's 1994 book Half-Time: Changing Your Game Plan
from Success to Significance, "worked as a catalyst to make
the large, pastoral churches work effectively, to identify their
main problems, to make them capable of perpetuating them-
selves (as no earlier pastoral church has ever been able to
do), and to focus them on their mission as apostles, witnesses,
and central community services." Modest, Buford says, "I'm
the legs for his brain."[247]

Who is Bob Buford? Until 1999, he was Chairman of the Board
of Buford Television, Inc., a nationwide network of stations and
media interests. Upon selling this business, Buford focused full-
time on philanthropy, writing and developing leadership tools
for Christian leaders, under the auspices of the organization he
founded in 1984, Leadership Network. According to an official bio
on Buford, Peter Drucker formally entered the picture in 1988:

> *In 1988, Dick Schubert, Frances Hesselbein and Bob Buford*
> *convinced Peter Drucker to lend his name, his great mind,*
> *and occasionally his presence to establish an operating*
> *foundation for the purpose of leading social sector organi-*
> *zations toward excellence in performance. Bob served as the*
> *Founding Chairman of the Board of Governors. Through*
> *its conferences, publications and partnerships, The Drucker*
> *Foundation (now titled Leader to Leader Institute) is helping*
> *social sector organizations focus on their mission, achieve*
> *true accountability, leverage innovation, and develop pro-*
> *ductive partnerships.*[248]

In 2008, Buford went on to establish The Drucker Institute
at Claremont College in California to house all of Drucker's writings, lectures and management ideas. Buford was subsequently
appointed Chairman of its Board of Advisors. Thus, the long and
close relationship between Peter Drucker and Bob Buford is well
documented. However, because of Buford's pre-existing activism
within the evangelical church in America, the following statement
on his bio describes him as "someone wanting to make a differ-

---

247   Jack Beatty, *The World According to Peter Drucker*, (New York: The Free Press,
1998), pp. 185-86.
248   Active Energy, About Bob Buford, (*http://www.activeenergy.net/about-bob/*).

ence through the application of his faith and resources under the general mission of transforming the latent energy of American Christianity into active energy."[249]

Herein is cause for great alarm. What does "transforming the latent energy of American Christianity into active energy" mean and where did this mandate come from? From a Biblical perspective, the only *energy* available to Christians and by extension, churches, is that which is supplied by the Holy Spirit. (See "For God hath not given us the spirit of fear; but of power, and of love, and of a sound mind." (2 Timothy 1:7) and "And Jesus returned in the power of the Spirit into Galilee" (Luke 4:14a.)

Remembering that Drucker had stated in 2001 that "*I am not a born-again Christian,*"[250] it was Drucker nonetheless who seeded Buford's mind with this "transforming the latent energy" doctrine, as he clearly stated in a 2014 interview:

> *Eight years into our work together Peter saw my mission in a single sentence: "To transform the latent energy of American Christianity into active energy."*[251]

It was life-changing for Buford at that point, ultimately leading him to structure his entire Leadership Network operation, which primarily served churches, around it. Buford explained,

> *Even then, I didn't get it right away. I was walking along a road in East Texas when I suddenly thought, "Whoa!" I stopped and wrote the words down. He had said, "At this stage in your life"—he was a great fan of innovation, so what works in one stage doesn't in another—"it's our job to release and direct energy, not to supply it."*[252]

Short of any clear explanation on the source of such energy, and considering it was Drucker's idea in the first place, the only possible conclusion is that both men are referring to a man-centered, rather than Holy Spirit-provided energy. To Drucker, the energy available to the church needed to be pumped into the social community (towns and cities) under the label of volunteerism, social

---

249 Halftime Institute, Faculty, Founder. www.halftimeinstitute.org

250 Claremont Colleges Digital Library, Drucker Archives, Interview with Peter Drucker, 2001-12-05.

251 Interview by Warren Bird (President, Leadership Network) with Bob Buford on his book, *Drucker and Me*, 2014.

252 Ibid.

action and other types of community involvement. The third leg of his three-legged stool could only be built in this manner, and he was very clear about it. In short, Drucker had succeeded in inserting a communitarian virus into America's remaining evangelical church movement. You might ask as this point, "How did it spread?" According to the same interview, Buford gives a hint:

> So his [Drucker's] influence on me and the church was a happy confluence of timing and readiness: of my pursing him and his genius for management, our growing friendship, my interest in the church, and the prepared minds of Bill Hybels and Rick Warren and other pastors. When Peter appeared, they were ready. Peter said to me once in an interview, "They didn't say, 'Look, leave us alone.' They said 'Give us more. Where is it? We need you.'"[253]

Thus, we see that Drucker mentored not only Bob Buford but soon-to-be megachurch pastors Rick Warren (Saddleback Church) and Bill Hybels (Willow Creek Association). The combination of Drucker's Communitarian philosophy and his massive collection of management resources thus became the new and fertile ground for America's megachurches and another postmodern phenomenon, the so-called emergent church. In short, this was the beginning of the "transforming" of the "latent energy of American Christianity". More importantly, it is what has filled the vacuum left by the waning of interest in Bible prophecy and the doctrine of Heaven as discussed earlier. Today, this newly transformed evangelical church is thoroughly focused on earthly, rather than heavenly, endeavors. This is clearly reflected in statements like these from churches (large and small) around the nation:

- *We are a family of faith, fully engaged, transforming our community and our world.* (Vancouver, Washington)
- *...dedicated to serving Jesus and people in the context of their local community.* (Seattle, Washington)
- *...partners with community minded individuals and organizations to serve and transform our community.* (Chapel Hill, North Carolina)

---

253   Ibid.

- *We are a movement of people who understand we are Jesus' plan to transform and heal communities.* (Granger, Indiana)

I am not taking issue with any other church doctrine here, but only pointing out the Communitarian influence that Drucker has brought into the church at large. The thought of renewing communities, transforming neighborhoods and more broadly, building the Kingdom of God on earth is now frequently seen as a reflection in contemporary music as well. One popular contemporary song pleads,

> *Build Your kingdom here.*
> *Let the darkness fear.*
> *Show Your mighty hand.*
> *Heal our streets and land.*
> *Set Your church on fire.*
> *Win this nation back.*
> *Change the atmosphere.*
> *Build Your kingdom here.*
> *We pray.*[254]

Of course, there is no Biblical mandate to heal our streets and land, to win our nation back or to bring the Kingdom of God here. The Bible is clear that the Kingdom of God is in Heaven where the King resides and that those who belong to Him are "strangers and pilgrims" (1 Pet 2:11) while on this earth. Elsewhere, Christians are also instructed to "not be conformed to this world" but rather be "transformed by the renewing of your mind" (Romans 12:2).

The result of this Communitarian error is having a profound impact on thousands of churches in America as the doctrine continues to be spread by Leadership Network and other organizations like it and by people like Bob Buford, Rick Warren and Bill Hybels. It is a pernicious error that redirects the believer's energy from heavenly things to earthly things, bringing about what the Bible labels as apostasy, or a "falling away".

Conclusion

There is little doubt historically, that Western thought and culture has been significantly influenced by the presence of the

254 *Build Your Kingdom Here lyrics*, Rend Collective Experiment band.

Christian church and the Bible. In our country, starting with the founding documents like the Declaration of Independence, the Bill of Rights and the Constitution, the founders were clearly immersed in Biblical thought and principles. That is not to say that they were all Christians, but even those who were not had great respect for those who were. The 20th century theologian and Christian philosopher Dr. Francis Schaeffer called this the "Christian consensus" and nothing more. It was a respect for and elevation of wisdom found rooted in the Bible rather than in humanistic man. In today's post-modern society, the Bible is completely irrelevant to those outside of the Church and unfortunately, it hasn't fared much better *within* the church. Whereas the Biblical mandate for Christians is to be "salt and light" to the world, led by pastors toward Godly living, many Christians instead have become little more than community reformers led by community organizers. And, of course, this is exactly what Peter Drucker desired more than anything else during the last quarter of his life.

As the Christian consensus fades into the shadows, the stage is set for a global sea change of unprecedented magnitude: A global authoritarian and totalitarian government is on the immediate horizon. Seeing this from a distance, this is exactly what Schaeffer concluded when he wrote in 1976,

> At that point the word left or right will make no difference. They are only two roads to the same end. There is no difference between an authoritarian government from the right or the left: The results are the same. An elite, an authoritarianism as such, will gradually force form on society so that it will not go on to chaos. And most people will accept it - from the desire for personal peace and affluence, from apathy, and from the yearning for order to assure the functioning of some political system, business, and the affairs of daily life. That is just what Rome did with Caesar Augustus.[255]

Of course, there is magnificent hope for all individual Christians who are rooted in the promises of Christ found in the Bible. Outside of that, the world and all who are in it, including

---

255   Francis Schaeffer, *How Should We Then Live: The Rise and Decline of Western Thought and Culture*, (Crossway Books, 1979), p. 244.

those Christians who are trying to reform it from within, may be in for a very rocky ride as the world hurdles toward Technocracy and Transhumanism and ultimately, toward totalitarian dictatorship.

At the same time and as an ending note, we must give space for God, who is able to intervene in the affairs of man. And He is able to do as He wishes. Christians can and should pray that He might exercise divine intervention to turn the tide of rebellion back, and perhaps He will. In the meantime, we all must answer Francis Schaeffer's urgent question, that in light of all these things, *"How Should We Then Live?"*

1979 INTERVIEW WITH GEORGE S. FRANKLIN, JR. COORDINATOR OF THE TRILATERAL COMMISSION

Introduction

In the original analysis of the Trilateral Commission in the 1970s, the only persons to actually interview and debate members of that elite group were Antony C. Sutton and me, Patrick Wood. From 1978 through 1981, we together or individually engaged at least seven different Commission members in public debate.

On July 27, 1979, Radio Station KLMG, Council Bluffs, Iowa aired a highly informative interview with George S. Franklin, Jr., Coordinator of the Trilateral Commission and long-time associate of David Rockefeller.

Joe Martin, the commentator on the program, invited authors Antony Sutton and Patrick Wood to participate in the questioning. The program was probably the most penetrating view of Trilateralism yet uncovered.

Only one complete transcript remains intact from those interviews, and it is reproduced below. Hopefully, this will give you some insight into the inner workings, attitude and mindset of Commission members.

Lest anyone make accusation that this transcript was selectively edited to show a "bad light" on the Commission, it is reprinted in full, without edit. Editor's comments are added in certain places to clarify the facts, when appropriate, and are clearly identified to the reader as such. Members of the Trilateral Commission are noted in bold type. The entire interview was first and only published in the *Trilateral Observer* in 1979, which was published by Patrick Wood and The August Corporation.

The Interview

Commentator: Hello.

Wood: Hello.

Commentator: Is this Mr. Wood?

Wood: Yes, it is.

Commentator: Patrick Wood, we have Antony Sutton on the other line. You two are there now, right?

Wood: Yes.

Commentator: Are you there too, Mr. Sutton?

Sutton: Yes.

Commentator: All right. Before we get Mr. Franklin on the phone, tell us, what is your concise opinion of the Trilateral Commission?

Sutton: It would seem that this is **David Rockefeller**'s concept, his creation; he financed it. The Trilateral Commission has only 77 or so American members. It's a closed elitist group. I do not believe that they in any way represent general thinking in the United States. For example, they want to restrict the rights of the media in violation of the Constitution.

> *[Ed: Compare this initial statement to Franklin's admissions during the interview.]*

Commentator: They want to restrict the rights of the media?

Sutton: Yes.

Commentator: All right, we have Mr. **George Franklin** on the phone right now, okay? Hang on, gentlemen. Hello, am I talking to Mr. **George S. Franklin**?

Franklin: That is right.

Commentator: You are coordinator of the Trilateral Commission?

Franklin: That is right.

Commentator: Mr. Franklin, my name is Joe Martin. I have two other gentlemen on the line and I have listeners on the line too, who would like to ask a few questions regarding the Trilateral Commission. Are you prepared to answer some questions, sir?

Franklin: I hope so.

Commentator: Is the Trilateral commission presently involved in any effort to make a one-world?

Franklin: Definitely not. We have not. We have no one-world doctrine. Our only belief that is shared by most of the members of the Commission itself is that this world will somehow do better if the advanced industrial democracy that serves Japan and the United States can cooperate and talk things out together and try to work on programs rather than at cross purposes, but definitely not any idea of a world government or a government of these areas.

[Ed: "Definitely not," says Franklin. Numerous statements in Trilateral writings show Franklin is in error. For example: "The economic officials of at least the largest countries must begin to think in terms of managing a single world economy in addition to managing international economic relations among countries," Trilateral Commission Task Force Reports: 9-14, page 268.]

Commentator: Why is it, in the Trilateral Commission that the name **David Rockefeller** shows up so persistently or [the name of] one of his organizations?

Franklin: Well, this is very reasonable. **David Rockefeller** is the Chairman of the North American group. There are three chairmen: one is [with] the North American group, one is [with]the Japanese group, and one is [with] the European group. Also, the Commission was really **David Rockefelle**r's original idea.

[Ed:Note that Franklin does not say (at this point) that the Trilateral Commission was financed and established by David Rockefeller.]

Commentator: On President **Carter**'s staff, how many Trilateral Commission members do you have?

Franklin: Eighteen.

Commentator: Don't you think that is rather heavy?

Franklin: It is quite a lot, yes.

Commentator: Don't you think it is rather unusual? How many members are there actually in the Trilateral Commission?

Franklin: We have 77 in the United States.

Commentator: Don't you think it is rather unusual to have 18 members on the Carter staff?

Franklin: Yes, I think we chose some very able people when we started the Commission. The President happens to think well of quite a number of them.

Commentator: All right, we would like to bring in our two other guests - men who have written a book on the Trilateral Commission. You may be familiar with Mr. Antony Sutton and Mr. Patrick Wood?

Franklin: I have not met them, but I do know their names, yes.

Commentator: Mr. Sutton and Mr. Wood, would you care to ask Mr. Franklin a question?

Sutton: Well, I certainly would. This is Tony Sutton. You have 77 members of which 18 are in the Carter Administration. Do you believe that the only able people in the United States are Trilateralists?

Franklin: Of course not, and incidentally, the 18 are no longer members of the Commission because this is supposed to be a private organization and as soon as anybody joins the government they no longer are members of the Commission.

Sutton: Yes, but they are members of the Commission when they join.

Franklin: That is correct.

Sutton: Do you believe that the only able people in the United States are Trilateralists?

Franklin: Of course not.

Sutton: Well, how come the heavy percentage?

Franklin: Well, when we started to choose members, we did try to pick out the ablest people we could and I think many of those that are in the Carter Administration would have been chosen by any group that was interested in the foreign policy question.

Sutton: Would you say that you have an undue influence on policy in the United States?

Franklin: I would not, no.

Sutton: I think any reasonable man would say that if you have 18 Trilateralists out of 77 in the Carter Administration you have a preponderant influence.

Franklin: These men are not responsive to anything that the Trilateral Commission might advocate. We do have about two reports we put out each year, and we do hope they have some influence or we would not put them out.

> [Ed: The Trilateral Commission puts out considerably more than two reports each year. In 1974 and 1976, it was four in each year plus four issues of "Trialogue"]

Sutton: May I ask another question?

Franklin: Yes.

Sutton: Who financed the Trilateral Commission originally?

Franklin: Uhh. . .The first supporter of all was a foundation called the Kettering Foundation. I can tell you who is financing it at the present time, which might be of more interest to you.

> [Ed: This is what Franklin said in another interview: *"In the meantime, David Rockefeller and the Kettering Foundation had provided transitional funding."*]

Sutton: Is it not the Rockefeller Brothers' Fund?

Franklin: The Rockefeller Brothers' Fund? The North American end of the Commission needs $1.5 million over the next 3 years. Of this amount, $180,000 will be contributed by the Rockefeller Brother's fund and $150,000 by David Rockefeller.

Commentator: Does that mean that most of it is being financed by the Rockefellers?

Franklin: No, it means that about one fifth of the North American end is being financed by the Rockefellers and none of the European and Japanese end.

Commentator: Do you have any further questions, Mr. Sutton?

Sutton: No, I do not.

Commentator: Do you have a question, Mr. Wood?

Wood: Yes, I have one question. In reading your literature and reports, there is a great deal of mention of the term "Interdependence".

Franklin: Right.

Wood: While we can see that there is some need for the world to cooperate in many areas, this system of interdependence seems to have some very profound effect on the United States structure as it is today. For instance, our national structure versus the interdependent structure in the world. Now, do you feel that this interdependent structure has been properly presented to the American public for approval or disapproval?

Franklin: Well, I don't think that it is a question of approval or disapproval altogether. For example, we get a great deal of our natural resources from abroad. Everybody knows that we get a great deal of oil from abroad. So, whether we like it or not, we are much more dependent on other nations that we used to be. Now, this does not mean that they make our decisions for us on what our policies are going to be, and our energy policies are made here by the President and Congress. Now, they do consult others about them because they have to, because unfortunately we are forced to become interdependent.

> *[Ed: The term "interdependent" is a key word in Trilateralism. Think for a moment: The known world has always been more or less interdependent. Trilateralists use "interdependence" in a manner analogous to the propaganda methods of Goebbels: if you repeat a phrase often enough people will begin to accept it automatically in the required context. The required context for Trilaterals is to get across the idea that "one-world" is inevitable."]*

Commentator: Does that answer your question, Mr. Wood?

Wood: Well, perhaps not completely, let me phrase that another way. Do you feel that your policy - that is, those who represent the Trilateral policy as well as interdependence - do you feel that that philosophy is in accord with the typical American philosophy of nationalism and democracy and so on?

Franklin: Well, I think I would answer that this way. First, we are in fact interdependent. I say, unfortunately, we depend on much more that we used to. Therefore, we have to cooperate far more than we used to. But, that does not mean that we are giving other people the right to determine our policy and we do not advocate that. You will not find that in any of our reports.

> *[Ed: Notice how Franklin ducks around the key issue presented by Wood, i.e., whether the concept as used by Trilaterals is inconsistent with generally accepted American ideals. Wood said nothing about "... giving other people the right to determine our policy." This is a straw man erected by Franklin to duck the issue.]*

Wood: Do you feel that the Trilateral Commission position has been publicized really at all around the country?

Franklin: We try to publicize it, we do not altogether succeed because there are so many other people who also want publicity, but we do try. Anything we do is open to public scrutiny.

> *[Ed: The August Corporation had recently commissioned a thorough search of the massive New York Times computerized data base. We came up with a very meager list of references to Trilateralism. Only 71 references in the past six years in all major U.S. and foreign publications. Many of these were no more than short paragraphs. We*

*know that the Trilateral Commission mailing list has only 4,000 names including all its 250 members and 600 or so Congressmen and elitists. In brief, media coverage has been - and is - extremely small. The 71 citations by the way include mostly critical articles from independent authors. It also includes such efforts as the Time front-page promotion of Jimmy Carter for President - probably the key effort on Carter's behalf. **Hedley Donovan** was then Editor-in-Chief of Time.]*

Commentator: Mr. Sutton?

Sutton: **Paul Volcker** was a member of the Trilateral Commission and has just been appointed Chairman of the Federal Reserve Board. Does **Paul Volcker** have any connection with Chase Manhattan which is dominated by Rockefellers?

Franklin: He was, quite a long time ago, on the staff of [Chase] Manhattan.

[Ed: **Paul Volcke**r has twice worked for Chase Manhattan Bank. In the 1950s as an economist and again in the 1960s as Vice President for Planning. We cannot deny that Volcker "knows about (Trilateral) financial policies" as stated by Franklin.]

Sutton: Don't you think that this is quite an unhealthy situation, where you have a man connected with Chase who is now Chairman of the Federal Reserve Board? Doesn't this give some credence to the criticism of elitism?

Franklin: Conflict of interest?

Sutton: Yes.

Franklin: It does give some credence to it. On the other hand, it is very important that the Chairman of the Federal Reserve Bank know about our financial policies and, therefore, will certainly have been connected to some financial institution. This has not always been the case. I think that anyone who knows **Paul Volcker**, knows that he is an extraordinarily objective person. I think if you would notice, that the editorial comments on his appointments were almost uniformly favorable, there must have been some that were unfavorable, but I have not seen them.

Sutton: May I ask another question?

Commentator: Go Ahead.

Sutton: Mr. **Donovan**, of Time-Life, has just been appointed Special Assistant to President Carter. Mr. Donovan is a member of your Commission.

Franklin: That is correct.

Sutton: Does this not emphasize the fact that the Carter Administration is choosing its administration from an extremely a narrow range. In other words, the Trilateral Commission?

Franklin: I do not think that that needs any confirmation. That is a matter of fact that he has chosen most of his main foreign policy people, I would have to say, from the people he got to know while he was on the Trilateral Commission.

[Ed: Franklin admits that the "Carter Administration is choosing its administration from an extremely narrow range."]

Sutton: Well, I can only make the statement that this leaves any reasonable man with the impression that the Carter Administration is dominated by the Trilateral Commission with your specific ideas which many people do not agree with.

Franklin: Well, I would certainly agree that people who were members of the Commission have predominant places in the foreign policy aspects of the Carter Administration. They are not, because they are members of the Commission, controlled in any sense by us. I do think that they do share a common belief that is very important that we work particularly with Europe and Japan or we are all going to be in trouble.

Sutton: But this common belief may not reflect the beliefs of the American people. How do you know that it does?

Franklin: I do not know that it does. I am no man to interpret what the people think about.

Sutton: In other words, you are quite willing to go ahead [and] establish a Commission which you say does not necessarily reflect the views of the people in the United States? It appears to me that you have taken over political power.

Franklin: I do not think this is true at all. Anybody who forms a group for certain purposes obviously tries to achieve these purposes. We do believe that it is important that Europe, Japan, and the United States get along together. That much we do believe. We also chose the best people we could get as members of the Commission. Fortunately, nearly all accepted. The President was one of them and he happened to have thought that these were very able people indeed, and he asked them to be in his government, it is as simple as that. If you are going to ask me if I am very unhappy about that, the answer is no. I think that these are good people.

Wood: May I ask a little bit more pointedly, if Carter got his education from the Trilateral Commission, was not his dean of students, so to speak, Mr. **Brzezinski**?

Franklin: I cannot tell you exactly what role Brzezinski had, but certainly he did have considerable effect on the education Carter received on foreign policy.

Wood: Mr. Brzezinski is on record in more than one of his books as being a proponent of rejuvenating or redesigning the U.S. Constitution, is this correct?

Franklin: I have not read all his books, I have not seen that statement, and I have worked with him very closely for three years and he has not said anything of that sort to me.

Wood: As a matter of fact, he is on record and in one of his books as indicating that the U.S. Constitution as it is today is not able to lead us into an interdependent world and that it should be redesigned to reflect the interdependence that we must move ahead towards.

Franklin: As I say, if you tell me that, I must believe it, and I have not read that book and I have never got any inkling of that between 1973 and 1976.

[*Ed: Here is what Brzezinski writes in one of his books Between Two Ages: America's Role in the Technetronic Era:*

Tension is unavoidable as man strives to assimilate the new into the framework of the old. For a time the established framework resiliently integrates the new by adapting it in a more familiar shape. But at some point the old framework becomes overloaded. The new input can no longer be redefined into traditional forms, and eventually it asserts itself with compelling force. Today, though, the old framework of international politics - with their spheres of influence, military alliances between nation-states, the fiction of sovereignty, doctrinal conflicts arising from nineteenth century crises - is clearly no longer compatible with reality."

and specifically on changing the U.S. Constitution:

The approaching two-hundredth anniversary of the Declaration of Independence could justify the call for a national constitutional convention to re-examine the nation's formal institutional framework. Either 1976 or 1989 - the two-hundredth anniversary of the Constitution could serve as a suitable target date culminating a national dialogue on the relevance of existing arrangements... Realism,

however, forces us to recognize that the necessary political innova-
tion will not come from direct constitutional reform, desirable as that
would be. The needed change is more likely to develop incrementally
and less overtly ... in keeping with the American tradition of blurring
distinctions between public and private institution.

Obviously Franklin is either unaware of the writing of his "close" as-
sociate Brzezinski or is evading the question.]

Commentator: I would like to interject a question if I could. Mr. Franklin, within the Trilateral Commission, are there any Trilateralists who have control of the energy resources in this world?

Franklin: No. We have no major oil companies represented on the Commission.

Commentator: I mean stockholders in oil companies.

Franklin: I am sure that **David Rockefeller** must have some stock in an oil company. I do not know.

Commentator: Doesn't **David Rockefeller** have stock in Chase National Bank?

Franklin: Definitely

Commentator: Doesn't Chase National Bank have stock in Exxon?

Franklin: Honestly, I do not know.

Commentator: Standard Oil? Mobil?

Sutton: Well, I do.

Franklin: I would be certain that some of their pension trusts and some of the trusts that they hold for individuals, undoubtedly do.

Commentator: So, the Trilateral Commission has no effect at all in the energy field at all?

Franklin: Yes, the Trilateral Commission has written a report on energy. There were three authors, there were always three authors. The American author was **John Sawhill**, who was formerly head of the Energy Administration and is now presently of New York University.

Commentator: I have read where the oil and gas world is dominated by seven major firms, do you agree with that?

Franklin: I do not have expertise in this field, but I think it sounds reasonable.

Commentator: Well, a listing of controlling ownership in these major oil and gas companies by banks - by Trilateral Commissioners - is listed as Manufacturer's Hanover, Chase Bank, Wells Fargo Bank, First National Bank of Chicago, and First Continental of Illinois. And these all supposedly are of Trilateral representation. Is that true, sir?

Franklin: No, sir, it is not true. Give me the list again. I think I can tell you which are and which are not.

Commentator: Manufacturer's Hanover.

Franklin: No, sir, it is not.

Commentator: There are no stockholders in that, who are members of the Trilateral Commission?

Franklin: Wait a minute. I cannot tell you whether there are no stockholders in Manufacturer's Hanover. I might even be a stockholder in Manufacturer's Hanover. I am not.

Commentator: Chase Manhattan figures prominently.

Franklin: Chase Manhattan certainly.

Commentator: ...which is David Rockefeller's Bank!

Franklin: There is no question about that.

Commentator: So there is some connection with the energy field.

Franklin: Well, yes.

Commentator: So, if Chase Manhattan has stock in Exxon, Mobil, and Standard Oil, then there is a direct connection there?

Franklin: I am sure that is true. Every bank runs pension trusts, so it must have some of its trust money in some of those companies.

Commentator: I have read, and I do not know if it is true, you may answer this, that Chase Manhattan is a number one stockholder in Exxon, number three in Mobil, and number two in Standard Oil.

Franklin: I just would not know.

Commentator: Do you have any questions, Mr. Sutton?

Sutton: Yes, the figures you have just quoted about Chase Manhattan stock ownership in the oil companies: these were published by the U.S. Senate some years ago. There is a series of these volumes. One, for example, is entitled *Disclosure of Corporate Ownership*.

[Ed: Any reader investigating further should note that the ownership is heavily disguised by use of nominee companies. For example "Cudd & Co." is a fictitious nominee name for Chase Manhattan Bank.]

A partial list of nominees which have been used by Chase Manhattan Bank includes the following:

Andrews & Co.	Elzay & Co.	Reeves & Co.
Bedle & Co	Gansel & Co.	Ring & Co.
Bender & Co.	Gooss & Co.	Ryan & Co.
Chase Nominees Ltd.	Gunn & Co.	Settle & Co
Clint & Co.	Kane & Co.	Taylor & Witt
Cudd & Co.	McKenna & Co.	Timm & Co.
Dell & Co.	Padom & Co.	Titus & Co.
Egger & Co.	Pickering Ltd.	White & Co.
Ehren & Co.		

Franklin: I am sure that these banks could run billions of dollars through trusts and some of the trusts must be invested in some of these major oil companies.

Commentator: Then the Trilateral Commission member who has stock in the bank and who is also a high-ranking Trilateral Commission member, would have some jurisdiction over energy?

Franklin: No, not really. I know some of the management of these companies. They are not controlled by the stockholders the way they used to be.

Wood: Let's put that question another way if we might. It perhaps would be erroneous to say Chase Manhattan Bank controlled Exxon, because in fact, they do not. However, Chase Manhattan Bank is the largest single shareholder that Exxon has. Considering the discussion going on about the major oil companies, and their part in this energy crisis, don't you think that it would be possible to exercise control from Chase Manhattan Bank to put pressure on Exxon to help alleviate the energy crisis?

Franklin: Well, I think you could answer that kind of question just as well, as I can. Everybody has their own views on these things.

Commentator: You must be familiar with the members of your

Commission, especially with Mr. Rockefeller and his various holdings?

Franklin: I am extremely familiar with Mr. Rockefeller. I have known him for nearly 50 years.

Commentator: ... and his holdings?

Franklin: I am not at all familiar with his holdings.

Commentator: I think everybody is familiar with his holdings. I thought everybody was familiar with his holdings, I know he owns Chase Manhattan Bank.

Franklin: No, that is not true.

Commentator: I mean, he is the largest stockholder.

Franklin: That, I would agree to. I would say that he has about five percent, I am not sure.

Commentator: Five percent? Would you agree with that, Mr. Sutton?

Sutton: Yes, plus he is chairman of the board.

Franklin: Yes, that is correct. I have no doubt that he does control Chase Manhattan Bank.

Commentator: You have no doubt about that?

Franklin: No, basically, no. Directors are important.

Commentator: Do you have any doubt that as chairman, he controls the bank and Chase Manhattan also controls or at least partly controls the American Electric Power [the utility company]?

Franklin: I do not know anything about it.

Commentator: You are not sure about that?

Franklin: I just don't know. These things do not ever really enter into consideration. If you look at our energy report that will tell you whether you think this is an objective or effective document or not.

> [Ed: Chase Manhattan Bank owns 1,646,706 shares of American Electric Power Company through two nominees, <Kane & Co. (1,059,967 shares) and Cudd & Co. (586,739 shares)>. This gives it a direct 2.8 percent of the total. However, numerous other holding in American Electric Power are maintained by banks and firms where Chase has some degree of control. For example, Morgan Guaranty has almost 500,000 shares and is dominated by J.P. Morgan; the second largest stockholder in J.P. Morgan is Chase Manhattan Bank.]

Commentator: Mr. Sutton?

Sutton: Can we go off energy for a while?

Commentator: Yes.

Sutton: I have a question for Mr. Franklin. Who chooses the members of the Trilateral commission?

Franklin: The Trilateral Commission's Executive Committee.

Sutton: Who comprises the committee?

Franklin: Who is on that committee?

Sutton: Yes.

Franklin: Okay. **William Coleman**, former Secretary of Transportation, who is a lawyer; **Lane Kirkland**, who is Secretary-General of the American Federation of Labor; **Henry Kissinger**, who does not need too much identification; **Bruce McLaury,** who is president of the Brookings Institution; **David Rockefeller**; **Robert Ingersoll**, who was formerly Deputy Secretary of State and Ambassador to Japan; **I. W. Able**, who was formerly head of United Steelworkers; and **William Roth**, who is a San Francisco businessman and was chief trade negotiator in the previous Kennedy trade round.

Sutton: May I ask a question? How many of these have a rather intimate business relationship with Mr. Rockefeller?

Franklin: **Henry Kissinger** is chairman of Mr. Rockefeller's Chase Advisory Committee.

Sutton: Coleman?

Franklin: Coleman, I don't think has any business relationship with him, he is a lawyer.

> *[Ed: In fact William Coleman is a Director of Chase Manhattan Bank which Franklin has already admitted to be controlled by **David Rockefeller**.]*

Sutton: Mr. Ingersoll?

Franklin: Mr. Ingersoll, I don't think has any business relationship.

Sutton: Isn't he connected with First Chicago?

Franklin: He is vice chairman of the University of Chicago.

Sutton: No, what about the First Bank of Chicago? [First Chicago Corp.]

Franklin: I don't believe that Ingersoll has any relationship with banks in Chicago, but I don't know for certain on that.

[Ed: Robert Stephen Ingersoll before joining the Washington "revolving door" was a director of the First National Bank of Chicago, a subsidiary of First Chicago Corp. The largest single shareholder in First Chicago is David Rockefeller's Chase Manhattan Bank. Ingersoll has also been a director of Atlantic Richfield and Burlington Northern. Chase Manhattan is also the largest single stockholder in these two companies. Thus, Ingersoll has a long standing relationship with Rockefeller interests.]

Commentator: We are adding another man to the interview, his name is Mr. John Rees, a very fine writer from the *Review of the News*, Washington, D.C., who is in the area right at this time to make some speeches.

Sutton: Mr. Franklin, do you believe in freedom of the press in the United States?

Franklin: Definitely, of course.

Sutton: Let me quote you from a book *Crisis In Democracy*, written by **Michel Crozier**, who is a Trilateral member.

Franklin: Correct.

Sutton: I am quoting from page 35 of his book: *"The media has thus become an autonomous power. We are now witnessing a crucial change with the profession. That is, media tends to regulate itself in such a way as to resist the pressure from financial or government interests."* Does that not mean that you want to restrict the press in some way?

Franklin: I can't quite hear you.

Sutton: Let me paraphrase this for you. I think I will be clear in my paraphrasing. The Trilateral Commission is unhappy with the press because it resists the pressure from financial or government interests. That is one of your statements.

Franklin: Now, let me say something about our book. The book that we put out, the report, is the responsibility of the authors and not of the Commission itself. You will find that in the back of a number of them, and that book is one of them, that other members of the Commission will hear dissenting views, and you will find dissenting views in the back of that book on the press question.

Sutton: I would like to quote a further statement from the same book and leave the questions at that point: "The media deprives government and to some extent other responsible authorities of the time lag and tolerance that make it possible to innovate and to experiment responsibly." What the book recommends is something like the Interstate Commerce Commission to control the press. This seems to me to be a violation of the Constitution.

Franklin: I would agree with you that we do not want something like the Interstate Commerce Commission to control the press.

> [Ed: **Michel Crozier**, et al, in Crisis In Democracy make the following statements with reference to the "Interstate Commerce Act and the Sherman Anti-trust Act":
>
> "Something comparable appears to be now needed with respect to the media.... there is also the need to assure to the government the right and the ability to withhold information at the source" (page 182).
>
> The authors go on to argue that if journalists do not conform to these new restrictive standards then "The alternative could well be regulation by the government."]

Sutton: I fail to understand why the Trilateral Commission would associate itself with such a viewpoint.

Franklin: As I just mentioned to you. We hired three authors for each report. The authors are allowed to say what they think is correct. What the Trilateral Commission does is this: It says we think this report is worthwhile for the public to see. This does not mean that all the members of the Commission agree with all the statements in the report and, in fact, a majority of them might disagree with certain things. Now, where a statement is one that many Commissioners seem to disagree with we then do put in the back a summary of the discussion. That book does have a summary of the discussion of our meeting which questions various things in the book, in the back of it.

Sutton: Would you say Mr. Franklin that the members of the Commission do have a common philosophy?

Franklin: Yes. I think a common philosophy. I think that all of them believe that this world will work better if the principal industrial powers consult each other on their policies and try to work them out together. This does not mean that they will agree on everything. Of course, they won't. But, at least they will know what the other countries feel, and why they feel it.

Sutton: *The Financial Times* in London -- the editor is **Ferdy Fisher**, a

Trilateralist. He fired a long time editorial writer, Gordon Tether, because Tether wanted to write articles criticizing the Trilateral Commission. Do you have any comments?

Franklin: I didn't know that at all. It sounds terribly unlikely, but if you say that it is so, probably it is.

> [Ed: See Chapter Seven "Trilateral Censorship: the case of C. Gordon Tether" in Trilaterals Over Washington. Trilaterals see the media as the "gatekeeper" and comment as follows:
>
> "Their main impact is visibility. The only real event is the event that is reported and seen. Thus, journalists possess a crucial role as gate-keepers of one of the central dimensions of public life."]

Rees: Frankly, Mr. Martin, with Antony Sutton on the line, I feel absolutely a novice, because Antony is a real expert on the Trilateral.

Sutton: Well, I am looking for information.

Commentator: Are you getting information?

Sutton: Yes, I am very definitely getting information.

Commentator: Do you have any other questions?

Sutton: Not at the moment. I'd rather hear someone else.

Commentator: All right.

Wood: I do have one question, if I might. You mentioned earlier that as you decided to issue a report, whether it reflected Trilateral policy or not, you felt that it was worthy to be shared with the public. Is that correct?

Franklin: We do not have a Trilateral policy, except for the very broad policy [which] is that each of these major areas ought to know what the other countries are doing and why and try to work things out as much as possible. That is our only Trilateral policy, I would say. We don't have a policy on energy and a policy on monetary reform and a policy on, etc.

> [Ed: The latest issue of Trialogue (Summer 1979) has an opening paragraph as follows:
>
> "The draft report presented in Tokyo by the Trilateral Task Force on Payments Imbalances analyzes the extreme payments imbalances which have marked the world economy throughout the 1970's and offers a series of broad policy recommendations..."
>
> Part II of the same issue has the following opening paragraph:

"The draft report presented in Tokyo by the Trilateral Task Force on Industrial Policy... reviews the desirable aims and criteria of trilateral industrial policies and their international implications."

Yet Franklin asserts "We don't have a policy on energy and a policy on monetary reform, etc."]

Wood: Okay, let me ask a question. Based on that then, what efforts have you made, if any, to publish these articles or these studies so they might be reviewed by the general American public? For instance, I have never seen one study published in any major popular magazine, whether it be *Time Magazine*, a newspaper -- in fact, there have been very few references. Over a period of six years now, there have been few mentions of the name "Trilateral Commission" in the nation's press. This is backed up by the *New York Times* data base, which is one of the most extensive in the world. Now if these are made public, can you tell me how these are made public?

Franklin: Yes. What we do is, that we have a list of about 4,000 people, some of whom request them and some of whom we thought would be interested if we sent them -- and we send them free -- and we would be glad to send them to you, for example, if you would like to have them. Now we also, when we publish, when we send them out to a considerable list of press correspondents. We also have press lunches and things. Because of the nature of this thing, it can't be printed in full, because they are just too long. No newspaper wants to print a 40- or 50-page study. But, there have been mentions of one or two of the studies in *Newsweek*. We would like to get more published, frankly, very much more than we have been getting. Now in Japan, for example, we have done much better. At our last plenary session in Tokyo, members of the Commission who were there, gave over 90 separate interviews to members of the Japanese press who were present. In fact, there were many more requests than that which we could not honor because there was not time. We have not done anything like as well in this country.

Wood: Allow me to ask you this. This takes specifically one case, the case of *Time Magazine*. **Hedley Donovan** is the former editor-in-chief of that magazine. I understand he is recently retired, and also you have as a member of your Commission, **Sol Linowitz**, also a director of *Time*. Now, Time-Life books, of course, you have *Time Magazine*, *Fortune*, *Money and People*. Now I would ask you -- considering the special advantage you have by having such a giant as **Hedley Donovan** and **Sol Linowitz** as well, both connected to *Time* -- don't you feel that if you really wanted to publicize these "position papers" that it would only take a scratch of the pen by Mr. Donovan?

Franklin: No, I don't, and I will tell you why. **Hedley Donovan** is not only a member of the Commission, but he is one of my close personal friends. **Hedley Donovan** is also a person of great integrity. He will not publish anything we do because he is connected with it. He looks out for the interest of *Time,* and he does not feel we were worth *Time* publicity, and I am sure he will be exactly the same way in the White House. He is going to be loyal to his President and to his job.

Wood: But *Time Magazine* is the largest news magazine in the country?

Franklin: Right. We only had a little publicity, but we had only what Hedley would have given, whether or not he was a member of the Commission.

Wood: So, he basically thinks that the Commission really does not matter.

Franklin: No. He does not, or he would not be a member of the Commission at all. *Time Magazine* does give us some money, not very much, but $2,500 a year to be exact. But, his editorial judgment is not biased by the fact that he is a member of the Commission.

Commentator: Mr. Rees, would you like to ask a question?

Rees: Yes, Mr. Franklin, I noticed that you were saying that the Trilateral Commission takes no responsibility for the use of the publisher's imprimatur, but I would be interested to know about how you go about selecting your writers to put out the various positions.

Franklin: Well that is a very interesting question. We have a meeting with the chairmen. The way the situation is organized is this. There are three chairmen, one from each of the three areas. Three secretaries, one from each of the three areas, and I have got an intermediate staff job called "coordinator." Now, the chairmen and secretaries meet with what they have jointly, will discuss not only topics they think will be useful to have, but also authors for these topics. The topics are then discussed by the whole Commission and approved or changed slightly. The authors are chosen by members of the staff and consultation with the chairmen.

Rees: So, although you do not take responsibility for the finished product you are responsible for the selection of the writers.

Franklin: Very much. No question about that.

Rees: So it does have your imprimatur stamp of approval each time?

Franklin: In that sense. We certainly choose the writers, and we choose them because we think they are very good, obviously. So far, every single report that has been written by the authors has, in fact, been accepted for publication by the Commission.

Rees: Then the report on the news media was accepted?

Franklin: It was accepted, but there was a lot of disagreement with that. It was felt that it was an important statement, with quite a lot of interesting new ideas in it. It was also a very strong opposition which was reflected in the back of the report in a section, I think it is entitled, "Summary of Discussion."

Commentator: Mr. Sutton, do you have any other questions?

Sutton: I have one more question, that goes to a new field entirely: taxation. We have established that **David Rockefeller** is chairman and the single most powerful influence in Chase Manhattan Bank. Now, do you happen to know the tax rate that Chase Manhattan pays in the United States?

Franklin: I don't know . . . happen to know -- it is about 50% [fifty percent].

Sutton: I will give you some figures. In 1976, Chase Manhattan Bank's tax rate was precisely zero. I am wondering why, if you are so influential politically, why at least you cannot pay a tax rate more equivalent to that of the average American Taxpayer, which is 15% or 20% or 30%?

Franklin: I have nothing to do with Chase Manhattan Bank. But if the tax rate was zero, it must have been because it had very large real estate losses in that year, I think.

Sutton: In 1975, it was 3.4%. It is always way under 10%.

Franklin: Well, that is extremely interesting. It is a new fact for me.

Sutton: Well, my point is this, that you are willing to guide the United States into the future, but apparently you are not willing to pay your fair share of the costs.

Commentator: You are talking about the Commission members as a whole?

Sutton: Yes.

Franklin: I think you will find that the Commission members pay whatever the laws says they are supposed to pay under the circumstances. I do not know what the particular reason was on Chase. They did have heavy losses. I am not familiar enough with their situation to be able to tell it to you.

Wood: May I ask another question along that same line, please?

Commentator: Go ahead.

Wood: In that same year, 1976, it is recorded that some 78% of Chase Manhattan's earnings came from International operations. That leaves 22% from the U.S... Don't you think perhaps this might be a conflict of interest, between choosing their international policy versus their domestic policy in the United States?

Franklin: Well, I think that is true of most of the major banks. Now, that does not answer your question, I recognize.

Wood: Where would their loyalty lie? If on one hand they are trying to look out for America, yet on the other hand they are trying to look out for their bread and butter, which is not America.

Franklin: First, in the long run, I think any of our major corporations must recognize, that unless the United States does well, they are going to be in the soup. Secondly, some of these people, you may or may not believe it, have enough integrity, they can divorce their interest, like Hedley Donovan could, on the question of publicity on the Trilateral Commission.

Commentator: Gentlemen, I think we are running out of time here. I think we have reached the end of the interview. We would like to thank you, Mr. Franklin, Mr. Wood, and Mr. Sutton. Thank you for being guests on our show.

THE EARTH CHARTER

Preamble

We stand at a critical moment in Earth's history, a time when humanity must choose its future. As the world becomes increasingly interdependent and fragile, the future at once holds great peril and great promise. To move forward we must recognize that in the midst of a magnificent diversity of cultures and life forms we are one human family and one Earth community with a common destiny. We must join together to bring forth a sustainable global society founded on respect for nature, universal human rights, economic justice, and a culture of peace. Towards this end, it is imperative that we, the peoples of Earth, declare our responsibility to one another, to the greater community of life, and to future generations.

Earth, Our Home

Humanity is part of a vast evolving universe. Earth, our home, is alive with a unique community of life. The forces of nature make existence a demanding and uncertain adventure, but Earth has provided the conditions essential to life's evolution. The resilience of the community of life and the well-being of humanity depend upon preserving a healthy biosphere with all its ecological systems, a rich variety of plants and animals, fertile soils, pure waters, and clean air. The global environment with its finite resources is a common concern of all peoples. The protection of Earth's vitality, diversity, and beauty is a sacred trust.

The Global Situation

The dominant patterns of production and consumption are causing environmental devastation, the depletion of resources, and a massive extinction of species. Communities are being undermined. The benefits of development are not shared equitably and the gap between rich and poor is widening. Injustice, poverty, ignorance, and violent conflict are widespread and the cause of great suffering. An unprecedented rise in human population has overburdened ecological and social systems. The foundations of global security are threatened. These trends are perilous—but not inevitable.

The Challenges Ahead

The choice is ours: form a global partnership to care for Earth and one another or risk the destruction of ourselves and the diversity of life. Fundamental changes are needed in our values, institutions, and ways of living. We must realize that when basic needs have been met, human development is primarily about being more, not having more. We have the knowledge and technology to provide for all and to reduce our impacts on the environment. The emergence of a global civil society is creating new opportunities to build a democratic and humane world. Our environmental, economic, political, social, and spiritual challenges are interconnected, and together we can forge inclusive solutions.

Universal Responsibility

To realize these aspirations, we must decide to live with a sense of universal responsibility, identifying ourselves with the whole Earth community as well as our local communities. We are at once citizens of different nations and of one world in which the local and global are linked. Everyone shares responsibility for the present and future well-being of the human family and the larger living world. The spirit of human solidarity and kinship with all life is strengthened when we live with reverence for the mystery of being, gratitude for the gift of life, and humility regarding the human place in nature.

We urgently need a shared vision of basic values to provide an ethical foundation for the emerging world community. Therefore, together in hope we affirm the following interdependent principles for a sustainable way of life as a common standard by which the conduct of all individuals, organizations, businesses, governments, and transnational institutions is to be guided and assessed.

PRINCIPLES

I. RESPECT AND CARE FOR THE COMMUNITY OF LIFE

1. **Respect Earth and life in all its diversity.**
   a. Recognize that all beings are interdependent and every form of life has value regardless of its worth to human beings.
   b. Affirm faith in the inherent dignity of all human beings and in the intellectual, artistic, ethical, and spiritual potential of humanity.

2. **Care for the community of life with understanding, compassion, and love.**
   a. Accept that with the right to own, manage, and use natural resources comes the duty to prevent environmental harm and to protect the rights of people.
   b. Affirm that with increased freedom, knowledge, and power comes increased responsibility to promote the common good.

3. **Build democratic societies that are just, participatory, sustainable, and peaceful.**
   a. Ensure that communities at all levels guarantee human rights and fundamental freedoms and provide everyone an opportunity to realize his or her full potential.
   b. Promote social and economic justice, enabling all to achieve a secure and meaningful livelihood that is ecologically responsible.

4. **Secure Earth's bounty and beauty for present and future generations.**
   a. Recognize that the freedom of action of each generation is qualified by the needs of future generations.
   b. Transmit to future generations values, traditions, and institutions that support the long-term flourishing of Earth's human and ecological communities.

In order to fulfill these four broad commitments, it is necessary to:

II. ECOLOGICAL INTEGRITY

5. **Protect and restore the integrity of Earth's ecological systems, with special concern for biological diversity and the natural processes that sustain life.**
    a. Adopt at all levels sustainable development plans and regulations that make environmental conservation and rehabilitation integral to all development initiatives.
    b. Establish and safeguard viable nature and biosphere reserves, including wild lands and marine areas, to protect Earth's life support systems, maintain biodiversity, and preserve our natural heritage.
    c. Promote the recovery of endangered species and ecosystems.
    d. Control and eradicate non-native or genetically modified organisms harmful to native species and the environment, and prevent introduction of such harmful organisms.
    e. Manage the use of renewable resources such as water, soil, forest products, and marine life in ways that do not exceed rates of regeneration and that protect the health of ecosystems.
    f. Manage the extraction and use of non-renewable resources such as minerals and fossil fuels in ways that minimize depletion and cause no serious environmental damage.

6. **Prevent harm as the best method of environmental protection and, when knowledge is limited, apply a precautionary approach.**
    a. Take action to avoid the possibility of serious or irreversible environmental harm even when scientific knowledge is incomplete or inconclusive.
    b. Place the burden of proof on those who argue that a proposed activity will not cause significant harm, and make the responsible parties liable for environmental harm.
    c. Ensure that decision making addresses the cumulative,

long-term, indirect, long distance, and global consequences of human activities.

d. Prevent pollution of any part of the environment and allow no build-up of radioactive, toxic, or other hazardous substances.

e. Avoid military activities damaging to the environment.

7. **Adopt patterns of production, consumption, and reproduction that safeguard Earth's regenerative capacities, human rights, and community well-being.**

a. Reduce, reuse, and recycle the materials used in production and consumption systems, and ensure that residual waste can be assimilated by ecological systems.

b. Act with restraint and efficiency when using energy, and rely increasingly on renewable energy sources such as solar and wind.

c. Promote the development, adoption, and equitable transfer of environmentally sound technologies.

d. Internalize the full environmental and social costs of goods and services in the selling price, and enable consumers to identify products that meet the highest social and environmental standards.

e. Ensure universal access to health care that fosters reproductive health and responsible reproduction.

f. Adopt lifestyles that emphasize the quality of life and material sufficiency in a finite world.

8. **Advance the study of ecological sustainability and promote the open exchange and wide application of the knowledge acquired.**

a. Support international scientific and technical cooperation on sustainability, with special attention to the needs of developing nations.

b. Recognize and preserve the traditional knowledge and spiritual wisdom in all cultures that contribute to environmental protection and human well-being.

c. Ensure that information of vital importance to human health and environmental protection, including genetic information, remains available in the public domain.

III. SOCIAL AND ECONOMIC JUSTICE

9. **Eradicate poverty as an ethical, social, and environmental imperative.**
    a. Guarantee the right to potable water, clean air, food security, uncontaminated soil, shelter, and safe sanitation, allocating the national and international resources required.
    b. Empower every human being with the education and resources to secure a sustainable livelihood, and provide social security and safety nets for those who are unable to support themselves.
    c. Recognize the ignored, protect the vulnerable, serve those who suffer, and enable them to develop their capacities and to pursue their aspirations.

10. **Ensure that economic activities and institutions at all levels promote human development in an equitable and sustainable manner.**
    a. Promote the equitable distribution of wealth within nations and among nations.
    b. Enhance the intellectual, financial, technical, and social resources of developing nations, and relieve them of onerous international debt.
    c. Ensure that all trade supports sustainable resource use, environmental protection, and progressive labor standards.
    d. Require multinational corporations and international financial organizations to act transparently in the public good, and hold them accountable for the consequences of their activities.

11. **Affirm gender equality and equity as prerequisites to sustainable development and ensure universal access to education, health care, and economic opportunity.**
    a. Secure the human rights of women and girls and end all

violence against them.

b. Promote the active participation of women in all aspects of economic, political, civil, social, and cultural life as full and equal partners, decision makers, leaders, and beneficiaries.

c. Strengthen families and ensure the safety and loving nurture of all family members.

12. **Uphold the right of all, without discrimination, to a natural and social environment supportive of human dignity, bodily health, and spiritual well-being, with special attention to the rights of indigenous peoples and minorities.**

a. Eliminate discrimination in all its forms, such as that based on race, color, sex, sexual orientation, religion, language, and national, ethnic or social origin.

b. Affirm the right of indigenous peoples to their spirituality, knowledge, lands and resources and to their related practice of sustainable livelihoods.

c. Honor and support the young people of our communities, enabling them to fulfill their essential role in creating sustainable societies.

d. Protect and restore outstanding places of cultural and spiritual significance.

IV. DEMOCRACY, NONVIOLENCE, AND PEACE

13. **Strengthen democratic institutions at all levels, and provide transparency and accountability in governance, inclusive participation in decision making, and access to justice.**

a. Uphold the right of everyone to receive clear and timely information on environmental matters and all development plans and activities which are likely to affect them or in which they have an interest.

b. Support local, regional and global civil society, and promote the meaningful participation of all interested individuals and organizations in decision making.

   c. Protect the rights to freedom of opinion, expression, peaceful assembly, association, and dissent.

   d. Institute effective and efficient access to administrative and independent judicial procedures, including remedies and redress for environmental harm and the threat of such harm.

   e. Eliminate corruption in all public and private institutions.

   f. Strengthen local communities, enabling them to care for their environments, and assign environmental responsibilities to the levels of government where they can be carried out most effectively.

14. Integrate into formal education and life-long learning the knowledge, values, and skills needed for a sustainable way of life.

   a. Provide all, especially children and youth, with educational opportunities that empower them to contribute actively to sustainable development.

   b. Promote the contribution of the arts and humanities as well as the sciences in sustainability education.

   c. Enhance the role of the mass media in raising awareness of ecological and social challenges.

   d. Recognize the importance of moral and spiritual education for sustainable living.

15. Treat all living beings with respect and consideration.

   a. Prevent cruelty to animals kept in human societies and protect them from suffering.

   b. Protect wild animals from methods of hunting, trapping, and fishing that cause extreme, prolonged, or avoidable suffering.

   c. Avoid or eliminate to the full extent possible the taking or destruction of non-targeted species.

16. Promote a culture of tolerance, nonviolence, and peace.

   a. Encourage and support mutual understanding, solidarity, and cooperation among all peoples and within and among nations.

b. Implement comprehensive strategies to prevent violent conflict and use collaborative problem solving to manage and resolve environmental conflicts and other disputes.

c. Demilitarize national security systems to the level of a non-provocative defense posture, and convert military resources to peaceful purposes, including ecological restoration.

d. Eliminate nuclear, biological, and toxic weapons and other weapons of mass destruction.

e. Ensure that the use of orbital and outer space supports environmental protection and peace.

f. Recognize that peace is the wholeness created by right relationships with oneself, other persons, other cultures, other life, Earth, and the larger whole of which all are a part.

THE WAY FORWARD

As never before in history, common destiny beckons us to seek a new beginning. Such renewal is the promise of these Earth Charter principles. To fulfill this promise, we must commit ourselves to adopt and promote the values and objectives of the Charter.

This requires a change of mind and heart. It requires a new sense of global interdependence and universal responsibility. We must imaginatively develop and apply the vision of a sustainable way of life locally, nationally, regionally, and globally. Our cultural diversity is a precious heritage and different cultures will find their own distinctive ways to realize the vision. We must deepen and expand the global dialogue that generated the Earth Charter, for we have much to learn from the ongoing collaborative search for truth and wisdom.

Life often involves tensions between important values. This can mean difficult choices. However, we must find ways to harmonize diversity with unity, the exercise of freedom with the common good, short-term objectives with long-term goals. Every individual, family, organization, and community has a vital role to play. The arts, sciences, religions, educational institutions, media, businesses, nongovernmental organizations, and governments are all called to offer creative leadership. The partnership of government, civil society, and business is essential for effective governance.

In order to build a sustainable global community, the nations of the world must renew their commitment to the United Nations, fulfill their obligations under existing international agreements, and support the implementation of Earth Charter principles with an international legally binding instrument on environment and development.

Let ours be a time remembered for the awakening of a new reverence for life, the firm resolve to achieve sustainability, the quickening of the struggle for justice and peace, and the joyful celebration of life.

BIBLIOGRAPHY

Primary

Akin, William E., Technocracy and the American Dream : The Technocrat Movement 1900 - 1941, ed. (Berkeley [u.a.], 1977).

Moller, Dr. Paul, 2006. *Holism and Evolution,* College of European and Regional Studies.

Technocracy, Inc., Technocracy Study Course (1934).

Adair, David, 'The Technocrats 1919-1967: A Case Study of Conflict and Change in a Social Movement', (Vancouver, BC, 1970).

Technocracy : Technological Continental Design. (Ferndale, WA, 2001).

Technocracy, Technological Social Design. (Savannah, Ohio, 1975).

Total Conscription! Your Questions Answered. (New York, N.Y., 1942).

Hubbert, Marion King, Man-Hours and Distribution (New York, N.Y., 1940).

Scott, Howard, [from old catalog], Technocracy. (New York, 1935).

Adamson, Martha, and Raymond I. Moore, Technocracy; Some Questions Answered. (New York, 1934).

Gernsback, Hugo, Technocracy Review. (Mount Morris, Ill., 1933).

Technocracy, The Magazine of the New Deal. (Los Angeles, Calif.).

Ackerman, Frederick Lee, The Facts Behind Technocracy (New York City, 1933).

Wilson, John Mills, Understanding Technocracy (San Diego, Calif., 1933).

Holder, William J. [from old catalog], Simplified Technocracy

(Salt Lake City, 1933).

Scott, Howard, Technocracy: Science Vs. Chaos (Chicago, 1933).

Smalley, Jack., The Technocrats' Magazine: Thirty Million Out of Work in 1933--or (Minneapolis, 1933).

Stabile, Donald R., Veblen and the Political Economy of Technocracy : The Herald of Technological Revolution Developed an Ideology of "scientific" Collectivism, ed. Don R. Stabile. y (In: The American Journal of Economics and Sociology, Malden, Mass.: Wiley, 1987).

Davis, Charles H., The American Technocracy Movement : A Case Study in the History of Economic Thought, ed. Charles H. Davis. y (1986).

Stabile, Donald., Prophets of Order : The Rise of the New Class, Technocracy and Socialism in America, ed. Stabile. Donald (Boston Mass., 1984).

Reed, John L., The Newest Whore of Babylon. The Emergence of Technocracy. A Study of the Mechanization of Man, ed. John L. Reed. y (Boston, 1975).

Technocracy Study Course : An Outline of Those Elements of Science and Technology Essential to an Understanding of Our Social Mechanism., ed. Inc. Technocracy (New York, NY, 1940).

Slocomb, Whitney Hart., How to Put Technocracy Into Practice, ed. Whitney H. Slocomb. y (Los Angeles, Calif, 1933).

Soule, George., A Critique of Technocracy's Five Main Points, ed. Soule. George (In: For and Against Technocracy, New York: Business Bourse, 1933).

Slocomb, Whitney Hart., The Causes and Cure of This Depression, or, How to Put Technocracy Into Practice, ed. Whitney Hart Slocomb. (Los Angeles, Calif., 1933).

Rautenstrauch, Walter., Technocracy's Views on Technological Development and Social Change, ed. Rautenstrauch. alter (In: For and Against Technocracy, New York: Business Bourse, 1933).

Laing, Graham Allan., and Charles Austin Beard, Towards Technocracy. (Los Angeles: The Angelus Pr., 1933).

Elsner, Henry, Messianic Scientism Technocracy, 1919-1960 (xii, 398 leaves., 1963).

Arkright, Frank., The A B C of Technocracy : Based on Authorized Material (New York and London, 1933).

The Technate of North America : The Minimum Area for the Maximum Defense and Efficiency. (New York, N.Y., 1941).

America Must Show the Way (New York, 1940).

The Energy Certificate. (New York, 1940).

Scott, Howard., The Evolution of Statesmanship & Science and Society. (New York, 1939).

Technocracy : Official Publication Technocracy, Inc. (New York, N.Y., 1935).

Cline, Martha Adamson and Raymond I. Moore, Technocracy: Some Questions Answered. (New York, 1934).

Zmavc, Ivan, Technocracy and Sociotechnics Dedicated With the Author's Compliments By the Institute for Technical Economy At Masaryk Academy of Work. (Prague, 1934).

Chase, Stuart, Technocracy an Interpretation. (vol. The John Day pamphlets. no. 19, New York, 1933).

Brandon, Joseph, Technocracy or Democracy Which Shall Govern Our Industries (Hollis, N.Y., 1933). Parrish, Wayne W., An Outline of Technocracy (New York, 1933).

Scott, Howard, Introduction to Technocracy (New York, 1933).

Smyth, William Henry, Technocracy Explained By Its Originator (Berkeley, Calif., 1933).

Fisher, Irving, A Word About Technocracy. (New Haven, 1933).

Sachs, Hans, Technocracy in Education By Hans Sachs (San Francisco).

Director, Aaron., The Economies of Technocracy (Chicago, Ill., 1933).

The Technocrat. (Pismo Beach, Calif., 1935).

Technocracy : Total Conscription: A Victory Program. (New York, N.Y., 1942).

Flying Wings for a Continental Offensive (New York, N.Y., 1943).

Continental Power for Continental Defense. (New York, N.Y., 1939).

Porter, Henry Alfred, Roosevelt and Technocracy (Los Angeles, Calif., 1932).

Supporting

B, R., Root Merrill, E., and Technocracy Langan, Inc., I Am the Price System and the Culture of Abundance (1945).

Bucchi, Massimiano, Beyond Technocracy : Science, Politics, and Citizens (Dordrecht, New York, 2009).

Crawford, Peter H., Technocracy -- an American Dogma for the Machine Age. (135 p., 1954).

Genoud, Christophe., Matthias Finger, and Maarten Arentsen, Energy Regulation: Convergence Through Mutlilevel Technocracy, ed. Genoud hristophe, Matthias Finger and Maarten Arentsen. (In: Reshaping European Gas and Electricity Industries, Amsterdam: Elsevier, 2004).

McDougall, Walter A., Technocracy and Statecraft in the Space Age. (In: The Global History Reader, New York: Routledge, 2005).

Burris, Beverly H., Technocracy At Work, (Suny Series, the New Inequalities, Albany, 1993).

Putt, Archibald., Putt's Law & the Successful Technocrat : How to Win in the Information Age (Hoboken, N.J., 2006).

Brown, William Glenn., The Dynamo & the Tree : My Twins and I Journeying in a Technate in the Year 1981 (Hicksville, N.Y., 1977).

Stabile, Donald R., Veblen and the Political Economy of Technocracy : The Herald of Technological Revolution Developed an Ideology of "scientific" Collectivism, ed. Don R. Stabile. y (In: The American Journal of Economics and Sociology, Malden, Mass.: Wiley, 1987).

Davis, Charles H., The American Technocracy Movement : A Case Study in the History of Economic Thought, ed. Charles H. Davis.

y (1986).

Fischer, Frank., Technocracy and the Politics of Expertise, ed. Fischer. rank (Newbury Park, Calif. [u.a.], 1990).

Day, Richard B., Ronald Beiner, and Joseph Masciulli, Democratic Theory and Technological Society, ed. by Richard B. Day. d. (Armonk, NY [u.a.], 1988).

Benard, Jean., From Political Bureaucracy to Economic Technocracy: A Transfer of Property Rights in a Socialist Economy Under Inverse Transition, eds. Jean, and Benard. (Vorträge, Reden Und Berichte // Universität Des Saarlandes, vol. 7, Saarbrücken: Europa-Institut, 1991).

Freeman, John R., Competing Commitments : Technocracy and Democracy in the Design of Monetary Institutions (In: International Organization, Cambridge, Mass.: Cambridge University Press, 2002).

Sartori, Giovanni., Market, Capitalism, Planning and Technocracy. (In: Markets, Hierarchies and Networks, London: Sage, 1998).

Centeno, Miguel Angel, The New Leviathan : The Dynamics and Limits of Technocracy, (In: Theory and Society, Dordrecht : Springer, 1993).

Ashcroft, David., Technocracy : A Discussion (In: Science Policy and Social Aspects of Science, Mons, 1979).

Simmons, Harry., System Dynamics and Technocracy (In: Futures, Amsterdam : Elsevier, 1973).

Shils, Edward A., The Social Control of Technocracy (In: Can We Survive Our Future, London [u.a.] : St. Martin's Pr., 1972).

Scott, Howard., Technocracy's Answer (In: Bingham : Alfred Mitchell, Freeport, N.Y : Books for Libraries Press, 1971).

Bell, Daniel., The Post-Industrial Society : Technocracy and Politics (In: Transactions of the World Congress of Sociology, Wechselnde Verlagsorte, 1970).

Back, Edith B., Technocracy and the Ethic of Social Work (In: The Social Service Review, Chicago, Ill.: Univ of Chicago Press, 1969).

Meynaud, Jean., and Paul. Barnes, Technocracy, Translated by

Paul Barnes. (Society Today and Tomorrow, London, 1968).

The Politics and Philosophy of Technocracy, ed. George Frederick. (In: For and Against Technocracy, New York: Business Bourse, 1933).

Money, Debt, and Price Under Technocracy, ed. George Frederick. (In: For and Against Technocracy, New York: Business Bourse, 1933).

An Examination Into Some of Technocracy's Examples, ed. George Frederick. (In: For and Against Technocracy, New York: Business Bourse, 1933).

The Background of Technocracy, ed. George Frederick. (In: For and Against Technocracy, New York: Business Bourse, 1933).

Frederick, Christine., The Psychology of Women Under Technocracy, ed. Frederick. Christine (In: For and Against Technocracy, New York: Business Bourse, 1933).

Doane, Robert R., Technocracy and the Maturity of the Chances (In: For and Against Technocracy, New York: Business Bourse, 1933).

Deventer, John H. van., The Weakness in the Technocracy Case (In: For and Against Technocracy, New York: Business Bourse, 1933).

Compton, Karl Taylor., Technology's Answer to Technocracy, (In: For and Against Technocracy, New York: Business Bourse, 1933).

Frederick, Justus George., What Are Technocracy's Assertions (In: For and Against Technocracy, New York: Business Bourse, 1933).

Holcomb, Hillman., Christian Technocracy. (Oakland, Calif., 1962).

Holcomb, Hillman., Gentiles Incorporated or International for Technocracy (Oakland, Calif., 1961).

Pamphlets on Technocracy. (New York, etc., 1932).

A Continental Hydrology : A Continental Design for Flood and Erosion Control, and Water for Power, Irrigation, Transportation, Recreation and Climatic Modification (Rushland, PA, 1970).

Technocracy, a New Challenge to Labor and Education : Address to the 52nd Convention of the American Federation of Labor, Cincinnati, Ohio, Nov. 23, 1932. (1932).

Murray, Alan Robert., and John Rodgers. King, The Facts About Technocracy (Los Angeles, 1932).

Cromie, Robert James, Technocracy From the Viewpoint of an Editor (Girard, Kan., 1933).

Total Conscription. (New York, N.Y., 1943).

Power for a Continent. (New York, N.Y., 1947).

Continentalism : The Mandate of Survival, (New York, 1947).

A Continental Hydrology, (Rushland, Pa., 1956).

Alchon, Guy, Technocratic Social Science and the Rise of Managed Capitalism, 1910-1933 (ii, 280 leaves, 1985).

Technocracy : Technological Social Design, (Savannah, Ohio, 1976).

Carleton, G., Technology and Humanism; Some Exploratory Essays for Our Time (Nashville, 1970). Technocracy Digest, (Vancouver, 1934).

The Northwest Technocrat, (Seattle, 1939).

Technocracy in Plain Terms : A Challenge and a Warning, (New York, N.Y., 1939).

Anderson, Stuart., Technocracy Passes, (1933).

The North American Technocrat. (Ferndale, WA, 2002).

Frederick, J. George, For and Against Technocracy, a Symposium, (New York, 1933).

Technocratic Trendevents. (Long Beach, Calif., 1950).

Bryson, Dennis Raymond., Lawrence K. Frank : Architect of Child Development, Prophet of Bio- Technocracy / By Dennis Raymond Bryson. (2 v. (v, 575 leaves), 1993).

Elsner, Henry., The Technocrats; Prophets of Automation. ([Syracuse, N.Y.], 1967).

Wilson, J. M., Tomorrow (San Diego, 1932).

Blanshard, Paul, Technocracy and Socialism (New York, 1933).

Darcy, Sam., and Lincoln Steffens, A Marxist Exposure of the Fallacy of Technocracy (San Francisco, 1930).

Mayers, Henry, The What, Why, Who, When, and How of Technocracy ; Amazing Revelations of Foremost U. S. Engineers and Economists Concerning Our Past Prosperity, Present Depression and Future Freedom. (Los Angeles, Calif., 1932).

International

Andreas, Joel., Rise of the Red Engineers : The Cultural Revolution and the Origins of China's New Class (Stanford, Calif., 2009).

Silva, Patricio., In the Name of Reason : Technocrats and Politics in Chile (University Park, Pa., 2008).

Elena, Eduardo., The Promise of Planning : Technocracy and Populism in the Making of Peronist Argentina (In: Fascismo Y Antifascismo, Peronismo Y Antiperonismo, Madrid : Iberoamericana, 2006).

Shiraishi, Takashi, Technocracy in Indonesia : A Preliminary Analysis (Rieit Discussion Paper Series, vol. 06,008, Tokyo).

Shiraishi, Takashi., and P. N. Abinales, After the Crisis : Hegemony, Technocracy and Governance in Southeast Asia (vol. Kyoto area studies on Asia, v. 11, Kyoto Melbourne, Vic., 2005).

Mizuno, Hiromi, Science for the Empire : Scientific Nationalism in Modern Japan (Stanford, Calif., 2009).

Radaelli, Claudio M., Technocracy in the European Union (Political Dynamics of the Eu Series, London [u.a.], 2008).

Bell, Stephen, The New Technocracy : Monetary Governance and the Reserve Bank of Australia (In: Economic Governance & Institutional Dynamics, South Melbourne, Victoria [u.a.] : Oxford Univ. Press, 2002).

Björkman, James Warner, and Kuldeep Mathur, Policy, Technocracy and Development : Human Capital Policies in the Netherlands and India (New Delhi, 2002).

Silva, Patricio, Studying Technocracy in Chile : What Can be Learned From the Mexican Case? (1996).

Dijkstra, A. Geske, Technocracy Questioned : Assessing Economic Stabilisation in Nicaragua (1999).

Shapiro, Martin M., Deliberative, Independent Technocracy V. Democratic Politics : Will the Globe Echo the E.U. (New York, NY, 2004).

Andersen, Svein S., and Tom R. Burns, Societal Decision-Making : Democratic Challenges to State Technocracy : Confrontations Over Nuclear, Hydro-Power and Petroleum Projects in Norway (Aldershot ; Brookfield, USA, 1992).

Rowney, Don Karl., Transition to Technocracy : The Structural Origins of the Soviet Administrative State (Studies in Soviet History and Society, Ithaca, NY , 1989).

Sicat, Gerardo P., National Economic Management and Technocracy in Developing Countries, ed. Gerardo P. Sicat. y (In: Economic Policy and Development, Dover, Mass.: Auburn House, 1985).

Andrade, Luis A. de, Technocracy and Development : The Case of Minas Gerais (1980).

de, Moraes, Martha Pimenta., The Controls of Technocracy : Seminar on Technocracy and Its Controls in Developing Countries (August 1978).

Dubsky, Roman., Social Development, Social Policy, and Technocracy : The Phillippine Experience (In: Philippine Journal of Public Administration, Manila, 1981).

Mai, Manfred., On the Relevance of the Technocracy Debate : An Essay on the Relationship Between Technology and Democracy. (In: Governance and Legitimacy in a Globalized World, Baden-Baden : Nomos, 2008).

Quick, Stephen A., Humanism or Technocracy? Zambia's Farming Co-Operatives 1965-1972. By Stephen a. Quick, (Zambian Papers, vol. No. 12, Manchester, 1978).

Moreira, Alves, Marcio., The Political Economy of the Brazilian Technocracy, ed. Moreira Alves. Marcio (In: Berkeley Journal of

Sociology, Berkeley, Calif., 1974).

Mallet, Serge., Bureaucracy and Technocracy in the Socialist Countries (European Socialist Thought, vol. 1, Nottingham, 1974).

Dimock, Marshall Edward, The Japanese Technocracy : Management and Government in Japan (New York, 1968).

Krämer, Erich., Was Ist Technokratie (Berlin, 1933).

Coston, Henry., Les Technocrates Et La Synarchie ([Paris], 1962).

Andrade, Luis Aureliano Gama de., Technocracy and Development the Case of Minas Gerais (xiii, 311 leaves., 1980).

Apter, David Ernest, Round Table on Technocracy and Its Controls : With Special Reference to Developing Countries : Rio De Janeiro 25-27 August, 1978. ([S.l.], 1979).

Martins, Carlos Estevam, Tecnocracia E Capitalismo : A Política Dos Técnicos No Brasil (São Paulo, 1974).

Malorny, Hans, Technokratie (Würzburg, 1937).

Druesne, Maurice., Les Problèmes Économiques Et La Technocratie (Paris, 1933).

Carrillo, Alejandro., La Tecnocracia; Bosquejo De Una Nueva Teoría Económico-Social. ([México?], 1934).

Baylis, Thomas A., The Technical Intelligentsia and the East German Elite; Legitimacy and Social Change in Mature Communism (Berkeley, 1974).

Doorn, Jacobus Adrianus Antonius van, The Engineers and the Colonial System Technocratic Tendencies in the Dutch East Indies (Rotterdam, 1982).

Bakken,, The Exemplary Society: Human Improvement, Social Control, and the Dangers of Modernity in China (Oxford [England] New York, 2000).

Bauchard, Philippe, Les Technocrates Et Le Pouvoir, X-Crise, Synarchie, C. G. T., Clubs (Paris, 1966).

Ascher, William Louis, Planners, Politics and Technocracy in Argentine [Sic] and Chile ([New Haven], 1997).

Centeno, Miguel Angel, The New Cientificos : Technocratic Politics in Mexico 1970-1990 (2 v. (iv, 513 leaves), 1990).

Brun, Gérard, Technocrates Et Technocratie En France, 1918-1945 (Paris, 1985).
Silva, Patricio, State Capacity, Technocratic Insulation, and Government-Business Relations in South Korea and Chile (vol. Nueva serie FLACSO. Relaciones internacionales y militares, Santiago, Chile, 2000).

Dubsky, Roman., Technocracy and Development in the Philippines (Diliman, Quezon City, 1993).

Website links

Technocracy Rising

    www.TechnocracyRising.com

The August Forecast

    www.AugustForecast.com

Freedom Advocates

    www.FreedomAdvocates.org

The Post Sustainability Institute

    www.PostSustainabilityInstitute.org

INDEX

For additional informaton and updates

www.TechnocracyRising.com

Made in the USA
Lexington, KY
27 August 2016